TRANSACTIONS

OF THE

AMERICAN PHILOSOPHICAL SOCIETY

HELD AT PHILADELPHIA
FOR PROMOTING USEFUL KNOWLEDGE

NEW SERIES—VOLUME 64, PART 1
1974

THE "REAL EXPEDICIÓN MARÍTIMA DE LA VACUNA" IN NEW SPAIN AND GUATEMALA

MICHAEL M. SMITH

Assistant Professor of History, Oklahoma State University

THE AMERICAN PHILOSOPHICAL SOCIETY
INDEPENDENCE SQUARE
PHILADELPHIA

February, 1974

The Ame   ociety

The publications   sist of PRO-
CEEDINGS, TRANSAC

THE PROCEEDING   fore the Society in addition to   blication by
the Committee on   t policy one
volume is issued e   rs, and the
price is $8.00 net per volume.

THE TRANSACTIONS, the oldest scholarly journal in America, was started in 1769 and is quarto size. In accordance with the present policy each annual volume is a collection of monographs, each issued as a part. The current annual subscription price is $20.00 net per volume. Individual copies of the TRANSACTIONS are offered for sale. This issue is priced at $4.00.

Each volume of the MEMOIRS is published as a book. The titles cover the various fields of learning; most of the recent volumes have been historical. The price of each volume is determined by its size and character.

The YEAR BOOK is of considerable interest to scholars because of the reports on grants for research and to libraries for this reason and because of the section dealing with the acquisitions of the Library. In addition it contains the Charter and Laws, and lists of present and former members, and reports of committees and meetings. The YEAR BOOK is published about April 1 for the preceding calendar year. The current price is $5.00.

An author desiring to submit a manuscript for publication should send it to the Editor, George W. Corner, American Philosophical Society, 104 South Fifth Street, Philadelphia, Pa. 19106.

TRANSACTIONS

OF THE

AMERICAN PHILOSOPHICAL SOCIETY

HELD AT PHILADELPHIA
FOR PROMOTING USEFUL KNOWLEDGE

NEW SERIES—VOLUME 64, PART 1
1974

THE "REAL EXPEDICIÓN MARÍTIMA DE LA VACUNA" IN NEW SPAIN AND GUATEMALA

MICHAEL M. SMITH

Assistant Professor of History, Oklahoma State University

THE AMERICAN PHILOSOPHICAL SOCIETY
INDEPENDENCE SQUARE
PHILADELPHIA

February, 1974

For
Susana, Marisol, Adriana, and Michael

Copyright © 1974 by The American Philosophical Society
Library of Congress Catalog
Card Number 73-92725
International Standard Book Number 0-87169-641-x
US ISSN 0065-9746

PREFACE

Perhaps the most unfortunate result of the Spanish Conquest of America was the subsequent decimation of indigenous populations. Modern scholarship has demonstrated that the leading killer of native inhabitants was epidemic disease. Smallpox, the most deadly of the recurrent epidemics, lashed the New World throughout the colonial period. Until 1798, with the discovery by Edward Jenner of smallpox vaccination, there had been no safe and effective method to protect against the disease.

Five years after Jenner's announcement, the Spanish government appointed Dr. Francisco Xavier de Balmis y Berenguer to lead the Royal Maritime Vaccination Expedition to the New World to introduce vaccination. As no means had yet been perfected to transport the vaccine safely, Balmis was forced to utilize a series of human repositories to maintain active virus through chain inoculations. This precarious method entailed the injection of cowpox virus into the arm of a young, non-immune child. When the vaccination lesion sufficiently developed, a portion of lymph was extracted from it and inserted into the arm of another non-immune child. Utilization of this "arm to arm" method, although awkard and expensive, safely conveyed smallpox vaccine to the New World, which had no supply of virus of its own.

Balmis, unquestionably an excellent and well-qualified physician, was proud and impressed with his own position. His haughty attitude provoked several disputes with leading colonial officials, most notably the Viceroy of Mexico, José de Iturrigaray, over alleged indifference, obstructionism, and lack of proper deference toward an emissary of the king.

Despite the quarrels and countless physical and technical difficulties, between 1803 and 1806, Balmis and his aides spread vaccine throughout the Caribbean Islands, northern South America, Mexico, Guatemala, the Philippine Islands, Macao, and even the Chinese mainland. The members of the expedition vaccinated tens of thousands of persons, established a network of vaccination boards and free clinics, and instructed hundreds of physicians, administrators, and laymen in the latest immunization techniques. This study focuses on the activities of the Royal Expedition essentially in Mexico and Guatemala, the area directly touched by that portion of the expedition led by the director himself. The story of the Royal Maritime Vaccination Expedition will perhaps further dispel the rapidly declining view that the Spanish colonial period in America was devoid of cultural, intellectual, and technical attainments. Indeed, the Royal Expedition was the most ambitious medical project conceived and carried out to its day. Its name should be written large on the pages of medical history.

To those who rendered aid, advice, and criticism goes my deepest appreciation. I am particularly grateful to Dr. Donald E. Worcester of Texas Christian University. Dr. R. Palmer Howard of the University of Oklahoma Medical Center provided invaluable critical comments. I wish to thank the directors and staffs of the Mexican Secretariat of Cultural Affairs and the Abraham Lincoln Fellowship Program for financial assistance during a year's stay in Mexico in 1969-1970. In Mexico I received every consideration and aid from Dr. Arturo Arnaiz y Freg and the staffs of the Archivo General de la Nación, the Biblioteca Nacional de México, the Hemeroteca Nacional, the Biblioteca Nacional de Antropología e Historia, and the Biblioteca del Colegio de México.

M. M. S.

Stillwater, Oklahoma
December, 1972

THE "REAL EXPEDICIÓN MARÍTIMA DE LA VACUNA" IN NEW SPAIN AND GUATEMALA

MICHAEL M. SMITH

CONTENTS

I. SMALLPOX IN NEW SPAIN AND GUATEMALA

THE INTRODUCTION OF SMALLPOX INTO AMERICA

When the Castilian *conquistadores* subjugated the Aztec empire in 1521, several factors contributed to their success. A proud martial tradition provided military techniques vastly superior to Aztec methods of fighting. Spanish technology supplied armaments such as fine steel swords and armor, as well as muskets and cannon from the foundries of Toledo. Handsome Andalusian horses, the pride of the Castilian gentleman, terrorized the Aztec warrior, who at first believed that horse and rider formed one terrible being.

But the arsenal of the conquistadores included another weapon, European disease, whose deadly ravages plagued New World inhabitants for centuries after the Conquest. The Conquest introduced a panorama of new infections which by the close of the Colonial Period were endemic, and even epidemic at times. Smallpox [1] was the most destructive of the new contagions. Measles,[2] scarlet fever, yellow fever, diphtheria, influenza, tuberculosis, cholera, mumps, chickenpox, and typhus joined native scourges such as *tabardillo, vómito prieto,* syphilis,[3] *matlazahuatl,*[4] pneumonia, and dysentery to torment the native population.

---

[1] The Aztecs referred to smallpox as *Hueyzahuatl: Huey* (great) *Zahuatl* (leprosy). The Mayas called smallpox *Kak, Ekpeckak* if it was incurable, and *Ixthuchkak* if it was easily cured.

[2] Measles was also a very destructive disease in the New World. The Aztecs named it *Zahuatl Tepiton* (small leprosy).

[3] The long discussed question as to whether syphilis originated in Europe or America has never been satisfactorily answered. Some Mexican historians are satisfied with the explanation that in return for the Old World disease of smallpox, the New World returned the favor with syphilis. See, for example, Guerra, 1953: p. 26.

[4] Matlazahuatl has never been clinically identified and may not have been a strictly indigenous affliction. Cooper is convinced that it was typhus. Cooper, 1965: p. 49. Gibson believes that it might have been either typhus or yellow fever. Gibson, 1964: p. 448. The most serious outbreaks of matlazahuatl noted by the chroniclers occurred in 1544–1546, in which perhaps eight hundred thousand died, and in 1577–1581, claiming approximately two million lives in Mexico, Michoacán, Puebla, and Oaxaca. Flores, 1886: 2: p. 214.

The early chroniclers [5] and most subsequent historians reiterated Bernal Díaz del Castillo's declaration that in 1520 Francisco de Eguía (or Guía),[6] a contaminated Negro slave from Pánfilo de Narváez's ship, communicated smallpox to the mainland from Hispaniola.[7] Although this is still the generally accepted version of the introduction of the disease into New Spain, recent scholars have questioned the thesis. José Alvarez Amezquita *et al.,* note that Diego de Landa's *Relación de las cosas de Yucatán* describes an infection in 1518 which bore all the characteristics of smallpox. They see a relationship between this epidemic and the arrival in Yucatán of Juan de Grijalva's expedition from Cuba in May of that year. The Grijalva group had to flee the region "debido a algunas enfermedades." The authors submit that these "enfermedades" could possibly have been smallpox.[8]

Horacio Figueroa Marroquín offers a much stronger refutation of Díaz del Castillo's assertion. He claims that the Negro actually had measles. He admits that smallpox might also have been introduced in 1520 as well, and makes no attempt to deny that the epidemic of 1520-1521 was smallpox. Figueroa Marroquín rejects the claim that the Negro had smallpox because no Spaniards were affected by the initial contagion, and he avers that it is highly doubtful that all had been previously exposed to the disease. He adds that the fact that approximately ninety per cent of them had prior exposure to measles would account for their immunity. Figueroa Marroquín also observes that the word "viruelas" employed by Díaz del Castillo does not necessarily signify smallpox. Until the eighteenth century, "viruelas" referred to a variety of eruptive fevers. Utilizing retroactive diagnosis based upon contemporary accounts, he affirms that the symptoms are those of measles, not smallpox.[9]

If Eguía (or Guía) did communicate smallpox to New Spain, he certainly did not introduce it into the New World. Smallpox existed in the Caribbean Islands years before the conquest of the mainland.[10] Between 1492 and 1520 Christopher Columbus and others reported smallpox epidemics in the newly discovered islands. Hispaniola experienced epidemics in 1507 and 1517.[11] On January 10, 1519, the governors of the Indies, Fray Luis de Figueroa and Fray Alonso de Santo Domingo, informed Carlos V that a smallpox infection had killed nearly one-third of the Indians on that island.[12]

Salvador Brau, the eminent Puerto Rican historian, claims that culpability for transmitting smallpox to the New World does not belong to the Spaniards at all, but to Genovese and Portuguese slave-traders who illegally introduced African slaves into Santo Domingo. He recalls that during the first few years after Discovery, all legal commerce with America was limited to the Sevillan market. Agents of the *Casa de Contratación* closely inspected all Spanish ships bound for the New World. The slave runners, who evaded cargo inspection, introduced infected slaves directly from Africa. As further proof that the Spaniards did not communicate the disease, Brau points out that virtually all epidemics originated in the mines of Santo Domingo, precisely where the slaves toiled, and from there spread to Puerto Rico and other islands. Since the Spanish Armada always stopped in Puerto Rico before continuing on to Santo Domingo, that island would have been the logical spawning ground of the infection if Spaniards had been the carriers.[13]

In view of the existence of the disease in the islands and contact with the mainland before the arrival of Cortez and Narváez—the expeditions of Hernández de Córdoba and Grijalva, for example—one cannot entirely dismiss the possibility of an earlier introduction, despite Spanish efforts to quarantine ships with cases of smallpox aboard.[14]

Smallpox struck the indigenous population with a virulency unmatched in the annals of European medicine.[15] Once infected, the Indian often experienced the initial symptoms of the disease within twenty-four hours. His body glistened with the moisture of an intense febrile sweat. Nightmares and delirium interrupted his already disturbed sleep. Nausea, vomiting, hemorrhaging at the nose, sore throat, acute thirst, aching body, and a racing pulse all contributed to his extreme inquietude. Children frequently went into convulsions. Intensification of these symptoms a few days after contagion plus the appearance of a cutaneous eruption on the face, neck, and breast made clear the severe nature of the disease. Finally putrid pustules covered his entire body causing a fiery pain and emitting a nauseous odor. If the victim recovered, the once smooth texture of his skin remained disfigured by deep pockmarks. Frequently the disease affected the eyes and blinded its victim.[16]

---

[5] Benavente, 1914: p. 13; Torquemada, 1943: **1**: p. 511; Herrera y Tordesillas, 1934–1952: **5**: p. 398; Sahagún, 1956: **1**: p. 285.

[6] Alvarez Amezquita, 1960: **1**: p. 46. This is the only source encountered which ventures to identify the culprit by name.

[7] Díaz del Castillo, 1928: p. 399.

[8] Alvarez Amezquita, 1960: **1**: p. 39.

[9] Figueroa Marroquín, 1957: pp. 49-67.

[10] Alvarez Amezquita, 1960: **1**: p. 51.

[11] Figueroa Marroquín, 1957: p. 51.

[12] Brau, 1966: p. 315.

[13] *Ibid.,* pp. 315–316.

[14] Alvarez Amezquita, 1960: **1**: p. 45.

[15] Guerra, 1953: p. 26.

[16] Francisco Gil, *Disertación físico-médica en la qual se prescribe un método seguro para preservar a los pueblos de viruelas hasta lograr la completa extinción de ellas en todo el reino. Su autor don Francisco Gil, Cirujano del Real Monasterio de San Lorenzo y su Sitio, e Individuo de la Real Academia Médica de Madrid. Reimpresa en México por D. Mariano de Zúñiga, y Ontiveros, calle de Espíritu Santo, Año de 1796. Archivo General de la Nación* (hereafter cited as AGN). "Impresos Oficiales," v. **21**, exp. 6, fs. 65–68.

MAJOR EPIDEMICS IN NEW SPAIN AND GUATEMALA

The first great epidemic in New Spain, 1520–1521, began in Cempoala [17] in May or June,[18] according to some chroniclers, or September, according to others.[19] From this point it spread to Tlaxcala, Tenochtitlán, and throughout the country.[20] Since the Indians were not acquainted with the disease, they could not adequately treat it. The measures they did take exacerbated the contagion. Their custom of frequent hot baths in *temazcalli*, where the sick mixed indiscriminately with the healthy, only served to spread the infection.[21]

With the indigenous population in a high state of receptivity and helpless to resist the disease, over half the population perished in many areas. Entire villages disappeared in a single contagion.[22] In Tenochtitlán and its contingencies, the most populous center of the Indian world, smallpox raged for sixty days soon after the Aztecs had expelled the Spaniards on the "Noche Triste." [23]

Descriptions of this first attack were vivid. Bernal Díaz del Castillo relates:

The whole country was stricken and filled with it, from which there was a great mortality, for according to what the Indians said they had never had such a disease, and as they did not understand it, they bathed very often, and on that account a great number of them died; so that dark as was the lot of Narváez, still darker was the death of so many persons who were not Christians.[24]

Toribio de Benavente (Motolinía) described ten plagues which afflicted New Spain after the Conquest. Smallpox, the first,

attacked the Indians, and sickness and pestilence were so great among them that in most provinces more than half the people died . . . many also died of hunger because all became sick at once and they could not help each other. . . . In many places whole families died. Because they could not bury all the dead, and in order to curtail the stench given off by the decomposing bodies, they tore down the houses on top of them, thus their own home became their sepulcher.[25]

Antonio de Herrera y Tordesillas recounts that

there were so many dead they could not bury them. The stench corrupted the air, and an even greater pestilence was feared. The smallpox epidemic spread throughout New Spain and caused an incredible mortality. It was a remarkable thing to see the Indians who were saved. The smallpox holes that disfigured their hands and faces were marks of their redemption.[26]

Clavijero notes that "those who because of their stronger constitution resisted the violence of the disease were so disfigured by the profound marks of the eruption that they horrified all who saw them." [27]

Bernardino de Sahagún narrates that

there occurred a great pestilence of smallpox in all the land, something which had never happened in Mexico nor in any other part of New Spain before, according to the ancients. And it deformed the faces of everyone, filling them with holes. So many died of the disease, that there was no one to bury them. In Mexico they threw corpses into the drainage ditches . . . and a great stench arose from the dead bodies.[28]

And he continues: "This pestilence killed countless people. Many died because there was no one left to feed them. Holes pocked the faces of those who escaped death. Others were blinded." [29]

Among the most famous victims of this infection was Cuitláhuac, the tenth lord of Tenochtitlán, who died after a reign of only eighty days.[30] The Tlaxcalan chieftain, Maxixcatzin, friend and ally of Cortez, also died during this plague.[31]

Recurring epidemics racked New Spain and Guatemala throughout the colonial period. Tabulating the principal contagions in the Valley of Mexico for this period, Charles Gibson lists sixteenth-century outbreaks in 1520–1521, 1531, 1532, and 1538. The seventeenth century brought new attacks in 1615–1616, 1653, 1663, and 1678, while in the eighteenth century, smallpox struck in 1711, 1734, 1748, 1761–1762, 1778–1780, and 1797–1798.[32]

Except for the accounts of the 1520–1521 epidemic, little is known about outbreaks definitely identified as smallpox between the sixteenth century and the second half of the eighteenth. After this period information largely concerns Mexico City.[33] In 1761–1762 both smallpox and typhus struck the capital. Since the last smallpox epidemic in Mexico City had occurred in 1737, thousands of children and young adults lacked immunity. Fatality estimates vary widely, ranging from 14,600 to twenty-five thousand.[34] The infection of 1779–1780 attacked over forty-four thousand in Mexico City. Perhaps as many as twenty-two thousand persons died in this epidemic.[35] The contagion of 1797–1798, although considerably milder than its immediate predecessors, still claimed the life of one out of every sixteen inhabitants of the capital, which had a population of approximately 125,000 persons.[36]

[17] Clavijero, 1844: 2: p. 84.
[18] Flores, 1866: 1: p. 46.
[19] Sahagún, 1956: 3: p. 58.
[20] Flores, 1886: 1: p. 46.
[21] Ocaranza, 1934: p. 83.
[22] Benavente, 1914: p. 14.
[23] Torquemada, 1943: 1: p. 512.
[24] Díaz del Castillo, 1928: p. 399.
[25] Benavente, 1914: p. 14.
[26] Herrera y Tordesillas, 1934–1952; 5: p. 398.

[27] Clavijero, 1844: 2: p. 84.
[28] Sahagún, 1956: 1: p. 285.
[29] *Ibid.*, p. 59.
[30] *Ibid.*, p. 285.
[31] Torquemada, 1943: 1: p. 523.
[32] Gibson, 1964: pp. 448-451.
[33] Cooper, 1965, is clearly the standard treatment of the Mexico City epidemics of 1761-1762, 1779-1780, and 1797-1798.
[34] *Ibid.*, pp. 53-54.
[35] *Ibid.*, p. 67.
[36] *Ibid.*, p. 154.

Much less is known about the history of smallpox in the Captaincy General of Guatemala. The disease evidently did not strike there until 1564. The first epidemic lasted into 1565 and, according to the Guatemalan medical historian, Carlos Martínez Durán, "killed many people." [37] In 1576 smallpox returned accompanied by measles and other afflictions. Reaching its peak in September, the infection decimated entire villages and prostrated the capital.[38] After 1705 smallpox repeatedly assailed Guatemala.[39] In 1733 the disease claimed the lives of 1,500 people in a single month in Guatemala City.[40] The most disastrous of all outbreaks occurred in 1780, striking especially hard in the poorest districts of the city. This epidemic severely crippled the capital, which had not yet completely recovered from a calamitous earthquake in 1773.[41] The simultaneous occurrence of the pestilence in both Mexico and Guatemala in 1779–1780 suggests a link between the epidemics.

After his visit to New Spain, Alexander von Humboldt observed that smallpox struck in seventeen- or eighteen-year cycles.[42] Although it is impossible to substantiate the claim for the entire colonial period, the intervals between the epidemics of 1761, 1779, 1797, and others in 1813 and 1830 support his observation.

The relatively dense indigenous population that Spaniards encountered at the Conquest declined rapidly during the first century of subjugation. Entire provinces were desolated, and indeed it seemed that the Indies were being destroyed. Spaniards, seeking explanations for the abrupt depopulation, blamed excessive labor requirements, inordinate tribute, mistreatment, Indian drunkenness and "weak constitutions," floods, droughts, and disease. Certainly labor in the mines, the *encomienda* regime, Spanish personal abuse of Indians, intertribal wars, disruption of the indigenous economy, and poor living conditions contributed to susceptibility and increased mortality rates.[43] Bartolomé de las Casas's zealous defense of the Indian from the white man's rapacity unintentionally created the "Black Legend." [44]

Yet recent scholarship, and not merely that of Spanish apologists, has discredited the Black Legend.[45] The view that Spanish cruelty and mistreatment of the Indian as the primary cause for the native population decline "has now lost much of its earlier acceptance.

Among all causes, epidemic disease is now recognized as paramount." [46] Certainly smallpox rates first place in these recurring waves of pestilential death.[47]

EARLY TREATMENT OF SMALLPOX

It is instructive to examine various methods employed to combat smallpox during the colonial period. As previously noted, the Indians at first tried to treat the illness with their traditional custom of frequent hot baths in the temazcalli. The heat and steam created by the baths intensified the discomfort, while contact with those already infected accelerated the contagion.

Sahagún described another native cure for the disease:

Pockmarks and asperity on the face which smallpox and other similar illnesses commonly cause are cured by drinking hot urine and washing one's face with it, and then applying ground yellow *chile* to the infected area. After this, wash again with urine or with incense, and continually cleanse the holes with the juice of the *azpan* herb. Later drink the juice of the herb called *tlatlauhqui* mixed with water.[48]

Martínez Durán notes that during the epidemic of 1733 in Guatemala City physicians were so ignorant of curative measures that, instead of prescribing medication for their patients, they simply recommended prayers and novenas as the only effective remedies.[49]

During Mexico City's epidemic of 1779, during which "only cadavers were seen in the streets, the only noises heard in the city were outcries and laments . . . ," [50] Dr. José Ignacio Bartolache composed an *Instrucción que puede servir para que se cure a los enfermos de viruelas epidémicas que ahora padecen en México, desde fines del estío, en el año corriente de 1779.* The work is perhaps representative of contemporary concepts of the disease and its treatment. Bartolache stated that smallpox was not endemic in Mexico, and only struck about every ten to fifteen years. Smallpox, in fact, was not an illness at all, he explained, but rather a remedy and agent which Nature employed to purge a certain amount of "bad humor" which each individual acquired at his mother's breast.

If Bartolache's perception of the nature and cause of the disease was erroneous, he was correct in explaining that the infection spread by contact, and that only quarantine would impede its dispersion. In fact, isolation of the infected was the only effective method employed to treat smallpox in the New World for over two and a half centuries.

Bartolache's instructions coincided with contemporary therapeutic practices. He recommended purges with

37 Martínez Durán, 1964: pp. 159–160.

38 *Ibid.,* p. 161.

39 Guerra, 1953: p. 163.

40 Martínez Durán, 1964: p. 238.

41 *Ibid.,* pp. 327–328.

42 Humboldt, 1941: **2**: p. 51.

43 Borah, 1951: p. 2; Rosenblat, 1954: pp. 73–75; Gibson, 1964: p. 136.

44 Las Casas, 1812.

45 *Cf.* Rosenblat, 1954: pp. 73–75; Gibson, 1964: p. 136; Borah, 1951: p. 2; Díaz de Iraola, 1947; p. 18. Among others who early recognized disease as the primary cause of depopulation in America was Humboldt, 1941: **2**: p. 51.

46 Gibson, 1964: p. 136.

47 *Cf.* Humboldt, 1941: **2**: p. 52; Guerra, 1943: p. 119; Flores, 1886: **2**: p. 214; Díaz de Iraola, 1947: p. 18; Alvarez Amezquita, 1960: **1**: p. 42; Alamán 1942: **1**: p. 115.

48 Sahagún, 1956: **2**: p. 171.

49 Martínez Durán, 1964: p. 283.

50 Fernández del Castillo, 1946: p. 312.

laxatives and strong saline solutions. He advised infected persons to drink water—as hot as they could stand it—clothe themselves warmly, and go to bed. He prescribed only water and *atole* as nourishment, while stressing extreme cleanliness for the victim and his surroundings. Soothing oils applied to the vesicles would diminish the pain. When the vesicles were mature, they could be lanced and squeezed clean with soft threads to accelerate healing and prevent scarring.[51]

On April 15, 1785, José de Gálvez, Spanish minister of state, sent the viceroy of New Spain [52] and the captain general of Guatemala [53] copies of a treatise recently published in Spain, Dr. Francisco Gil's *Disertación físico-médica en la qual se prescribe un método seguro para preservar a los pueblos de viruelas hasta lograr la completa extinción de ellas en todo el reyno.* Gálvez forwarded the viceroy 150 copies of the work and ordered their distribution to clergymen, physicians, and leading citizens.[54]

Although there is no evidence that either the viceroy or the captain general immediately complied with this order, a twelve-page extract of the dissertation was published in Mexico City in May, 1788.[55] On August 6, 1796, after measures recommended in a circular issued the previous month had failed to halt the spread of an epidemic in southern New Spain,[56] and facing possible contamination of the capital, Viceroy Branciforte ordered that Bartolache's entire work be reprinted and distributed throughout the viceroyalty. The Royal Order of April 15, 1785, served as a prologue for the new edition.[57]

The Royal Order related the measures Gálvez had adopted during an earlier epidemic in the Province of Louisiana. His instructions stressed quarantine. Gálvez's major suggestion was that infected persons be interned in a lazaretto placed at a sufficient distance from the town and located so that the prevailing winds could not communicate the disease to the local population.[58]

Gil's thesis suggested similar measures. He declared, however, that smallpox was a disease communicated only by contact. To avoid contamination, one must avoid those who were already infected. Although variolization was being practiced in many parts of the world at that time, Gil doubted its efficacy and warned that it could spread the infection. He recommended that if variolization was utilized, inoculated persons should be quarantined until completely recovered.[59]

Gil prescribed the establishment of lazarettos staffed by physicians at public expense. Medical attendants should wear clean gowns and exercise the utmost sanitary precautions. All bedclothing and clothing of the sick and their attendants should be treated with a solution composed of resin, lavander, rosemary, sweet marjoram, and juniper. Local authorities should prohibit all commerce and traffic with the contaminated village.[60]

Despite these directives and other measures to contend with an epidemic in the Oaxaca-Tehuantepec area, the contagion persisted. On February 28, 1797, aware of the imminent danger to the capital, Branciforte composed a new circular. The thirteen-point decree, distributed throughout the viceroyalty, outlined the new procedure. Branciforte ordered the construction of a lazaretto in each village to house all victims of the contamination. Priests, physicians, and public officials were to report immediately any new cases. Patients and attendants would be placed in strict quarantine. Towns were to be divided into districts under the charge of *regidores* (councilors), minor city officials, and leading citizens who would coordinate health services in each area. If required, a cordon of troops would isolate the town. Bonfires built at all entrances to the city would purify the air. Letters dispatched from the infected area should be treated with sulphur, while mail carriers must change clothing before entering non-infected towns. Charitable societies would collect funds to aid the poor, usually the most severely afflicted during any epidemic. The circular prohibited burial of variolous corpses in churches or in the regular cemeteries and advised church officials to provide new burial grounds away from normal transit. If the charitable societies' funds proved insufficient, Branciforte authorized utilization of the city's *fondos de propios* (income from public lands) and *bienes de communidad* (community property). As a last resort, Branciforte permitted variolization; but inoculated persons must submit to quarantine until their complete recovery. When all else failed, he suggested prayer.[61]

[51] José Ignacio Bartolache's *Instrucción,* reprinted in the *Suplemento a la Gaceta de México* (Mexico City), 23 Septiembre 1797: pp. 341–344, under the title *Instrucción sobre el método de curar.*
[52] José de Gálvez to Viceroy of New Spain, Aranjuez, 15 Abril 1785, AGN, "Reales Cédulas," v. 130, exp. 168, fs. 263–264.
[53] José de Gálvez to President of Guatemala, Aranjuez, 15 Abril 1785, Biblioteca Nacional de Antropología e Historia (México), Fondo de Microfotografía, Serie "Guatemala," Primera Serie, #51, 2 fs.
[54] José de Gálvez to Viceroy of New Spain, Aranjuez, 15 Abril 1785, AGN, "Reales Cédulas." v. 130, exp. 168, fs. 263–264.
[55] *Extracto de la obra publicada en Madrid el año pasado de 1784 con el título Disertación físico-médica en la qual se prescribe un método seguro para preservar a los pueblos de viruelas, compuesta por D. Francisco Gil, Cirujano del Real Sitio y Monasterio de San Lorenzo.* AGN, "Epidemias," v. 12, exp. 1, fs. 1–12.
[56] *Circular,* México, 14 Julio 1796, AGN, "Epidemias," v. 3, exp. 1, fs. 2–2v.
[57] Gil, *Disertación,* fs. 24–75.

[58] *Ibid.,* fs. 25–26v.
[59] *Ibid.,* fs. 27, 40v–41.
[60] *Ibid.,* fs. 47–51.
[61] *Circular,* México, 28 Febrero 1797, AGN, "Epidemias," v. 16, exp. 2, fs. 26v–27v.

On November 22, the Conde de Cadena, governor-intendant of Puebla, published an edict similar to Branciforte's circular. He ordered the establishment of charitable societies and divided the city into wards, providing each with a physician to treat the sick. He prohibited the sale or exchange of clothing worn by contaminated persons and ordered the burning of bonfires on every street corner to purify the air. The prelate declared that cadavers should be covered with quicklime. He prohibited wakes and suggested that the dead be buried as soon as possible.[62]

Measures adopted in port cities included the establishment of health inspections to examine all arriving ships. Agents would inspect crew, passengers, and cargo while the vessel was anchored at a safe distance from the port. No cargo or baggage could be unloaded, no passengers could disembark, nor could anyone but authorized personnel board the ship until it was cleared for landing. Appropriate locations were chosen to quarantine contaminated vessels.[63]

Despite sponsoring such protective measures, physicians in New Spain and Guatemala, like their colleagues in Europe, were unable to combat the periodic incursions of smallpox. Vaguely aware of the causal relationship between micro-organisms and infection, they usually attributed the primary origin of disease to contamination of the air. Although ignorant of the nature and cause of smallpox, they did attempt to treat its symptoms. Unfortunately, useless and even dangerous remedies such as bleeding, purgatives, and scatalogical prescriptions counteracted their beneficial suggestions of rest, special diets and medicinal teas.[64]

VARIOLIZATION

If traditional methods of combating smallpox were insufficient, a useful though potentially dangerous preventative was available. Variolization, or inoculation with the matter extracted directly from a smallpox vesicle, had been practiced in various parts of the world for centuries. In 1721 Lady Mary Wortley Montague, wife of the English ambassador to Constantinople, introduced the method into Europe. One of her own children had been successfully inoculated in Constantinople, and upon her return to London she convinced the Princess of Wales of its efficacy. In July, 1721, the princess ordered the inoculation of five condemned prisoners according to the instructions of Lady Wortley Montague. When this experiment proved satisfactory, the princess had her own children inoculated. The courtiers quickly imitated the practice and the method

eventually spread throughout Europe.[65] Among those who submitted to variolization were Catherine II and the grand dukes of Russia, the kings of Sweden and Denmark, the archdukes and archduchesses of Austria, and Louis XVI of France.[66]

Variolization was a simple procedure and was relatively safe during the first stages of an epidemic. A successful inoculation induced a mild case of smallpox and rendered lifetime immunity. Yet variolization could be dangerous. It might immunize one person but induce the disease in its full force in another. An inoculated person could also infect the non-immune.[67]

Variolization was an elementary operation. The most common method of inoculation was to extract a quantity of fluid from a smallpox vesicle with a lancet and transfer it to the arm (or arms) or the hand, between the index finger and the thumb, of the recipient. After inoculation, the recipient was confined to bed. Within a few days the virus reacted. If inoculation was successful, symptoms were mild. Pustules were few and, after lancing and cleansing, would dry quickly without disfigurement. Pregnant women, the infirm, the very young or very old, and children with worms or in dentition should not be inoculated. Yet despite its dangers, variolization was capable of saving human life.[68]

Variolization was not utilized in New Spain or Guatemala until the epidemics of 1779–1780. Although Dr. José Ignacio Bartolache usually receives credit for introducing the practice, in October, 1779, Dr. Esteban Morel performed the first authenticated operation in New Spain. Morel received the cautious approval of the viceroy and the *Real Protomedicato* (Royal Medical Board) to continue inoculations, but only upon request. He immediately established an inoculation center in the Hospital de San Hipólito and prepared for the multitude—no one came.[69]

Dr. José Felipe de Flores had substantially more success with inoculation in Guatemala. When all other methods failed to impede the epidemic of 1780, Flores requested permission from Captain General Matías de Gálvez to employ variolization. Despite divided counsel from the *Ayuntamiento* (municipal council), the *Fiscal* (attorney), and various physicians, Gálvez gave his approval. Flores's activities proved the utility of variolization. Few of the thousands inoculated suffered a malign form of the disease, and no fatalities resulted

[62] *Bando*, Puebla, 22 Noviembre 1797, AGN, "Epidemias," v. 6, exp. 5, f. 195.
[63] Ayuntamiento de Veracruz to Félix Berenguer de Marquina, Veracruz, 22 Agosto 1801, AGN, "Epidemias," v. 2, exp. 3, fs. 40v–41.
[64] Cooper, 1965: p. 191.

[65] Gil, *Disertación*, f. 39v.
[66] Fernández del Castillo, 1960: p. 51.
[67] Hayward, 1956: p. 50.
[68] José de Flores, *Instrucción sobre el modo de practicar la inoculación de las viruelas y método para curar esta enfermedad, acomodado a la naturaleza, y modo de vivir de los indios, del Reyno de Guatemala. Impreso de orden del Superior Gobierno, en la Oficina de Don Ignacio Beteta, Año de 1794*. Biblioteca Nacional de Antropología e Historia (México), Fondo de Microfotografía, Serie "Guatemala," Primera Serie, #51, 17 pp.
[69] Cooper, 1965: pp. 64–66.

from the operation. The percentage of deaths was minimal in districts where variolization was employed. Flores, in the face of virtually unanimous opposition of his fellow physicians, placed complete faith in inoculation; success silenced his critics.[70]

Variolization deserves primary credit for moderating the 1797–1798 epidemic in New Spain. At first, however, Viceroy Branciforte hesitated to approve early and widespread use of inoculation. Smallpox, which had existed in pockets throughout the country since the early years of the decade, reached epidemic proportions in the southern regions of the viceroyalty by 1796.[71] In August, 1796, Branciforte ordered the reprinting of Gil's *Disertación,* which stressed the traditional method of quarantine and discreetly avoided mention of variolization. Branciforte's previous circular of July 14, 1796, had recommended variolization only when all other efforts failed. On August 31, 1797, however, after the disease reached Mexico City, he authorized a program of free, voluntary inoculation.[72]

Variolization gained widespread popularity in 1797–1798. The areas of greatest activity were Mexico City and its environs and the Bishopric of Michoacán. In the Bishopric of Michoacán, Juan Antonio Riaño, intendant of Guanajuato, and Manuel Abad y Queipo, governor and vicar general of the bishopric, energetically fought the epidemic and supported variolization. Abad y Queipo directed the inoculation of nearly 6,800 persons in Valladolid. Of that number only 170 died, and many of them had been exposed to the disease before the operation. Thus only two and one-half per cent of those treated perished, while fourteen per cent of the non-inoculated succumbed. An estimated fifty to sixty thousand persons received variolization in the viceroyalty.[73]

Inoculation did not enjoy unanimous support. Cosme de Mier y Trespalacios, who played the leading role in fighting the epidemic in Mexico City, reported to the viceroy on September 20, 1797, that a paper containing verses impugning and satirizing variolization was circulating throughout the capital.[74] Although the verses are decidedly inferior, they do indicate sentiments critical of inoculation. Written as lyrics for *boleros,* they are arranged in alternating four- and three-line stanzas. The following stanzas have been translated literally with no attempt at rhyme:

> The poorest and most
> destitute doctors
> have invented
> the inoculation.

> But it must be pointed out
> that those who are inoculated
> are traveling with death.

> Those who are inoculated
> do not know what they are doing;
> they think they will be safe,
> but it is only a ruse.

> But this is certain,
> some will be left pocked
> and some dead.

> . . . .

> Grieving Mexico
> has already complained
> that indigent doctors
> have infected her.[75]

EDWARD JENNER AND PREVENTATIVE INOCULATION

Smallpox constantly threatened Europe through the eighteenth century as well. The most perilous of contagious diseases, it erupted intermittently in epidemic form.[76] The disease attacked sixty per cent of the population, causing approximately ten per cent of the total deaths.[77] The most common practices employed to treat smallpox were quarantine, variolization, and self-exposure to a mild case of the disease. None of these methods offered an assurance of success, while the latter two could even extend the contagion.[78]

In 1798 Edward Jenner, a rural physician in Berkeley, Gloucestershire, England, published *An Inquiry into the Causes and Effects of the Variolae Vaccinae*—the results of twenty years of observation and experimentation. Jenner had studied the folk belief that if one contracted cowpox, he would never suffer smallpox. Cowpox is a disease similar to, but much less dangerous than smallpox. Humans usually contract the infection during milking by contact with vesicles which erupt on the udder and teats of the infected animal. Cowpox causes slight inconvenience and its vesicles quickly disappear. On May 14, 1796, Jenner submitted his theory to a practical test. He vaccinated eight-year-old James Phipps with cowpox virus. Six weeks later he inoculated young Phipps with matter taken from a smallpox vesicle. Jenner's theory was confirmed when the disease did not occur.[79]

Preventative vaccination is a simple operation. The cowpox matter is introduced into the recipient's arm by making several superficial incisions with a lancet or a needle. Within three or four days a papule appears and is surrounded by a reddish zone. On the fifth or sixth day a definite vesicle appears, the margins of

[70] Martínez Durán, 1964: pp. 329–330.
[71] Cooper, 1965: p. 87.
[72] *Ibid.,* pp. 116–117.
[73] Humboldt, 1941: **2**: pp. 51–52.
[74] Cosme de Mier, "Auto," México, 20 Septiembre 1797, AGN, "Historia," v. **65,** exp. 14, f. 1.

[75] "Boleros," AGN, "Historia," v. **65,** fs. 1v–4. An investigation to determine the author's identity was unsuccessful.
[76] Hayward, 1956: p. 33.
[77] Fernández del Castillo, 1960: p. 48.
[78] Hayward, 1956: p. 50.
[79] Jenner, 1798.

which are raised while the center is depressed. By the eighth day the vesicle has attained its maximum size. It is round and distended with limpid fluid. By the tenth day the virus reaches its peak of reaction. The areola forms and the vesicles contain their greatest amount of lymph. By the eleventh or twelfth day the vesicles usually begin to desiccate. At the end of the second week, the vesicle is converted into a brownish scab, which gradually becomes dry and hard. About three weeks after vaccination, the scab separates and leaves a circular pitted scar. Vaccination is effective as long as the recipient is non-immune and the virus used is not past its peak of potency.[80]

News of Jenner's discovery quickly spread throughout Europe. His publications generated enthusiasm in some scientific circles and skepticism in others. The Prince of Wales was Jenner's most energetic supporter in England. Thomas Jefferson sent him a letter of congratulation. Napoleon immediately commanded that his troops be vaccinated. The Empress of Russia ordered that the first child vaccinated in Russia should thereafter be called "Vaccinoff" and enjoy a life pension from the imperial government.[81]

Jenner did not escape criticism. Some opponents sincerely believed that it was immoral, even sacrilegious, to infect perfectly healthy persons with "repugnant, dirty material" extracted from an animal. Others charged that vaccination caused tuberculosis, degeneration of the blood, cancer, and other fatal diseases. One detractor assured that vaccination would cause bovine horns to sprout on the recipient's forehead.[82]

Despite the criticism of his contemporaries, Jenner gave the world the first effective means to eradicate smallpox epidemics and substantially increased understanding of the principle of immunization. Although it was not known until some time later, vaccination could not offer lifelong immunization as Jenner at first believed. The degree of protection diminishes after a few years, making revaccination necessary.[83]

Although New World gazettes, especially after 1800, carefully chronicled European developments of vaccination, port regulations, isolation of infected persons, and variolization were the only means to combat the disease. Expeditions in search of cowpox repeatedly failed. An examination of the *Gazeta de Guatemala* for this period reveals that almost every issue described frustrated attempts to acquire the virus from Spain or the United States,[84] the latest vaccination instructions,[85] excerpts from European journals discussing the serum,[86]

and articles extolling its benefits.[87] But lacking the precious cowpox, the Spanish American colonist could only hope that vaccine would somehow arrive before the next epidemic.

Various means to transport the fluid were in vogue at the time. One method, the "in vitro" technique, consisted of vacuum-sealing active cowpox virus between glass slides or in vials. Another was to impregnate cloth or silk threads with active matter and allow it to dry. A drop of water would dissolve the encrusted vaccine and prepare it for use. Both of these methods lacked aseptic precautions and the virus often quickly deteriorated, especially in the hot climates of Spanish America. The surest way, although awkward and expensive, was to utilize a series of human repositories. This "in vivo" method consisted of vaccinating a young, non-immune person with a potent preparation of cowpox. On the ninth or tenth day after vaccination, when the virus reached its peak of reaction, a doctor would extract a quantity of the lymph and transmit it to another individual. A continual succession of similar operations could conserve the vaccine indefinitely. The obvious weaknesses in this system were immune reactions, destruction of the vesicle before its employment, or any other break in the chain of inoculations.

II. FORMATION OF THE "REAL EXPEDICIÓN MARÍTIMA DE LA VACUNA"

THE INITIAL STEPS

Only chance would have brought the life-preserving vaccine to Spanish America if on June 19, 1802, the Ayuntamiento of Santa Fé de Bogotá, facing a new epidemic, had not sought the intercession of Carlos IV. The Ayuntamiento had previously requested the viceroy's help, explaining that the city's only hospital was inadequate and the Ayuntamiento's resources were limited. They asked that he authorize use of various unappropriated funds and the creation of another hospital in one of the Dominican convents. At first the viceroy merely took measures to forestall the spread of the infection. He forbade the Ayuntamiento to spend additional public funds to fight the epidemic, but he did, however, accede to the creation of a new hospital. To provide for the hospital's immediate expenses, he allotted six hundred *pesos* raised earlier in a lottery to finance the construction of a house of correction for women. When this sum proved insufficient, he permitted further disbursements.[1]

Dissatisfied with the viceroy's behavior, the Ayuntamiento petitioned the king to specify procedures for

[80] Osler, 1927: pp. 335–336.
[81] Bermúdez, 1946: pp. 300–301.
[82] *Ibid.*, p. 301.
[83] Hayward, 1956: p. 57.
[84] See: *Gazeta de Guatemala,* 30 Agosto 1802: p. 212; 27 Septiembre 1802: p. 239; and 31 Enero 1803: p. 5.
[85] *Ibid.,* 7 Febrero 1803: pp. 11–12.
[86] *Ibid.,* 27 Septiembre 1802: pp. 239–241.
[87] *Ibid.,* 11 Julio 1803: pp. 281–282.
[1] "Extracto del expediente general de la vacuna en ultramar," (Hereafter cited as "Extracto") Cádiz, 12 Marzo 1813, *Archivo General de Indias* (hereafter cited as AGI), "Indif. Gen.," Leg. 1.558, II, fs. 1–3.

similar situations in the future, reprimand the viceroy for illegally prohibiting use of municipal revenues, and order him to reimburse the lottery fund.[2]

In December, 1802, the king forwarded the Ayuntamiento's letter to the Council of the Indies for a decision.[3] On February 19, 1803, the Council declared that the Ayuntamiento's information was inadequate.[4] The Council could not discern whether the epidemic had spread throughout the city, whether it had been curtailed, or whether any prophylactic measures had been employed to impede its extension. Nor did the Council know whether the viceroy had sufficient resources with which to reimburse the lottery fund. To judge the viceroy's actions it needed a full report from all concerned. With complete information the Council could make recommendations for future procedures.[5]

The king approved the Council's decision, and at this point correspondence on the subject between the Ayuntamiento and the Council of the Indies terminated. In a separate note to the Council on March 13, however, Carlos IV expressed his concern over the ravages of smallpox in his American dominions and ordered the Council to investigate the possibility of introducing the vaccine into the colonies.[6]

The popular image of Carlos IV would belie such an altruistic interest in his American subjects' health. He is usually characterized as an incompetent, blundering cuckold, manipulated by Napoleon and deceived by his queen and his prime minister, Manuel Godoy. Yet during the first ten years of his reign, medical sciences in Spain gained new impetus. The Real Colegio de Medicina and a school of veterinary medicine were established in Madrid. The study of "practical medicine" was begun in the Hospital General. A "decent" medical library was founded. All of this activity added new stimuli to the study of medicine, pharmacology, chemistry, experimental physics, and botany, and encouraged the publication and acquisition of books dealing with the sciences.[7]

Carlos IV had personally experienced the tragedy of smallpox in 1798 when the disease struck his daughter, María Luisa. As a result he ordered the first physician of the Royal Chamber, Francisco Martínez Sobral, aided by Antonio Gimbernat and Ignacio Lacaba, surgeons of the King's Chamber, to inoculate the princess and the king's two sons, Carlos and Fernando. The princess fully recovered by November, 1798. The king and queen, delighted by the results of variolization,

resolved that it be put into practice in the hospitals, orphanages, poorhouses, and other charitable institutions dependent upon Their Royal Munificence. It was not the desire of Their Majesties to oblige all of their subjects to follow this method, but it was Their desire that the happy example of the Royal Family would encourage its general adoption and diminish the disasters that this calamity so commonly cause in Their dominions.[8]

The January, 1800, issue of the *Gaceta de Madrid* reported that an Italian physician, identified only as Careno, had sent Carlos IV a copy of Jenner's treatise along with some threads encrusted with cowpox virus. This gift probably marked the introduction of preventative vaccination into Spain.[9]

THE FLORES REPORT

Don Francisco Requena, a member of the Council of the Indies, had also perceived the utility of dispatching the vaccine by a maritime expedition. He asked Dr. José Felipe de Flores, physician of the King's Chamber, to study the matter and inform the Council of his findings.[10] This was the same José de Flores who had successfully introduced variolization into Guatemala during the epidemic of 1780. In 1797 he had received a royal pension and thereafter lived, traveled, and practiced in Europe.[11]

On February 28, 1803, Flores presented his report. Emphasizing the need to eradicate smallpox in the New World, he declared that the disease was the "first and principal cause of the depopulation of America." He suggested a two-part expedition led by the most learned doctors from the Medical School of Cádiz. The ships would carry cows infected with cowpox, a sufficient number of young boys for successive vaccination during the trip, and a quantity of vaccine sealed between glass slides. One or more of these methods of conveyance would insure the safe arrival of active virus in the New World. One vessel would proceed to New Spain via Havana, Puerto Rico, Guatemala, and Yucatán. The other would anchor in Cartagena and dispatch the fluid to Santa Fé de Bogotá, La Guayra, Montevideo, Portobello, Panama, and the other southern dominions. Once the vaccine reached the several capitals, the ayuntamientos, principal citizens, and selected physicians could supervise its conservation and propagation. Provincial capitals and municipalities would adopt a similar procedure.[12]

Recognizing the influence of the Church in America and predictable popular opposition to any novelty,

[2] *Ibid.*, fs. 3v–4.

[3] Cavallero to Marqués de Bajamar, Cartagena, 25 Diciembre 1802, AGI, "Indif. Gen.," Leg. 1.558, I, f. 1.

[4] "Consulta," 19 Febrero 1803, AGI, "Indif. Gen.," Leg. 1.558, I, f. 1.

[5] "Extracto," fs. 5–6v.

[6] Cavallero to Bajamar, Aranjuez, 13 Marzo 1803, AGI, "Indif. Gen.," Leg. 1.558, I, fs. 1–2.

[7] Lafuente, 1930: **15**: pp. 296–297.

[8] *Mercurio de España* (Madrid), Noviembre, 1798: pp. 284–286.

[9] Fernández del Castillo, 1960: p. 64.

[10] "Consulta," Madrid, 22 Marzo 1803, AGI, "Indif. Gen.," Leg. 1.558, I, f. 1.

[11] Díaz de Iraola, 1947: p. 26.

[12] José de Flores, "Establecimiento de la vacuna en América," Madrid, 28 Febrero 1803, AGI, "Indif. Gen.," Leg. 1.558, I, fs. 4–17.

Flores endowed vaccination with a religious quality to facilitate its acceptance. He suggested that when an infant was baptized, the priest should require the godparents to return the child within six months for vaccination. A unique prayer and solemn indulgence especially authorized by the Pope would sanctify the ceremony. A physician, or perhaps even the priest himself, would perform the operation and record it in a special parochial registry.[13]

Flores recommended several measures to insure compliance with vaccination regulations. Bishops would inspect parish records during their diocesan visits. Viceroys, governors, and other colonial officials would encourage the acceptance of vaccination by both example and decree. Assuming ultimate responsibility for the preservation and propagation of vaccine within its jurisdiction, each Audiencia would require priests to submit an annual report on the progress of immunization in each parish. After collecting all reports the Audiencia could present an exact accounting to the king.[14]

On March 22 the Council approved Flores's recommendations. The Council suggested that a physician and some young boys from the *Casa de Desamparados* (Foundling Home) in Madrid accompany the regular packet ship to Veracruz. After stopping in the Canary Islands, Puerto Rico, and Havana they would proceed to New Spain. Once the vaccine reached Mexico the viceroy and provincial governors would supervise its propagation throughout the kingdom. Flores could join the ship directed to Cumaná, Caracas, and Cartagena and from these points dispatch vaccine to Peru, Costa Rica, Nicaragua, and Guatemala. The Council suggested that Francisco Xavier de Balmis y Berenguer, who had recently translated a treatise concerning vaccination and who had resided many years in New Spain, command the Mexican portion of the expedition. If the king did not wish to employ packet ships it would cost little, considering the benefits, to outfit two small vessels of the Armada especially for the expedition. If Flores and Balmis declined the commission, or if the king disapproved of their selection, the Council would accept any other physicians with equivalent credentials. The Council further suggested the formulation of complete instructions to guide and govern any projected expedition.[15]

On April 6, before ruling upon these suggestions, the king ordered that the Council determine a method to finance the undertaking.[16] Indeed there was doubt that Spain could afford such a vast enterprise. By the spring of 1803 her economic condition was desperate. The Peace of Amiens in March, 1802, had granted a temp-

orary respite from more than a century of calamitous warfare. Successive loans, exhausted credit, endemic poverty, poor harvests, natural disasters, and epidemics produced a staggering annual budgetary deficit. In 1797 alone the deficit reached eight hundred thousand reales.[17] Seeking expert advice, the Council sent the file to the General Accounting Office and the fiscal for their opinions. But since the tribunal had adjourned for vacations, they took no immediate action.[18]

Coincidental with this activity, however, Don Lorenzo Berges, physician to the royal family, solicited a license to go to Santa Fé de Bogotá to continue his study of chemistry and botany. Aware that the vaccine had not yet reached that viceroyalty, he offered to introduce it. Berges requested only that the king continue his present salary as physician to the royal family. He offered to pay from his own resources any expenses incurred during his mission. He had previously received permission to accompany the newly appointed viceroy, Don Antonio Amar, to Santa Fé de Bogotá. Amar had offered his help and would lodge Berges in his own home while he was engaged in propagating the vaccine.[19] On April 20 the king granted Berges's request, stipulating that he submit periodic reports on his progress.[20]

The Council of the Indies finally presented its reply to the king on May 22. It noted that the Accounting Office reported that the Protomedicato was studying the project but did not know whether any specific instructions had been formulated. The fiscal declared that two other doctors should be sent to South America because Berges alone was insufficient. But neither made any recommendations concerning financial arrangements for the expedition. Nevertheless the Council suggested that the Royal Treasury suffer the initial expenses. It could be reimbursed later from the municipal funds of the towns which directly benefited from the expedition. The colonial governments could then determine the means to continue the financing.[21]

In a separate opinion the Marqués de Bajamar, Governor of the Council of the Indies, expressed his disagreement with the Council majority.[22] He suggested sending an expedition to each of the four viceroyalties, thus taking advantage of existing political divisions and organization. Three doctors, in addition to Berges, directing separate groups, could depart for Mexico, Lima, and Buenos Aires in packet ships. Working with the viceroys and the protomedicatos in

[13] *Ibid.,* fs. 17–18.
[14] *Ibid.,* fs. 18–19.
[15] "Consulta," Madrid, 22 Marzo 1803, AGI, "Indif. Gen.," Leg. 1.558, I, fs. 8–14.
[16] Cavallero to Bajamar, Aranjuez, 6 Abril 1803, AGI, "Indif. Gen.," Leg. 1.558, I, f. 1.
[17] Lafuente, 1930: **16**: p. 288. In Spanish monetary terms, thirty-four *maravedies* = one real; eight reales = one peso.
[18] "Extracto," f. 12.
[19] Lorenzo Berges, "Statement," Madrid, 12 Abril 1803, AGI, "Indif. Gen.," Leg. 1.558, I, fs. 1–2.
[20] Cavallero to Berges, Aranjuez, 20 Abril 1803, AGI, "Indif. Gen.," Leg. 1.558, I, f. 1.
[21] "Consulta," 22 Mayo 1803, AGI, "Indif. Gen.," Leg. 1.558, I, f. 2.
[22] Bajamar to Cavallero, Madrid, 26 Mayo 1803, AGI, "Indif. Gen.," Leg. 1.558, I, f. 1.

the several capitals, the Spanish physicians would instruct local practitioners and facilitate extension of the vaccine to the provinces.[23]

The expedition to New Spain would transmit the vaccine to Havana, Puerto Rico, and Guatemala. The Peruvian mission would first stop in Cartagena, Portobello, and Panama. The other delegation would proceed directly to Buenos Aires. Although Bajamar stipulated that the expedition carry "legitimate pus" from Spain, he did not indicate a mode of transportation of the fluid.[24]

Bajamar noted that epidemics often decimated one-third to one-half of a province. As a result of the decreased population, tribute diminished, commerce stagnated, fields lay unattended, and mine production declined with consequent reduction in royal income. He proposed, therefore, that the Royal Treasury absorb all expenses for the expedition. Long-range benefits would ultimately repay the investment.[25]

The king approved Bajamar's suggestions and on June 6 instructed the *Junta de Cirujanos de Cámara* (Council of Chamber Surgeons), composed of Antonio Gimbernat, Ignacio Lacaba y Vila, and Leonardo Galli, to select three physicians to direct expeditions to Buenos Aires, Mexico, and Lima. The Junta, together with these appointees, should then determine salaries and immediate funds required to begin organization of the expedition.[26]

To transport the vaccine, the royal instructions continued, each physician should take a sufficient number of non-immune boys from the *Casa de Niños Expósitos* (Foundling Home) and the Casa de Desamparados in Madrid. These children would remain in the care of the viceroys until they found a suitable position or reached legal age.[27]

The Spanish physicians would instruct local practitioners in vaccination techniques and dispatch the virus to the provincial capitals and principal cities of each viceroyalty. A royal order would impress the viceroys with the importance of the mission and encourage bishops and other clergy to give it their complete support.[28]

On June 7 José Antonio Cavallero, minister of the Office of Grace and Justice, who assumed ultimate charge of the expedition, wrote to Don Lorenzo Berges in Cádiz. Cavallero explained that since the king was sending three more physicians to the other viceroyalties, Berges should postpone his trip and join the rest of the expedition in Madrid. Such action would insure uniformity of procedure throughout the American colonies.[29] The order reached Cádiz on June 14, but by that time Berges had already sailed for Santa Fé de Bogotá.[30]

BALMIS'S "REGULATION" AND "ITINERARY"

Soon after Cavallero communicated the Royal Order of June 6 to the Junta, Dr. Francisco Xavier de Balmis volunteered to serve as director of the expedition and presented to Cavallero the rough drafts of a "Regulation" and "Itinerary" which he had formulated to guide its organization. In March the Council of the Indies had requested the Protomedicato to seek a complete set of instructions to guide and govern the organization of the expedition.[31] Balmis's plan was one of the few submitted. Impressed with the project, Cavallero suggested that Balmis send him a copy of the final draft.[32]

On June 18 Cavallero received Balmis's project,[33] and after dicussing it with the king, forwarded it to the Junta de Cirujanos de Cámara. He requested that the Junta determine the plan's feasibility and Balmis's qualifications for the position of director.[34] This project, although slightly altered later, provided the technical data required to complete steps in the formation of the expedition.

The "Regulation" provided for a director, two assistants, two male nurses, and fifteen to twenty non-immune boys for progressive inoculation during the voyage. Since Balmis's plan indicated that the expedition would leave from La Coruña, the Casa de Niños Expósitos and the *Hospicio de Pobres* (Poorhouse) in Santiago de Compostela could provide the young boys.[35]

The "Regulation" also outlined the duties of each member of the expedition. The director would assume full responsibility for the success or failure of the venture; therefore, he would exercise complete authority. His duties were manifold. Besides supervising the

---

[23] Marqués de Bajamar, "Dictamen del Gobernador del Consejo de Indias en el Expediente de extender en América el uso de la vacuna, en el que S.M. ha mandado al Consejo proponga los arbitrios que estime conveniente así para costear los profesores que deben ejecutar esta operación, como acerca del modo de verificarla," Madrid, 26 Mayo 1803, AGI, "Indif. Gen.," Leg. 1.558, I, f. 1.

[24] *Ibid.*, fs. 1–2.

[25] *Ibid.*, fs. 2–3.

[26] Cavallero to Antonio Gimbernat, Aranjuez, 6 Junio 1803, AGI, "Indif. Gen.," Leg. 1.558, I, fs. 2–3.

[27] *Ibid.*, fs. 3–4.

[28] *Ibid.*, fs. 4–5.

[29] Cavallero to Berges, Aranjuez, 7 Junio 1803, AGI, "Indif. Gen.," Leg. 1.558, I, fs. 1–2.

[30] A photostatic copy of the above-mentioned letter shows that Berges left Cádiz for Santa Fé de Bogotá on June 14. AGI, "Indif. Gen.," Leg. 1.558, I, f. 1.

[31] *Supra*, n. 1, p. 12.

[32] Cavallero to Junta de Cirujanos de Cámara, Aranjuez, 20 Junio 1803, AGI, "Indif. Gen.," Leg. 1.558, I, fs. 1–3.

[33] Balmis to Cavallero, Madrid, 18 Junio 1803, AGI, "Indif. Gen.," Leg. 1.558, II, fs. 1–3.

[34] Cavallero to Junta de Cirujanos de Cámara, Aranjuez, 2 Junio 1803, AGI, "Indif. Gen.," Leg. 1.558, I, f. 2.

[35] Francisco Xavier de Balmis, "Reglamento que deberán observar los empleados en la expedición destinada a conducir y propagar la inoculación de la verdadera vacuna en los Quatro Virreinatos de América, Provincias de Yucatán y Caracas, y en las Islas Antillas," Madrid, 18 Junio 1803, AGI, "Indif. Gen.," Leg. 1.558, I, f. 1.

vaccination of all who desired it, he would instruct physicians in the operation and distribute copies of Balmis's *Tratado histórico y práctico de la vacuna* to serve as a vaccination manual. He would keep a complete record of his operations and the effects upon the vaccination vesicle produced by changing climates, altitudes, temperatures, and race mixtures. After his return to Spain, the director would publish a complete account of his experience for the public's enlightenment.[36]

The assistants, his principal lieutenants, were to be sufficiently instructed in vaccination procedures to assume leadership of secondary expeditions or to replace the director if necessary. During subsidiary missions they would compile minute records of their activities and later incorporate them into the director's general report. Besides supervising the expedition's dispensary and instruments, they would serve as surgeons for all employees.[37]

The male nurses would assume direct responsibility for the children's cleanliness and good health. They were to watch the boys constantly and prevent them from accidentally destroying their vesicles.[38]

According to Balmis's "Itinerary," the expedition would sail from La Coruña to Veracruz via Tenerife, Puerto Rico, La Guayra, Havana, Campeche, and Mérida. From Veracruz the expedition would continue on to Mexico, passing through Xalapa and Puebla. After establishing a reserve of vaccine in the capital and provincial centers, the expedition would proceed to Lima from Acapulco. A sufficient number of boys would be gathered from the Real Hospicio de Pobres in Mexico to transmit the vaccine to Lima. From Lima three subdivisions would spread the preservative to Buenos Aires, Quito, and Chile. Balmis suggested that if the king so desired, a portion of the expedition could proceed from Acapulco to the Philippine Islands and introduce vaccination into Spain's oriental dominions.[39]

On June 23 the Junta de Cirujanos de Cámara reported that it had approved Balmis's project and recommended that he direct the expedition. His plan, the Junta noted, promised the greatest chance of success and was, in fact, quite similar to one which they themselves had envisioned. The Junta especially praised the advantages of a single, unified expedition over three separate ones. The members did, however, offer a few minor modifications.[40]

The Junta's major revisions included the addition of two assistants. Since the trip would be long and hazardous, one or more of the members might become ill or die, thus handicapping the expedition or frustrating it entirely. In addition, the Junta believed that the personnel recommended by Balmis was inadequate to staff the several subdivisions he had mentioned in his "Itinerary." The Junta also proposed that the expedition always carry some vaccine "in vitro" to insure a constant supply of virus. The expedition could distribute three or four hundred pairs of glass slides containing vaccine among physicians in the various American ports and in this way transmit the lymph where it was impossible to do so arm to arm.[41]

The Junta appointed José Salvany, Ramón Fernández de Ochoa, and Manuel Julián Grajales as assistants. Salvany, surgeon of the Real Sitio de Aranjuez and a graduate of the Real Colegio de Barcelona, was to serve as assistant director. The assistants would receive an annual salary of one thousand pesos, beginning with their departure from Madrid and continuing until their return. The Junta also noted that, since Balmis was not personally acquainted with his assistants, he should be allowed to choose men of his own confidence as male nurses.[42]

FRANCISCO XAVIER DE BALMIS Y BERENGUER

Balmis's experience thoroughly prepared him to direct the expedition. The fifty-year-old native of Alicante was honorary physician of the King's Chamber, honorary consulting surgeon of the Royal Armies, professor of medicine, and corresponding member of the Royal Medical Academy of Madrid. In 1775 he had accompanied the punitive naval expedition led by General Alejandro O'Reilly against the Algerian pirates. After this adventure he returned to the Real Colegio de Valencia, from which he was graduated in 1778.[43] In 1780, during the siege of Gibraltar, he served as first army surgical assistant.[44]

Upon his return to Spain, Balmis joined the First Infantry Battalion of Zamora in the Army of Operations, which had been ordered to America under the command of Bernardo de Gálvez. After a brief tour in Guarico, Balmis moved with his battalion to Havana where he helped organize the new Hospital General. He performed his duties so well that Gálvez personally commended him to King Carlos III. In September, 1783, Balmis's battalion was transferred to Veracruz to reinforce the Spanish garrison.[45]

[36] *Ibid.*, fs. 2–5.

[37] *Ibid.*, fs. 6–7.

[38] *Ibid.*, f. 8.

[39] Francisco Xavier de Balmis, "Derrotero para conducir con la más posible brevedad la verdadera vacuna y asegurar su feliz propagación en los Quatro Virreinatos de América, Provincias de Yucatán y Caracas, y en las Islas Antillas," Madrid, 18 Junio 1803, AGI, "Indif. Gen.," Leg. 1.558, I, fs. 1–4.

[40] Junta de Cirujanos de Cámara to Cavallero, Aranjuez, 23 Junio 1803, AGI, "Indif. Gen.," Leg. 1.558, I, fs. 1–2.

[41] *Ibid.*, fs. 2–3.

[42] *Ibid.*, fs. 6–8.

[43] Díaz de Iraola, 1947: p. 6.

[44] Ildefonso Arias de Saavedra to Matías de Gálvez, México, 12 Noviembre 1783, AGN, "Historia," v. 195, exp. 2, fs. 4–4v.

[45] Balmis to Martín de Mayorga, México, 17 Enero 1784, AGN, "Historia," v. 195, exp. 2, fs. 7–7v.

From November, 1787, to April, 1788, at the request of Archbishop Alonzo Núñez de Haro y Peralta of Mexico, Balmis served as chief surgeon in Mexico City's Hospital del Amor de Dios, which specialized in the treatment of syphilitics.[46] In late 1788 Balmis retired from the army and traveled throughout Mexico studying indigenous plants and investigating the curative qualities of medicinal herbs.[47]

Coincidental with Balmis's experiments with native plants, Nicolás Viana, "El Beato," a healer from Pátzcuaro, was promoting an Indian remedy for venereal disease in Mexico City. Viana claimed that he had successfully employed the concotion, whose principal ingredients were the roots of the begonia and maguey plants, for thirty-six years. A series of experiments under the careful observation of the Protomedicato in the Hospital de San Juan de Dios convinced medical authorities of the remedy's value.[48]

Balmis had learned of the native treatment soon after his arrival in Veracruz, but he doubted its efficacy. In late 1790 Núñez de Haro y Peralta appointed Balmis to supervise the syphilitic ward in the Hospital de San Andrés. Experimenting with Viana's remedy, by June, 1791, Balmis claimed to have cured 323 patients afflicted with various venereal diseases. In the meantime he had perfected and simplified the method by eliminating most of Viana's questionable ingredients such as sundry appendages of frogs and insects and other non-medicinal additives.[49]

In November, 1791, the archbishop commissioned Balmis to introduce the new treatment into Spain. Balmis requested a license from the viceroy on November 12,[50] and in January, 1792, sailed for the peninsula. Among his baggage were one hundred arrobas[51] of maguey and thirty arrobas of begonia. In July, 1792, he received permission from the king to begin his experiments, under the supervision of the Protomedicato, in Madrid's Hospital de San Juan de Dios, Hospital General, and the Hospital de la Pasión.[52]

Although Balmis believed that his experiments conclusively proved the plants' therapeutic value, a special commission appointed to examine his work denounced him as a charlatan.[53] Balmis answered his critics with an extensive dissertation entitled *Demostración de las eficaces virtudes nuevamente descubiertas en las raíces de dos plantas de Nueva España, especies de agave y de begonia para la curación del vicio venéreo y escro-*

fuloso y de otras graves enfermedades que resisten al uso de mercurio, y demás remedios conocidos. Basically a procedural instruction, it contained detailed case studies of Balmis's work in Madrid. Although twentieth-century physicians find it difficult to accept Balmis's claims for the plants' curative powers,[54] his method did gain some contemporary acceptance. The Pope ordered that the treatment be employed in at least one hospital in Rome.[55] Some physicians who had utilized the remedy claimed that in addition to curing syphilis, the begonia and maguey would cure a variety of cutaneous eruptions, gout, arthritis, dropsy, and visceral obstructions.[56] In recognition of Balmis's efforts in bringing the begonia to Europe and his extensive writings on its medicinal value, the plant was officially designated as the *Begonia balmisiana* in the botanical dictionary, *Flora mexicana*.[57]

Balmis continued his experiments and returned to Mexico three times to further his study.[58] In 1795 he was named honorary surgeon of the Chamber of Carlos IV, and in 1799 received his degree as doctor of medicine.[59] Balmis had quickly accepted Jenner's theory and was soon one of the most famous vaccinators in Madrid. In early 1803 he gained further acclaim for his *Tratado histórico y práctico de la vacuna*. A translation of J. L. Moreau de la Sarthe's work, it was the most complete study of vaccination at that time.

ORGANIZATION AND DEPARTURE OF THE ROYAL EXPEDITION

On June 28, 1803, Balmis received the appointment as director of the "Real Expedición Marítima de la Vacuna" with an annual salary of two thousand pesos.[60] His assistants were also notified of their selection,[61] and the minister of the navy was ordered to prepare a ship for the transportation of the expedition.[62]

In his letter of acknowledgment of July 2 Balmis named Basilio Bolaños, Angel Crespo, and Pedro Ortega as male nurses. He also requested three additional aides, suggesting Antonio Gutiérrez y Robredo as a fourth assistant, and Francisco Pastor y Balmis and Rafael Lozano y Pérez as practitioners. Gutiérrez, a graduate of the Colegio de San Carlos, and Pastor, Balmis's nephew, had assisted him in Madrid. Lozano

[46] Balmis to Manuel Antonio Flores, México, 21 Enero 1789, AGN, "Historia," v. 233, exp. 12, f. 2.
[47] Balmis to Conde de Revillagigedo, México, n.d., AGN, "Historia," v. 233, exp. 14, f. 3v.
[48] Balmis, 1794: pp. 1–2.
[49] Ibid., p. 19.
[50] Balmis to Conde de Revillagigedo, México, 12 Noviembre 1791, AGN, "Historia," v. 460, f. 108.
[51] An arroba equals approximately twenty-five pounds.
[52] Balmis, 1794: pp. 19–21.
[53] Ibid., pp. 20–23.
[54] Fernández del Castillo, 1960: p. 25.
[55] Gaceta de México, 12 Noviembre 1795: p. 498.
[56] Ibid., 13 Julio 1796: pp. 115–116.
[57] Balmis, 1794: p. 343.
[58] Díaz de Iraola, 1947: p. 15.
[59] Martínez Durán, 1964: p. 477.
[60] Balmis to Cavallero, Madrid, 2 Julio 1803, AGI, "Indif. Gen.," Leg. 1.558, I, fs. 1–3.
[61] Cavallero to Pedro Ceballos, Palacio, 30 Junio 1803, AGI, "Indif. Gen.," Leg. 1.558, I, f. 1.
[62] Cavallero to Grandallana, Palacio, 30 Junio 1803, AGI, "Indif. Gen.," Leg. 1.558, I, fs. 2–3.

y Pérez also had considerable experience with vaccination.[63]

Balmis complained that the Junta had been extremely frugal in its salary allotments. His experience in America, where everything was much more expensive than in Spain, convinced him that the pay was entirely inadequate. He suggested doubling the salaries of the director and assistants. The practitioners should receive one thousand pesos and the male nurses eight hundred.[64]

Balmis further requested a complete dispensary, a number of thermometers and barometers to make daily meteorological observations, two thousand vials, and a pneumatic machine to vacuum-seal the vials. He suggested that his assistants wear the uniform used in the army hospitals and the male nurses, those worn by the porters of the Royal Botanic Garden and the Natural History Laboratory. In view of the voluminous correspondence he would maintain during the course of the expedition, he requested franking privileges.[65]

To insure the quality of the vaccine, Balmis suggested that the five boys from the Casa de Desamparados in Madrid, who would form the first links in the chain of inoculations from Spain to America, be vaccinated with lymph extracted from children whom he himself had previously immunized.[66]

Balmis also revised his original "Itinerary" to include Santa Fé de Bogotá. He doubted that Berges alone could have successfully introduced the vaccine into that viceroyalty. Evidently Berges had attempted to transport the lymph in vials, a practice which had repeatedly failed in the past.[67]

Although the king granted most of Balmis's requests, he did not increase the salaries.[68] The director's salary remained two thousand pesos, beginning with his departure from Madrid until his return. Thereafter, until he secured a position appropriate to his standing, he would receive half-pay in addition to an immediate subsidy of two hundred doubloons to purchase a suitable outfit. Assistants would earn exactly one half of what the director received. Practitioners enjoyed a salary of six hundred pesos, male nurses five hundred. They also would receive half-pay after their return to Madrid and until they were established, together with an immediate fifty doubloons for personal equipment.[69]

Since the expedition was scheduled to depart from La Coruña in early August, Balmis spent July making the final preparations.[70] He directed the printing of five hundred copies of his *Tratado histórico,* which he would distribute to physicians in the New World. He supervised the collection of medical supplies, construction of the instruments for meteorological observation, production of the vials, provision of outfits for the children, and preparation of transportation from Madrid to La Coruña. Directors of the Casa de Desamparados in Madrid and the Casa de Niños Expósitos in Santiago selected the boys who would accompany the expedition. Isabel Gómez y Cendala, rectoress of the latter institution, was chosen to care for the children during the journey to America.[71] And the *Gaceta de Madrid* publicly announced the formation of the Royal Expedition.[72]

An immediate problem arose concerning the selection of a ship. Domingo Grandallana, minister of the navy, had been instructed on June 30 to provide a vessel from the Royal Armada. He replied on July 4 that the only available ships of the type required by the expedition were packet ships and that even those were scarce. Grandallana believed that a merchant craft would be more satisfactory and cost far less to maintain than a fully armed vessel of the Armada.[73] Therefore, on July 27 Cavallero ordered the port judge of La Coruña to secure a merchant ship of approximately 250 tons. He was to negotiate a contract as soon as possible under the terms most advantageous to the Royal Treasury.[74]

On July 29 Cavallero communicated a series of instructions to Miguel Cayetano Soler, minister of the Royal Treasury, and informed him of the current status of the preparations. He also ordered Soler to arrange payment of the expedition's immediate expenses and notify the viceroys of its impending departure.[75] After reducing these instructions to a circular on August 4, Soler communicated the first official announcement of the expedition to the colonies.[76]

On September 1 Cavallero dispatched detailed directives to the viceroys of New Spain, Peru, Buenos Aires, and Santa Fé; the commandant general of the Interior Provinces; the captains general of the Canary Islands, Philippine Islands, and Caracas; and the governors of Havana and Puerto Rico. The orders contained a

[63] Balmis to Cavallero, Madrid, 2 Julio 1803, AGI, "Indif. Gen.," Leg. 1.558, I, f. 13.

[64] *Ibid.,* fs. 2–13.

[65] *Ibid.,* fs. 15–21.

[66] *Ibid.,* fs. 15–17.

[67] Francisco Xavier de Balmis, "Suplemento al Derrotero dado para propagar la vacuna desde la América Septentrional a la meridional, y las Islas Filipinas," Madrid, 2 Julio 1803, AGI, "Indif. Gen.," Leg. 1.558, I, fs. 1–4.

[68] Cavallero to Balmis, Palacio, 28 Julio 1803, AGN, "Epidemias," v. 17, fs. 333–334v.

[69] Cavallero to Soler, Palacio, 29 Junio 1803, AGI, "Indif. Gen.," Leg. 1.558, I, f. 4.

[70] Cavallero to Grandallana, Palacio, 30 Junio 1803, AGI, "Indif. Gen.," Leg. 1.558, I, f. 4.

[71] Díaz de Iraola, 1947: p. 35.

[72] "Decreto," Palacio, 31 Julio 1803, AGI, "Indif. Gen.," Leg. 1.558, I, f. 3.

[73] Grandallana to Cavallero, Palacio, 4 Junio 1803, AGI, "Indif. Gen.," Leg. 1.558, I, fs. 1–3.

[74] "Extracto," fs. 36–38.

[75] Cavallero to Soler, Palacio, 29 Julio 1803, AGI, "Indif. Gen.," Leg. 1.558, I, fs. 1–3.

[76] Miguel Cayetano Soler, *Circular,* San Ildefonso, 4 Agosto 1803, AGI, "Indif. Gen.," Leg. 1.558, I, fs. 1–2.

basic text followed by precise instructions to meet local conditions.[77]

Delayed by the many unforeseen obstacles which could be expected in an undertaking of such magnitude, Balmis was still in Madrid by late August. On August 24, however, he announced that the expedition was fully equipped and ready to begin the trip to La Coruña.[78] He presented a list of his staff and their salaries, noting a monthly allotment for support of their families in Spain.[79] Balmis declared that he needed his full salary, but would assign his income as honorary consultant to the royal armies to maintain his wife. He also reported that Angel Crespo was unable to accompany the expedition and nominated Antonio Pastor y Balmis to replace him as male nurse.[80] Finally he requested lodging for his entire retinue in the Augustinian Convent in La Coruña.[81]

Still in Madrid on September 7, Balmis noted the state of war between France and Great Britain and solicited passes of safe-conduct from each of the belligerents to insure the expedition's unmolested travel. The king informed him that safe-conducts would be provided as soon as Balmis presented the names of the ship and its owner.[82]

Balmis finally reached La Coruña on September 21.[83] On October 1 he presented a formal bill of 94,853 reales for the expedition's preparatory expenses.[84] However, he still faced a series of problems and nearly two months of further delay before the expedition actually sailed.

The principal difficulty was the lack of a ship. The port judge had been instructed on July 27 to secure an appropriate vessel and prepare it for the expedition's departure. On August 1 he presented the proposals of José de Becerra, owner of the four-hundred-ton frigate *Silph,* and Tavanera y Sobrinos, owners of the *María Pita,* a 160-ton corvette. The *Silph* did not qualify because it was too large, but the port judge was instructed

to lease the *María Pita* or any other ship he deemed suitable.[85] Inexplicably, by the end of September he still had not acquired a vessel. In the meantime Balmis arrived in La Coruña and sought a ship on his own. Balmis stated on October 1 that of all the vessels he had inspected, none was more suited for the expedition than the frigate *San José,* owned by Manuel de Goycoechea. Goycoechea had bid two thousand pesos per month less than anyone else and offered the lowest prices for passenger accommodations. He would not, furthermore, begin charges until the ship actually embarked. Under these circumstances Balmis signed a contract obliging Goycoechea to present his craft in La Coruña by October 8. The owner assured him that after some minor repairs the *San José* would arrive promptly.[86] The king approved the transaction and authorized the port judge to finalize negotiations.[87]

The *San José* did not reach La Coruña by the stipulated date, however, and Balmis immediately instructed the port judge to engage the *María Pita,* which after the *San José* presented the most advantageous conditions. The port judge submitted this new contract for royal approval on October 12.[88] On October 21 the king authorized these arrangements and at the same time instructed the minister of the Royal Treasury to advance the ship-owners three months' pay to outfit and provision the vessel. He also ordered Soler to secure the safe-conducts.[89]

Lodging in La Coruña presented another difficulty. Balmis had earlier requested that his entire staff be lodged in the Augustinian Convent.[90] Arriving in La Coruña, he found that the governor had arranged for them to stay in the Charity Hospital. Balmis, who detested the conditions which existed in establishments of public charity, refused to stay there. He left only the children from Madrid and Santiago in the hospital and sought more suitable accommodations for himself and his staff in private homes.[91]

On November 2 Balmis reported that the contemptuous attitude of Ramón Fernández de Ochoa toward his colleagues and his open disrespect for the director were causing dissension within the staff. Fernández de Ochoa was evidently angry because Salvany, not he, would serve as assistant director. Carlos IV authorized Balmis to dismiss Fernández de Ochoa immediately and require him to repay any advance salary he had received. The king further declared that Balmis could take similar action against any other member who was dissatisfied

[77] José Antonio Cavallero, original draft of "La resolución del Rey sobre la propagación de la vacuna en aquellos dominios y medios adaptados para conseguir el objeto," San Ildefonso, 1 Septiembre 1803, AGI, "Indif. Gen.," Leg. 1.558, II, 34 fs.

[78] "Extracto," fs. 32–33v.

[79] Francisco Xavier de Balmis, "Lista de los empleados en la expedición de la vacuna, sus dotaciones y asignaciones que dejan a sus familias en España con expresión de sus nombres, Pueblos de su residencia en donde las han de percibir, y el líquido haber que deberá recibir en América cada individuo," Madrid, 21 Agosto 1803, AGN, "Epidemias," v. 10, exp. 7, f. 5.

[80] It is not clear why Crespo did not retain his original appointment since he did accompany the expedition. Miguel Lerdo de Tejada, who knew Crespo personally, states that he served as Balmis's secretary and kept the diary of the expedition. He did receive a belated appointment as male nurse just prior to the trip to the Philippines. Lerdo de Tejada, 1850: 1: p. 342.

[81] "Extracto," fs. 32–33v.

[82] *Ibid.,* fs. 52–53v.

[83] *Ibid.,* f. 38.

[84] *Ibid.,* f. 53v.

[85] *Ibid.,* f. 37.

[86] *Ibid.,* fs. 38–39.

[87] *Ibid.,* f. 39v.

[88] *Ibid.,* fs. 40–40v.

[89] *Ibid.,* f. 41.

[90] *Ibid.,* f. 33v.

[91] *Ibid.,* fs. 34–35.

with the existing arrangements. Fernández de Ochoa was formally dismissed on November 29.[92]

On November 30, 1803, the Balmis expedition, composed of the director, three assistants, two practitioners, three male nurses, a secretary, the ex-rectoress, and twenty-two young boys, sailed from La Coruña in the *María Pita,* which was commanded by Pedro del Barco. Of the twenty-two children who accompanied the expedition to New Spain, the names of twenty-one are known. Since all were taken from the Casa de Niños Expósitos in Santiago, few had surnames. Their names and ages upon arrival in Mexico are as follows: Vicente Ferrer (seven), Pascual Aniceto (three), Martín (three), Juan Francisco (nine), Tomás Metitón (three), Juan Antonio (five), José Jorge Nicolás de los Dolores (three), Antonio Veredia (seven), Francisco Antonio (nine), Clemente (six), Manuel María (three), José Manuel María (six), Domingo Naya (six), Andrés Naya (eight), José (three), Vicente María Sale y Vellido (three), Cándido (seven), Francisco Florencio (five), Gerónimo María (seven), and Jacinto (six).[93] Benito Vélez, the adopted son of Isabel Gómez y Cendala, was the other identified child.[94] These twenty-two innocents formed the most vital element of the most ambitious medical enterprise any government had ever undertaken.[95]

III. THE VOYAGE FROM SPAIN TO AMERICA

THE CANARY ISLANDS

According to the "Itinerary" the expedition's first stop would be Santa Cruz de Tenerife in the Canary Islands. In addition to the numerous official entourage, the party included a variety of menials to service the compartments and attend members of the expedition, especially the children.[1] Since the 160-ton *María Pita* was considerably smaller than the 250-ton vessel envisioned for the voyage, conditions aboard were crowded.[2]

The most vital concern during the crossing was sustaining the chain of inoculations. Two boys would be vaccinated every ninth or tenth day; thus if one destroyed his vaccination vesicle or otherwise rendered it ineffective, the other was available for subsequent inoculations. Twenty-two boys were sufficient to transmit the vaccine to America, but they did require con-

stant attention. The children would be sorely tempted to scratch the itching vaccination. Besides, the virus could be transferred by accidental contact with one of the non-immune boys, especially as they slept in their congested quarters. To protect the vaccine and the supply of repositories, members of the expedition maintained a day and night vigil over them.[3]

Little record exists of the expedition's activities in the Canaries. Documents in the Sevillan archives do not indicate when the expedition arrived or what it accomplished. Balmis later informed Benito Pérez y Valdelomas, captain general of Campeche, that the captain general of the Canary Islands, Marqués de Casa-Cagigal, and an enthusiastic public cordially received the mission. He reported only that he had "satisfactory results."[4] In Tenerife Balmis realized that five hundred copies of his *Tratado histórico* were insufficient for the entire trip. He requested that Juan Lázaro, his attorney in Madrid, order two thousand more copies printed at Balmis's expense and forward them to Havana with the next mail. On the afternoon of January 6, 1804, the expedition departed for the Antilles.[5]

PUERTO RICO: THE FIRST CONFRONTATION

Thirty-four days later, on February 9, 1804, the expedition anchored in Puerto Rico. An aide of the governor, Brigadier General Ramón de Castro, welcomed Balmis and accompanied the delegation to the accommodations prepared by the Ayuntamiento. In spite of the paucity of city funds, the municipal council liberally provided members of the expedition with houses, servants, and food.[6] The vaccine had arrived in optimum conditions, and Balmis eagerly anticipated the triumph of being the first physician to vaccinate in Spanish America.

One can imagine Balmis's shock when he discovered that the vaccine had preceded him. In 1803, with a new epidemic threatening the island, Governor Castro learned that encrusted lymph had been taken from England to the Danish island of St. Thomas. After several unsuccessful attempts, he obtained the virus from the neighboring island by means of a recently vaccinated two-year-old slave girl. Castro immediately commissioned Dr. Francisco Oller, a surgeon in the Military Hospital, aided by Dr. Tomás Prieto, to propagate the preservative. Within twenty-three days the two physicians had vaccinated 1,557 persons, including Oller's own son, the Bishop-Elect Juan Alejo Arizmendi, and

[92] *Ibid.,* fs. 51–52.
[93] Pascual Portillo, "Lista de los Niños que por Real Orden de S.M. vinieron de España con la Expedición de la Vacuna," México, 27 Junio 1809, AGN, "Filipinas." v. **53**, exp. 15, fs. 374–374v.
[94] Antonio Batres to Viceroy, México, 8 Agosto 1811, AGN, "Epidemias," v. **17**, f. 327.
[95] Fernández del Castillo, 1960: p. 21.
[1] Balmis to Cavallero, Madrid, 4 Diciembre 1806, AGI, "Indif. Gen.," Leg. 1.558, II, f. 2.
[2] "Extracto," f. 47v.

[3] Balmis to Iturrigaray, México, 14 Enero 1805, AGN, "Epidemias," v. **4**, exp. 13, f. 30.
[4] Balmis to Benito Pérez, Puerto Rico, 28 Febrero 1804, AGN, "Epidemias," v. **4**, exp. 10, fs. 3v–4.
[5] "Extracto," fs. 68v–69. In a letter to Cavallero, Balmis later reported that he had actually printed seven hundred copies. Balmis to Cavallero, Madrid, 4 Diciembre 1806, AGI, "Indif. Gen.," Leg. 1.558, II, f. 2.
[6] Brau, 1966: pp. 530–532.

Governor Castro's two young daughters.[7] On December 21, 1803, Castro proudly informed the Spanish government of Oller's achievements.[8]

Deprived of his glory, Balmis reacted with anger and suspicion. After a perfunctory examination, he denounced Oller's vaccine as spurious and derided the physician as the most incompetent person possible to assume such a grave responsibility.[9] He charged, furthermore, that the governor's only interest in securing the vaccine was to gain merit in Madrid.[10] Balmis then distributed placards denouncing Oller's operations.[11]

Oller, however, stoutly defended his vaccine and challenged Balmis to prove his accusations by revaccination with his own lymph. Balmis's vaccine failed to react in Oller's son and the bishop-elect, and he refused to continue the test.[12]

Irritated by his tardy arrival and the increasing coolness of his hosts, Balmis prepared to leave the island. He reneged on his promises to extend the protection to parts of the island where the disease was still active and to offer public lectures explaining vaccination.[13] On March 12, 1804, after entrusting his remaining vaccine to the governor, he departed for La Guayra.[14]

Balmis's four-week stay in Puerto Rico had been a total failure. He failed to introduce vaccine into the island. He failed to establish an agency to conserve and propagate the virus. And he failed to instruct the local physicians in the techniques of vaccination. He did, however, totally alienate the local government and medical community. In addition Balmis revealed an egotism and vindictiveness which augered ill for the remainder of his mission and diminished the stature of the expedition. Instead of departing from Puerto Rico with the gratitude of its people, Balmis left behind the indelible image of "a man more swelled with his own official position than identified with the beneficent significance of his task." [15]

PUERTO CABELLO, CARACAS, AND LA GUAYRA

On March 20, after an uneventful eight-day voyage, the expedition reached Puerto Cabello. Balmis reported that the entire mission was in jeopardy since only one vaccinated boy remained, and he was ready to transmit the virus at the time of their arrival. He blamed the shortage of carriers on Governor Castro's refusal to provide the boys he had requested in Puerto Rico.[16]

Fortunately, favorable winds had accelerated their trip, and upon arrival Balmis immediately vaccinated twenty-eight children of the Venezuelan port's leading families.[17]

To complete his mission more quickly, especially after learning of the death of Lorenzo Berges in Santa Fé de Bogotá, Balmis decided to divide the expedition when it reached La Guayra. One portion, under the direction of José Salvany, would travel throughout the viceroyalties of Santa Fé, Peru, and Buenos Aires. Balmis would lead the other half from La Guayra to New Spain via Cuba.[18]

In the meantime Balmis dispatched Manuel Grajales with part of the expedition to La Guayra in order to introduce the vaccine along the coast. The director, Salvany, and most of the other members went on to Caracas. On April 3 the captain general of Caracas, Manuel Guevara Vasconcelos, and the Ayuntamiento enthusiastically received Balmis and his party. The Ayuntamiento had generously allotted eight thousand pesos to pay the expedition's expenses during its stay in the province. It had also sent deputies to accompany Grajales during his journey to La Guayra.[19]

Balmis's sojourn in Caracas was pleasant and productive. On April 5, when the children's vesicles had matured, inoculations commenced. In three days Balmis and Salvany vaccinated 2,064 persons. After the first vaccination session the Ayuntamiento arranged an elaborate celebration in honor of the expedition. An orchestra, composed of "all individuals in the city who had, or claimed to have, musical talent," provided the entertainment.[20]

When more lymph was available, inoculations continued. Practitioners from surrounding villages observed Balmis's operations and took vaccinated children back to their own towns to spread the preservative. Balmis conducted sessions to instruct local physicians in the method of inoculation and the conservation and propagation of the virus.[21]

In accordance with a plan submitted by Balmis, the first *Junta Central de la Vacuna* (Central Vaccination Board) in America was established in Caracas. The Junta, composed of leading civil and ecclesiastical personalities, was charged with the perpetuation of the vaccine and its propagation to all parts of the province.[22] The formation of the Junta was celebrated in the cathedral on April 22 with a solemn *Te Deum*. The captain

[7] *Ibid.*
[8] "Extracto," fs. 76–76v.
[9] Brau, 1966: p. 531.
[10] "Extracto," f. 77.
[11] Brau, 1966: p. 531.
[12] *Ibid.*
[13] *Ibid.,* p. 532.
[14] "Extracto," f. 78v.
[15] Brau, 1966: p. 530.
[16] Brau on the other hand claims that Balmis had obtained a sufficient number of children in San Juan under the pretext of

taking them only to Mexico. Once aboard the ship, however, Balmis announced his intention of going to La Guayra. At this point the parents protested and refused to allow the children to accompany the expedition. *Ibid.,* p. 532.
[17] "Extracto," fs. 81v–82.
[18] *Ibid.,* fs. 82v–83v.
[19] *Ibid.,* fs. 83v–84v.
[20] Manuel Guevara Vasconcelos to Soler, Caracas, 9 Mayo 1804, AGI, "Indif. Gen.," Leg. 1.558, I, fs. 1–4.
[21] *Ibid.,* fs. 4–6.
[22] The composition and obligations of the juntas will be discussed in full below.

general, Audiencia, and all leading corporations of the capital took part in the ceremonies.[23]

By April 29 Balmis reported that he and Salvany had vaccinated over twelve thousand persons in Caracas and announced that he was preparing to go on to La Guayra. When he left Caracas on May 6 his recent success had erased the chagrin of his venture in Puerto Rico. In recognition of Balmis's achievements in Caracas the Ayuntamiento named him an honorary regidor.[24]

The expedition divided in La Guayra as planned. Manuel Grajales, Rafael Lozano, and Basilio Bolaños accompanied Salvany. Before their separation Balmis gave Salvany a detailed set of instructions. He advised his assistant director to establish juntas in each viceregal and provincial capital, patterning them after the Junta Central in Caracas. He recommended union and *esprit de corps* among members of the mission, efficiency and exactitude in the performance of their duties, and deference to colonial administrators. He suggested that Salvany devise a complete itinerary of each province and confer with local officials concerning the best means to distribute the vaccine. Salvany should study the effects of vaccination on other diseases and record in detail the natural history, industry, arts, flora and fauna, medicine, and disease of each area he visited.[25] Balmis then turned northward toward Cuba, while Salvany embarked for the southern regions of the Spanish American Empire. They never saw each other again.[26]

CUBA

Balmis originally planned to sail from La Guayra to Santiago de Cuba, but tempestuous weather forced him on to Havana where the *María Pita* anchored on May 26. The difficult trip had broken the children's health. Once again Balmis found that the vaccine had preceded him.[27]

On February 4, 1802, the Economic Society of Havana had received a copy of Pedro Hernández's *Origen y descubrimiento de la vacuna* from Madrid. The Society sent the copy to Tomás Romay y Chacón, a prominent physician of the capital, for his opinion of its value. Romay highly praised the work, noting that it was the first treatise on vaccination ever received in the island. He proposed an immediate search for the cowpox in order to begin inoculations as soon as possible. The governor and captain general of Cuba, Salvador Muro Salazar, Marqués de Someruelos, enthusiastically supported Romay's suggestions and provided ample funds for his experiments. Romay

requested the lymph from Spain and the United States and initiated a search for cowpox virus on the island. A year passed without results. On March 23, 1803, however, Don Felipe Facio gave Someruelos three vials containing vaccine he had brought from Philadelphia. Romay immediately vaccinated his own children, but by that time the virus had deteriorated. Another year passed in a fruitless search for the preservative.[28]

The vaccine arrived in Havana quite by chance, however, on February 10, 1804. Doña María Bustamante had left Aguadilla, Puerto Rico, on February 2. The day before her departure her ten-year-old son and two young mulatto maids had been vaccinated. When they reached Havana the virus was in an ideal condition for transmission. On February 12, Romay inoculated his own five children and thirty-five others with lymph from the three carriers.[29] By March 26 he had vaccinated nearly four thousand people in Havana and had sent encrusted lymph to the diocesan bishop in Santa Clara and several interior cities.[30]

When skeptics questioned the efficacy of the new preservative, Romay immediately set about to prove its value. On March 23 he inoculated his own sons, six-year-old Tomás and four-year-old Pedro, with matter extracted from a smallpox vesicle. The operation took place before representatives of the Real Protomedicato and leading physicians of the city. His sons suffered no ill effects and the witnesses pronounced Romay's vaccinations an unqualified success.[31]

Balmis, abandoning his arrogant and tactless attitude of Puerto Rico, readily accepted Romay's work and converted his own quarters into a vaccination center. According to his own account, Balmis's mastery of the operation and deft public instructions "quickly decided the vacillating attitude of many practitioners, rectified the misconceptions of others, destroyed the arguments of the vaccination's most vociferous enemies, and dissipated the fears of many persons who had previously refused vaccination." [32]

Balmis, Gutiérrez, and Romay also inoculated a number of cows in an effort to induce the disease and establish a reservoir of virus. The method had previously failed in Madrid, La Coruña, and Caracas, while Romay's experiments soon after receiving the virus suffered a similar fate. Once again the technique failed.[33]

On June 7, however, Balmis presented to Governor Someruelos his plan for the formation of a Central Vaccination Board to insure the perpetuation of vaccine. He recommended that Romay be charged with conserving the virus until the junta was established. At the

[23] Vasconcelos to Soler, Caracas, 9 Mayo 1804, AGI, "Indif. Gen.," Leg. 1.558, I, fs. 7–11.
[24] "Extracto," fs. 88–88v.
[25] *Ibid.,* fs. 88v–90.
[26] For a detailed account of the Salvany expedition, see Díaz de Iraola, 1947.
[27] "Extracto," f. 113.

[28] Sánchez López, 1950: pp. 115–122.
[29] *Ibid.,* pp. 123–124.
[30] "Extracto," fs. 108–109.
[31] *Suplemento al Periódico Número 34,* Havana, 16 Abril 1804, AGN, "Epidemias," v. 12, exp. 6, f. 50.
[32] Sánchez López, 1950: p. 132.
[33] *Ibid.*

same time he congratulated the governor and Romay on their accomplishments before his arrival and thanked them for their cooperation with the expedition. He also sent the Economic Society several copies of his *Tratado histórico* which were later placed in their library for public consultation. In recognition of his dedicated service the Society named Balmis an honorary member in the quality of "distinguished professor." [34]

By mid-June, Balmis was ready to continue his voyage to Mexico. On June 17 he reported that he had just received news that the *San Luis,* carrying the Salvany expedition, had been shipwrecked in the Magdalena River. Fortunately no one was injured and the vaccine was salvaged.[35] On June 18 the *María Pita* weighed anchor for the southeastern coast of New Spain. Before his departure Balmis found it necessary to purchase four young slaves to transport the vaccine since the boys promised by the governor failed to arrive on time. Balmis later complained that he had to sell the slaves in Mexico at a personal loss of 250 pesos.[36]

IV. THE ROYAL EXPEDITION ANTICIPATED

INITIAL EFFORTS TO SECURE THE VACCINE

On June 25 the expedition anchored at Sisal, about ten leagues northwest of Mérida, the capital of Yucatán. Once again Balmis was denied the honor of introducing his precious preservative. As in Puerto Rico and Cuba, the vaccine had preceded the expedition by several weeks.[1] Residents of New Spain had sought the fluid for a number of years. In December, 1802, when José de Iturrigaray arrived in New Spain to replace Félix Berenguer y Marquina as viceroy, he brought a portion of cowpox vaccine in vials. Dr. Alejandro García Arboleya accompanied Iturrigaray to Mexico City and immediately vaccinated several children in the Casa de Niños Expósitos. Unfortunately, the vaccine failed to take effect, having lost its potency during the voyage from Spain.[2]

Undaunted by this initial failure, Iturrigaray commissioned García Arboleya and Dr. Antonio Serrano, director of the *Hospicio Real* (Royal Orphan Asylum), to investigate the possible existence of cowpox in the viceroyalty. At the same time he suggested that they inoculate some cattle with the vitiated fluid, hoping it would induce the disease. All attempts to find or induce cowpox in Mexico failed. Although the royal circulars announcing the formation of the Royal Expedition assured residents of New Spain that the preservative would inevitably arrive, the search for vaccine continued.[3]

Iturrigaray sought the virus in the Caribbean Islands after learning from Havana newspapers that it was available in Puerto Rico and Cuba. He read with interest the descriptions of the vaccine's introduction into Havana and the success of Romay's operations. Both the viceroy and García Arboleya repeatedly requested that physicians in the Antilles dispatch vaccine to Veracruz in mail ships.[4]

ACHIEVEMENTS OF THE AYUNTAMIENTO OF VERACRUZ

The insistent petitions from Mexico City were answered in the spring of 1804. Bernardo de Cozar, physician of the Royal Armada, who had maintained correspondence with García Arboleya, vaccinated eighteen members of the crew of the war frigate *Anfitrite* and several others on the *Nuestra Señora de la O* a few days before their scheduled departure from Havana. Cozar selected the *Anfitrite's* physician to care for the seamen until they reached Veracruz, from where the lymph could be dispatched to the capital.[5] Unfortunately, however, Cozar's inoculations uniformly produced immune reactions.[6]

At the same time, however, José Angel de Zumaran, second officer of the *Nuestra Señora de la O,* received from Bachiller Marcos Sánchez Rubio some vaccine which had been encrusted on silk threads shortly before his vessel sailed on April 3. Zumaran would conserve the lymph until the ship reached Veracruz. Since he had assisted Sánchez Rubio in some of the latter's vaccinations in Havana, Zumaran was familiar with the operation.[7]

On April 7 Zumaran, fearing that the lymph would deteriorate, informed Captain Miguel de Palacios that he wanted to employ the vaccine immediately. The captain ordered all non-immune crew members to report to the ship's doctor, Miguel Angel Pérez Carrillo, who

[34] Benigno Duque de Heredia to Balmis, Havana, 13 Junio 1804, AGN, "Epidemias," v. 4, exp. 13, fs. 1–2.

[35] "Extracto." fs. 114–114v.

[36] Balmis to Cavallero, Madrid, 4 Diciembre 1806, AGI, "Indif. Gen.," Leg. 1.558, II, f. 2.

[1] According to Humboldt, 1941: 2: p. 52, a certain Don Tomás Murphi, a resident of Veracruz, introduced the vaccine into that city in January, 1804. He had received the vaccine from the United States. Humboldt, however, is the only contemporary source which mentions Murphi. He does not include the extent of Murphi's activities.

[2] Alvarez Amezquita, 1960: 1: p. 180; Lerdo de Tejada, 1850: 1: p. 342; Iturrigaray to Cavallero, México, 26 Junio 1804, AGI, "Indif. Gen.," Leg. 1.558, I, f. 1; *Gaceta de México,* Suplemento al núm. 12, 26 Marzo 1804, p. 93.

[3] *Gaceta de México,* Suplemento al núm. 12, 26 Mayo 1804, p. 94.

[4] Iturrigaray to Romay, México, 22 Marzo 1804, AGN, "Epidemias," v. 12, exp. 6, f. 1; Cozar to Iturrigaray, La Habana, 29 Marzo 1804, AGN, "Epidemias," v. 10, exp. 8, f. 1.

[5] Cozar to Iturrigaray, Havana, 29 Marzo 1804, AGN, "Epidemias," v. 10, exp. 8, fs. 1–1v.

[6] Ayuntamiento de Veracruz to Iturrigaray, Veracruz, 28 Abril 1804, AGN, "Epidemias," v. 10, exp. 10, f. 15.

[7] Sánchez Rubio to Iturrigaray, Havana, 12 Mayo 1804, AGN, "Epidemias," v. 10, exp. 8, fs. 3–3v; Zumaran to Iturrigaray, Veracruz, 12 Abril 1804, AGN, "Epidemias," v. 12, exp. 6, fs. 4–5.

selected two seamen for immediate inoculation. Three other men were held in reserve in case the ship's arrival in Veracruz was delayed. Pérez Carrillo vaccinated the two sailors, Manuel Serra and Francisco Montero, and assigned them a separate cabin for the remainder of the voyage.[8]

Owing to the lack of adequate winds, the *Nuestra Señora de la O* was forced to anchor on a reef outside the harbor of Veracruz. Zumaran received permission to go ashore and deliver the vaccine to Governor García Dávila. He assured the governor that Pérez Carrillo was willing to employ it if the governor so desired. García Dávila, however, decided to summon a special council meeting for the following morning in order to discuss propagation of the vaccine.[9]

The next morning Zumaran and Pérez Carrillo again visited the governor. Since the Ayuntamiento had not yet convened, they asked permission to vaccinate a few townspeople before the virus deteriorated. They would utilize the remaining vaccine when the Ayuntamiento assembled. After receiving the governor's approval, Pérez Carrillo vaccinated five children in the home of Francisco de la Torre y Sánchez, a local merchant. Zumaran and José María Pérez, surgeon of the Royal Armada, witnessed the operations. In this manner Pérez Carrillo performed the first successful smallpox vaccinations in New Spain.[10]

Later that morning the Ayuntamiento, joined by the physicians of Veracruz, met in the main council room. Dr. Florencio Pérez y Comoto, a staff member of the Hospital de San Sebastián, also presented some vaccine which Pérez Carrillo had brought him from Havana in four glass containers.[11] In the presence of the Ayuntamiento and representatives from the medical community, Pérez Carrillo and Pérez y Comoto performed simultaneous vaccinations between noon and 1:00 P.M. Pérez Carrillo vaccinated twelve children with the lymph Zumaran had brought from Cuba while Pérez y Comoto inoculated thirteen others with the virus he had obtained in vials. Although Pérez y Comoto's vaccine ultimately failed to produce the desired effects, Zumaran's was of excellent quality.[12]

Sufficiently impressed with the operation, the Ayuntamiento ruled that vaccinations should continue when more lymph was available and appointed three of its members to witness future inoculations. The Ayuntamiento and Pérez y Comoto immediately notified the viceroy of the day's events and promised to keep him fully informed of the results.[13]

Since the vesicles of Serra and Montero gave every indication of containing active virus, the two sailors were taken to Veracruz and placed in a private home under the care of Zumaran. On April 15, when their vesicles had matured, the first arm-to-arm inoculations began. By order of the Ayuntamiento, only the vesicles of Manuel Serra would be utilized the first day, reserving Montero's lymph for the next.[14]

On April 15 Pérez Carrillo and Pérez y Comoto vaccinated thirteen children with the active material obtained from two of Serra's four vesicles. On the following day they inoculated forty children with the lymph extracted from Montero, for they found Serra's remaining two vesicles completely desiccated. They later discovered that, without the Ayuntamiento's authorization, Zumaran had permitted José María Pérez to vaccinate seven children with Serra's fluid the previous evening. In all, however, the sailors provided vaccine to inoculate sixty persons.[15] In addition to its gratitude, the Ayuntamiento gave Zumaran one hundred pesos and Montero and Serra fifty pesos each for conveying the preservative to Veracruz.[16]

After the initial vaccinations, the Ayuntamiento created a medical board to determine both the vaccine's effectiveness and an efficient method of propagating it. Each Thursday the board would submit to the representatives of the Ayuntamiento a list of all persons vaccinated during the week. The Ayuntamiento could examine the report on Friday and formulate a complete account for the viceroy.[17]

The Ayuntamiento enthusiastically directed extension of the virus to all districts of the city. On April 25 it informed the viceroy that the medical board had reported that "legitimate" vaccine was effectively established in Veracruz. By May 5 Doctors Miguel Angel Pérez Carrillo, Florencio Pérez y Comoto, José María Pérez, and Francisco Hernández had vaccinated nearly one thousand persons.[18]

In addition to the understandable zeal of the Ayuntamiento to disseminate the vaccine throughout Veracruz, its extraordinary energy in dispatching the lymph

---

[8] Zumaran to Iturrigaray, Veracruz, 12 Abril 1804, AGN, "Epidemias," v. 12, exp. 6, fs. 5–5v.

[9] *Ibid.*, fs. 5v–6.

[10] *Ibid.*, f. 6v.

[11] Pérez y Comoto to Iturrigaray, Veracruz, 18 Abril 1804, AGN, "Epidemias," v. 12, exp. 6, f. 14.

[12] Ayuntamiento de Veracruz to Iturrigaray, Veracruz, 11 Abril 1804, AGN, "Epidemias," v. 21, exp. 6, fs. 2–2v.

[13] Ayuntamiento de Veracruz to Iturrigaray, Veracruz, 11 Abril 1804, AGN, "Epidemias," v. 12, exp. 6, fs. 2–3; Pérez y Comoto to Iturrigaray, Veracruz, 11 Abril 1804, AGN, "Epidemias," v. 12, exp. 6, f. 4.

[14] Ayuntamiento de Veracruz to Iturrigaray, Veracruz, 18 Abril 1804, AGN, "Epidemias," v. 12, exp. 6, f. 16.

[15] Pérez y Comoto to Iturrigaray, Veracruz, 18 Abril 1804, AGN, "Epidemias," v. 12, exp. 6, fs. 14–14v.

[16] Ayuntamiento de Veracruz to Iturrigaray, Veracruz, 21 Abril 1804, AGN, "Epidemias," v. 10, exp. 6, f. 7.

[17] Ayuntamiento de Veracruz to Iturrigaray. Veracruz, 21 Abril 1804, AGN, "Epidemias," v. 10, exp. 10, f. 6.

[18] This figure was reached by examining the following Ayuntamiento reports to the viceroy: Ayuntamiento de Veracruz to Iturrigaray, 11 Abril 1804, AGN, "Epidemias," v. 12, exp. 6, fs. 2–3v; 14 Abril 1804, v. 10, exp. 10, fs. 1–2; 21 Abril 1804, v. 10, exp. 10, fs. 6–7v; 24 Abril 1804, v. 10, exp. 10, fs. 4–4v; 25 Abril 1804, v. 10, exp. 10, fs. 8–10; 27 Abril 1804, v. 10, exp. 10, f. 14; 5 Mayo 1804, v. 10, exp. 10, fs. 22–22v.

to other localities, at its own expense, merits special attention. When Iturrigaray learned that the fluid had arrived in Veracruz, he immediately ordered Pérez y Comoto to forward to him some of the virus by a special messenger.[19] On April 23 Pérez y Comoto dispatched a portion of the vaccine in slides and impregnated into silk cloth, along with brief instructions.[20] The Ayuntamiento soon learned of Pérez y Comoto's action, but aware that the fluid deteriorated rapidly, commissioned Dr. José María Pérez to convey virus "in vivo" to the capital without awaiting the results of the previous shipment.[21]

Pérez left Veracruz for Mexico City on the morning of April 25, accompanied by José Froconi, José María Romero, Manuel Lucio Pifano, and Mariano Perdegón, members of the local garrison. Fronconi had been inoculated on April 20, and the others were vaccinated the day before their departure. As an added precaution, Pérez carried some virus encrusted on silk threads. After stopping in Jalapa and Puebla, the group expected to reach Mexico City on April 30.[22]

Without the direct intervention of the Ayuntamiento, the preservative reached the Captaincy General of Guatemala. The captain general and the protomedicato of Guatemala had sent repeated requests for the fluid to Veracruz. In early May the Ayuntamiento replied that it would dispatch the lymph as soon as possible. In the meantime, however, Don Ignacio Pavón y Muñoz, a native Guatemalan residing in Veracruz, obtained a portion of the vaccine and on April 28 sent the fluid enclosed in vials, along with a vaccinating needle and new instructions, by a special messenger. On May 20 the virus reached Guatemala.[23]

On May 2 the Ayuntamiento of Veracruz dispatched surgeon Miguel José Monzón in the brigantine *Saeta* to perform the operation throughout Campeche and Yucatán. José Velasco, Mateo Vargas, Matías Gonzales, José Carmona, and Ignacio de la Torre, musicians attached to the Veracruz garrison, accompanied Monzón. The young men were successively vaccinated until the expedition reached Campeche, where Monzón began his operations.[24]

On May 9 lymph was sent by special courier to the Ayuntamiento of Oaxaca. The remittance included vaccine in vials and silk threads, along with instructions to guide local practitioners. By the time the lymph arrived on May 22, however, it had deteriorated.[25] A short time later the *practicante mayor* (ranking staff member) of the Hospital Real of Veracruz, a certain Pages, along with four boys, led a more successful mission to the neighboring cities of Orizaba and Córdoba.[26]

Discovering that Pérez's vaccinations in Jalapa on his way to Mexico City produced only immune reactions, the Ayuntamiento sent a young girl to transmit the vaccine to the neighboring city, but the excessive heat desiccated her vesicles. A second mission composed of two young boys was canceled when it was found that a recently vaccinated girl had successfully transmitted the virus to Jalapa.[27]

The Ayuntamiento also took measures to prevent loss of the vaccine. It asked the governor to order all local officials in the *tierra caliente* and along the coasts to send boys from their districts for vaccination. The boys would then return to their villages and continue to propagate the lymph, creating a steady supply of vaccine around the port.[28]

Despite such efforts, however, the vaccine lasted only a little over two months. But by the time it was lost on approximately June 20, 1,350 persons in the city had received immunization. In a letter to the viceroy, the Ayuntamiento described the difficulty of perpetuating the virus. Most residents had been exposed to the disease during the epidemic 1797–1798 and were already immune. Many others had suffered smallpox in Europe. It also noted that since the last epidemic, 1,562 children had been born in the city. When from that number were deducted those who died, the 1,350 already vaccinated, and others who spent the summer outside Veracruz, by the end of June there was no one left to immunize. Veracruz physicians were clearly unaware of the technique of conserving the vaccine by maintaining a reserve of non-immune children for sequential vaccination. Their eagerness to vaccinate everyone destroyed the potential reserve. The Ayuntamiento, however, could claim credit for a total of 3,027 vaccinations, mostly in the southeastern region of the

[19] Iturrigaray to Pérez y Comoto, México, 17 Abril 1804, AGN, "Epidemias," v. 12, exp. 6, fs. 9–9v.

[20] Pérez y Comoto to Iturrigaray, Veracruz, 23 Abril 1804, AGN, "Epidemias," v. 12, exp. 6, f. 9.

[21] Ayuntamiento de Veracruz to Iturrigaray, Veracruz, 25 Abril 1804, AGN, "Epidemias," v. 10, exp. 10. f. 8v.

[22] *Ibid.*, fs. 9–9v.

[23] *Gazeta de Guatemala*, 25 Julio 1804: pp. 338–339.

[24] Miguel José Monzón, "Relación circunstanciada de la Expedición filantrópica que por disposición del M.Y.A. de Veracruz y del Sor. Dn. Ciriaco Cevallos salió para este Puerto de Campeche bajo mi dirección in 2 de Mayo del Presente año con el objeto de propagar la vacuna en toda la provincia de Yucatán," Campeche, 25 Julio 1804, AGN, "Epidemias," v. 4, exp. 10, f. 14.

[25] Ayuntamiento de Veracruz to Iturrigaray, Veracruz, 19 Mayo 1804, AGN, "Epidemias," v. 10, exp. 9, f. 3; Izquierdo to Iturrigaray, Oaxaca, 22 Mayo 1804, AGN, "Epidemias," v. 4, exp. 6, f. 1; Iturrigaray to Balmis, México, 6 Septiembre 1804, AGN, "Epidemias," v. 4, exp. 6, f. 3.

[26] Ayuntamiento de Veracruz to Iturrigaray, Veracruz, 9 Mayo 1804, AGN, "Epidemias," v. 10, exp. 10, f. 24.

[27] Ayuntamiento de Veracruz to Iturrigaray, Veracruz, 9 Mayo 1804, AGN, "Epidemias," v. 10, exp. 10, f. 24; Ayuntamiento de Veracruz to Iturrigaray, Veracruz, 19 Mayo 1804, AGN, "Epidemias," v. 10, exp. 9, f. 3v; Ayuntamiento de Veracruz to Iturrigaray, Veracruz, 9 Junio 1804, AGN, "Epidemias," v. 10, exp. 9, f. 9.

[28] Ayuntamiento de Veracruz to Iturrigaray, Veracruz, 5 Mayo 1804, AGN, "Epidemias," v. 10, exp. 10, f. 22.

viceroyalty.[29] The productive expeditions sent from Veracruz to Campeche and Mexico City merit closer consideration.

MIGUEL JOSÉ MONZÓN IN CAMPECHE

On May 1 Ciriaco de Cevallos, port commander of Veracruz, notified the Ayuntamiento of Campeche that Miguel José Monzón had been commissioned to introduce the virus into that province.[30] As previously mentioned, Monzón and his party departed the following day. Prior to his embarkation he had vaccinated José Velasco and Mateo Vargas. On May 6 he inoculated the three remaining musicians, Matías Gonzales, José Carmona, and Ignacio de la Torre, and gathered the excess lymph into glass containers. The mission reached Campeche on May 9 and met with the Ayuntamiento.[31] Monzón immediately dispatched a letter to Captain General Benito Pérez y Valdelomas, who resided in Mérida, and presented his credentials from the Ayuntamiento of Veracruz.[32]

Pérez y Valdelomas himself was extremely interested in propagating the vaccine throughout his jurisdiction. On April 3 he had created a medical board, composed of Antonio Poveda, José Bates, and Carlos Escofiet, to seek cowpox in the province. He had also solicited the preservative in the neighboring districts but without success. A short time later he received a portion of the virus enclosed in vials, a French-made vaccinating needle, and a set of instructions from Dr. Francisco Isla y Solórzano, general administrator of royal income in Havana. Pérez y Valdelomas entrusted this material to Poveda, who, assisted by Bates and Escofiet, immediately began the inoculations.[33] They soon discovered, however, that the lymph had already lost its potency.[34]

On April 18 Pérez y Valdelomas received a letter from Balmis, written in Puerto Rico on February 28, informing him that the Royal Expedition would stop in Campeche and Mérida sometime in June before continuing on to Veracruz. Balmis also mentioned that when he arrived in Puerto Rico vaccination was already being practiced, but he soon discovered that Oller's fluid was ineffective.[35]

On May 11 Pérez y Valdelomas acknowledged Monzón's letter, expressed his gratitude to the Ayuntamiento of Veracruz, and enclosed an extract of Balmis's letter. He also mentioned that a "German doctor" claimed to have found cowpox in the province and requested that Monzón inform him of the details of this discovery. After promising Monzón sufficient financial assistance, Pérez y Valdelomas reminded him to send complete reports on his progress.[36]

On May 10, in the presence of the Ayuntamiento of Campeche, Monzón had vaccinated six individuals with the lymph he had stored in vials during the voyage from Veracruz. Five days later, when the vesicles of Ignacio de la Torre had matured, he began arm to arm inoculations. Monzón soon noted a declining public interest in vaccination. He even found it necessary to go to the homes of the people and implore them to submit to the operation. Some days no one at all responded to his request.[37] He soon discovered the cause of popular resistance. Dr. Carlos Escofiet, who had not even witnessed Monzón's vaccinations, was publicly denying the vaccine's utility and criticizing local officials for allowing its propagation.[38] Escofiet had read Balmis's letter to Pérez y Valdelomas impugning Oller's vaccinations in Puerto Rico. He surmised that the vaccine from Veracruz must be equally inferior since it had come from the same ultimate source.[39]

Monzón bitterly complained to an *alcade* (magistrate), who issued an order for Escofiet's imprisonment.[40] Monzón also explained the situation to the captain general,[41] who censured Escofiet and threatened "disagreeable consequences" if he did not cease his criticism.[42] When Pérez y Valdelomas later discovered that Escofiet had been imprisoned, however, he immediately ordered his release and confiscated the case records.[43]

Despite these obstacles, Monzón's mission produced excellent results. By July 9, only one month after his arrival in the province, he had vaccinated 1,227 persons. Most of his vaccinations were performed in private

---

[29] This total included 1350 in Veracruz, 1366 in Campeche, 151 in Córdoba, 49 in Orizaba, 24 in Puebla, 4 in Jalapa, and 83 in Mexico City. Ayuntamiento de Veracruz to Iturrigaray, Veracruz, 12 Septiembre 1804, AGN, "Epidemias," v. 10, exp. 11, fs. 2–3.

[30] Cevallos to Ayuntamiento de Campeche, Veracruz, 1 Mayo 1804, AGN, "Epidemias," v. 10, exp. 10, f. 19.

[31] Miguel José Monzón, "Relación circunstanciada," Campeche, 25 Julio, AGN, "Epidemias," v. 4, exp. 10, f. 14.

[32] Monzón to Pérez y Valdelomas, Campeche, 9 Mayo 1804, AGN, "Epidemias," v. 4, exp. 10, f. 1.

[33] Benito Pérez y Valdelomas, Antonio Poveda, José Bates, Carlos Escofiet, "Auto," Mérida, 18 Abril 1804, AGN, "Epidemias," v. 4, exp. 10, fs. 1–3.

[34] Pérez y Valdelomas to Monzón, Campeche, 11 Mayo 1804, AGN, "Epidemias," v. 4, exp. 10, f. 1.

[35] Balmis to Pérez y Valdelomas, Puerto Rico, 2 Febrero 1804, AGN, "Epidemias," v. 4, exp. 10, fs. 3v–4.

[36] Pérez y Valdelomas to Monzón, Campeche, 11 Mayo 1804, AGN, "Epidemias," v. 4, exp. 10, fs. 1–1v. Monzón later reported all experiments with the lymph obtained from these animals failed to produce an effective vaccine. Monzón to Pérez y Valdelomas, Campeche, 5 Junio 1804, AGN, "Epidemias," v. 4, exp. 10, f. 6v.

[37] Miguel José Monzón, "Realción circunstanciada," Campeche, 25 Julio 1804, AGN, "Epidemias," v. 4, exp. 10, f. 14.

[38] Monzón to Pérez y Valdelomas, Campeche, 25 Mayo 1804, AGN, "Epidemias," v. 4, exp. 10, f. 4.

[39] Miguel José Monzón, "Relación circunstanciada," Campeche, 25 Julio 1804, AGN, "Epidemias," v. 4, exp. 10, f. 14v.

[40] *Ibid.*

[41] Monzón to Pérez y Valdelomas, Campeche, 25 Mayo 1804, AGN, "Epidemias," v. 4, exp. 10, f. 5.

[42] Pérez y Valdelomas to Monzón, Mérida, 29 Mayo 1804, AGN, "Epidemias," v. 4, exp. 10, f. 5v.

[43] Miguel José Monzón, "Relación circunstanciada," Campeche, 25 Julio 1804, AGN, "Epidemias," v. 4, exp. 10, f. 15.

homes, while the others took place in various municipal buildings.[44]

THE FIRST VACCINATIONS IN MEXICO CITY

It will be remembered that on April 23, at the request of the viceroy, Dr. Florencio Pérez y Comoto sent vaccine to Mexico City, where it arrived two days later.[45] Within an hour Dr. Alejendro García Arboleya and Lic. José María Navarro vaccinated five children in the Casa de Niños Expósitos. Accompanied by Dr. Antonio Serrano, García Arboleya returned to the Casa the next morning where he vaccinated two more children. The lymph produced the desired results in five of the seven, assuring the existence of the virus in the capital.[46]

While these events were occurring, another shipment of vaccine had been dispatched to Mexico City. José María Pérez, commissioned by the Ayuntamiento of Veracruz, had departed for the capital on the morning of April 25 along with five young men who were to be vaccinated at various intervals. On April 26 the party reached Jalapa, where Pérez paused just long enough to vaccinate four recruits of the infantry regiment quartered there. Two hours later he left for Puebla. The expedition reached the City of the Angels on the morning of April 28 and received a warm welcome from the governor-intendant, the Conde de Cadena. Taking advantage of the vaccine's unexpected arrival, the governor requested that Pérez vaccinate citizens of Puebla that same afternoon. Pérez inoculated twenty-four persons, the first eight of whom were the prolific governor's own children. The expedition departed the following morning and reached Mexico City on April 30. Although Pérez's vaccine was now superfluous, it did add to the capital's reserve.[47]

Spurred by reports of smallpox in Veracruz,[48] the viceroy initiated procedures to facilitate vaccine distribution throughout the capital. He commissioned Alejandro García Arboleya, Antonio Serrano, and José María Pérez to direct vaccination.[49] The three decided to assemble daily at a scheduled hour during which time they could review what each had accomplished that day, exchange observations, and formulate precise

reports for the viceroy.[50] They agreed to meet in the Casa de Niños Expósitos from 10:00 A.M. to 1:00 P.M. and in the Royal Palace from 6:00 until 8:00 P.M.[51]

The commissioners also formulated rules for dissemination of the virus and instructions to local physicians. No other practitioners could vaccinate in the Casa unless one of the three commissioners was present. Every day from ten o'clock in the morning to one o'clock in the afternoon doctors could examine the vaccine, observe inoculations, and gain practical experience by vaccinating children they might bring for that purpose. All physicians were required to give a complete daily account of their operations and observations to the commissioners, who in turn would add them to their report to the viceroy.[52]

On May 4 Pérez performed his first arm-to-arm operation in Mexico City. That same day Serrano and García Arboleya examined the seven children inoculated on April 25 and 26 and decided that the vesicles of five had sufficiently matured to transmit the lymph. They notified the viceroy that they would begin public vaccination on the following day.[53]

The question as to who would have the honor of performing the first operation provoked a petty disagreement among the three commissioners. The first inoculation session would take place in the Royal Palace, utilizing lymph obtained from Pérez's patients. Serrano announced that it was highly probable that the viceroy's own son would be the first person vaccinated. Although they would be using Pérez's lymph, it was only proper that García Arboleya perform the initial operation since he was the viceroy's family physician. Pérez could then immediately perform the second. Pérez replied, however, that it would be a personal affront if he were not permitted to initiate the inoculations. The others then tried to placate him by suggesting that all three take part in a simultaneous operation, but again Pérez refused. They finally agreed that, if the viceroy's son did not attend, Pérez would vaccinate first, and the others would follow in rotation. On May 5 inoculations began in the Royal Palace. Since the viceroy's son did not appear, Pérez proceeded with the first operation as planned. But much to the chagrin of García Arboleya and Serrano, he continued to vaccinate the other twenty-two children in attendance without giving them a chance to perform.[54]

The second session, held at the Casa de Niños Expósitos that afternoon, was celebrated amidst great ceremony. Iturrigaray decided that to impress the populace with the importance of vaccination, a member of his own family would receive the first inoculation.

[44] Miguel José Monzón, "Estado que manifesta los días en que hice las 55 vacunaciones; casa en que las hice; número de vacunados en cada una; Individuos de quien se tomó el fluído, sus edades y día en que se vacunaron," Campeche, 25 Julio 1804, AGN, "Epidemias," v. 4, exp. 10, fs. 10–10v.

[45] Iturrigaray to Pérez y Comoto, México, 25 Abril 1804, AGN, "Epidemias," v. 12, exp. 6, f. 21.

[46] García Arboleya and Serrano to Iturrigaray, México, 3 Mayo 1804, AGN, "Epidemias," v. 10, exp. 12, f. 2.

[47] Pérez to Iturrigaray, México, 5 Mayo 1804, AGN, "Epidemias," v. 12, exp. 6, f. 28.

[48] Reports concerning a new outbreak in Veracruz were mentioned with the first notice of the arrival of the vaccine and continued until the end if the year.

[49] Pérez to Iturrigaray, México, 5 Mayo 1804, AGN, "Epidemias," v. 12, exp. 6, f. 28.

[50] García Arboleya and Serrano to Iturrigaray, México, 4 Mayo 1804, AGN, "Epidemias," v. 10, exp. 12, fs. 3v–4.

[51] García Arboleya and Serrano to Iturrigaray, México, 6 Mayo 1804, AGN, "Epidemias," v. 12, exp. 6, f. 32.

[52] Ibid.

[53] Ibid.

[54] Ibid., fs. 32–32v.

He sent his youngest son, Vicente, who was twenty-one months old, in an elegant coach replete with guards and personal attendants.[55] Five children were vaccinated that afternoon by García Arboleya and Serrano in alternate operations. Pérez did not attend. The youngsters were members of the capital's first families, including, besides the viceroy's son, children of the secretary of the viceroyalty and the assessor general.[56]

The following day García Arboleya and Serrano lodged new complaints against their colleague. Besides Pérez's attitude of the previous morning and his absence at the afternoon vaccination session, they found that he was performing operations without reporting them according to their agreement. They also discovered that some of Pérez's vaccinations on May 4 had resulted in immune reactions, and they feared that the inferior virus might be propagated throughout the city. They requested that Iturrigaray admonish Pérez for his lack of cooperation and order him to report all vaccinations to the other members of the commission.[57]

Despite the personal differences among the commissioners, vaccination continued almost daily. Iturrigaray had informed the archbishop,[58] the Ayuntamiento,[59] and the Protomedicato[60] of the creation of the commission and requested that they give complete support to its work. Broadsides advised the public to attend daily 9:30 to 11:00 A.M. sessions in the Casa de Niños Expósitos and explained that vaccination was entirely gratis.[61]

On May 17 Iturrigaray took action to reorganize administration of the vaccine. He appointed García Arboleya, Serrano, and José Ignacio García Jove, president of the Real Protomedicato, to formulate a plan which would indicate: (1) an effective metod of establishing a supply of the vaccine in the Casa de Niños Expósitos; (2) means to disseminate the fluid throughout the capital; and (3) the manner by which the virus could be communicated to the entire viceroyalty.[62] At the same time Iturrigaray notified the Ayuntamiento of Veracruz [63] and its representative in Mexico City, Francisco Marián y Torquemada,[64] that he was relieving José María Pérez of his commission. Since the vaccine was now fully established in the capital, there was no reason for the Ayuntamiento to continue to support an additional expedition.[65]

The committee submitted its proposal a week later. In reference to the first point, it decided that since only a deposit of the vaccine was required, there was no need to provide for daily operations. It suggested that four children be vaccinated every nine days and remain under constant medical observation in the Casa de Niños Expósitos. This method involved fewer children and reduced the cost of caring for them during their internment. Only 164 non-immune children would be required each year to maintain the supply, and only children six years and four months old or younger could be utilized since it had been that long since the last epidemic exposed the entire city. The Casa de Niños Expósitos and the Hospicio de Pobres contained only a limited number of children; therefore, the city's poor families must provide the remainder.[66]

Mexico City was divided into eight *cuarteles mayores* (major wards), each containing four *cuarteles menores* (minor wards). The 164 children per year—preferably less than one year old—would be divided among the cuarteles menores. Thirty-one cuarteles menores would furnish five children annually, and one would supply ten. Upon the order of the alcalde of a cuartel mayor, one of the cuarteles menores would supply four children to the Casa de Niños Expósitos on a specified day and hour. With each cuartel providing its quota in rotation, the capital would have a constant reserve of vaccine.[67]

In regard to the second point, the commissioners stated that Mexico City physicians could vaccinate as often as they chose since the continual existence of the preservative was already assured by point one. When a physician acquired vaccine he should convoke the residents of his district and vaccinate all non-immune per-

[55] Iturrigaray to Cavallero, México, 26 Junio 1804, AGI, "Indif. Gen.," Leg. 1.558, I, f. 3. Although it is often asserted that the viceroy's son was the first person vaccinated in Mexico City, he was actually the thirty-third. After eleven days his vaccination still had failed to produce the desired results. "Estado que manifesta a los que se les ha prendido la vacunación de los inoculados los días 4, 5, 6, 7 de Mayo de 1804, con la especificación de cada Professor," México, 15 Mayo 1805, AGN, "Epidemias," v. 10, exp. 12, f. 11.

[56] Pérez, García Arboleya, and Serrano to Inturrigaray, México, 5 Mayo 1804, AGN, "Epidemias," v. 10, exp. 12, fs. 5–5v.

[57] Serrano and García Arboleya to Iturrigaray, México, 6 Mayo 1804, AGN, "Epidemias," v. 12, exp. 6. fs. 33–33v.

[58] Iturrigaray to Archbishop of México, México, 5 Mayo 1804, AGN, "Epidemias," v. 12, exp. 6, fs. 30–30v.

[59] Iturrigaray to Ayuntamiento de México, México, 5 Mayo 1804, AGN, "Epidemias," v. 10, exp. 6, fs. 31–31v.

[60] Iturrigaray to Real Protomedicato, México, 6 Mayo 1804, AGN, "Epidemias," v. 6, exp. 6, fs. 26–26v.

[61] Aviso al Público, México, 1804, AGN, "Impresos Oficiales," v. 26. exp. 42, f. 148.

[62] Iturrigaray to Serrano and García Arboleya, México, 17 Mayo 1804, AGN, "Epidemias," v. 12, exp. 6, fs. 43–44.

[63] Iturrigaray to Ayuntamiento de Veracruz, México, 17 Mayo 1804, AGN, "Epidemias," v. 12, exp. 6, f. 48.

[64] Iturrigaray to Marián y Torquemada, México, 18 Mayo 1804, AGN, "Epidemias," v. 12, exp. 6, f. 49.

[65] Pérez later notified Iturrigaray that he had decided to remain in Mexico City and had volunteered to lead an expedition to Zacatecas and Durango. Although this expedition never took place, Pérez remained in Mexico City and continued to work with García Arboleya and Serrano at least until August.

[66] Antonio Serrano, Alejandro García Arboleya, and José Ignacio García Jove, "Los medios más sencillos, para establecer para siempre la inoculación de la vacuna, en la Casa de la Cuna, como depósito, para la segura existencia del fluído en este Reyno nos parece el Siguiente," México, 24 Mayo 1804, AGN. "Epidemias," v. 12, exp. 6, fs. 55–55v.

[67] *Ibid.,* fs. 55v–56.

sons more than one year old. After the cuartel menor had provided the five children required of that district, physicians could then vaccinate children under one. A new reserve would thus be available for the coming year. When a doctor needed vaccine he could obtain it from the deposit in the Casa de Niños Expósitos, but he was expected to maintain his own supply. Recourse to the deposit was only a last resort.[68]

All practitioners must report their operations to the commission and submit a complete list to the administrative chaplain of the Casa de Niños Expósitos. These rosters would include the name of the doctor, the date of vaccination, and the name, age, and parents of the vaccinated child. The physician was also to present a description of the development of each vesicle, carefully explaining any abnormalities.[69]

Propagation of the vaccine in the provinces would follow the basic pattern established for the capital except that children under one could be vaccinated. The commission would assign physicians and itineraries for each intendancy. Each expedition would include a physician and three non-immune children. The commissioners reported, however, that thus far only Dr. García Arboleya and Lic. José María Navarro were willing to lead provincial missions. García Arboleya offered to introduce the vaccine into San Luis Potosí and Guanajuato, while Navarro volunteered to go to Guadalajara. They suggested that the viceroy put the plan into practice as soon as possible and determine a source of finance.[70]

A supplement to the *Gaceta de México* of May 26 gave a complete account of developments concerning vaccination in Mexico from the time of Iturrigaray's arrival and of accomplishments to date. To inform the public and instruct local physicians, the *Gazeta* reprinted in full Dr. Pedro Hernández's *Origen y descubrimiento de la vacuna.*[71]

Although no immediate action was taken to dispatch formal expeditions to the provinces, on June 8 Iturrigaray did appoint García Arboleya to propagate the vaccine in the towns immediately surrounding Mexico City. He also ordered local officials and clergymen to give García Arboleya their full support.[72] García Arboleya's principal labors were concentrated in Coyoacán and Tacuba, where he reportedly found a sufficient number of children to insure the existence of the vaccine for as long as it was needed. In addition to propagating the virus, he taught the local public

officers to conserve the lymph by arm-to-arm inoculations.[73]

Financing propagation of the vaccine was a difficult problem, for the Royal Treasury was already heavily burdened. Iturrigaray even believed that the Royal Expedition was impractical under the circumstances. Fortunately, upon the viceroy's request,[74] the archbishop of Mexico, Francisco Xavier Lizanza, offered to maintain from funds at his disposal the four children continually housed in the Casa de Niños Expósitos.[75]

Although provincial expeditions were never organized, the vaccine did reach some north central districts through private initiative. On May 21 the commandant general of the Internal Provinces, Brigadier General Numesio Salcedo, received vaccine in Chihuahua from some unidentified source in Mexico City. Army surgeon Jaime Gurza then successfully vaccinated a non-immune child. From the active lymph of these first few vesicles, Gurza vaccinated Salcedo's six-month-old daughter and many other children. Since Gurza was the only practitioner in the whole province, Salcedo could not immediately dispatch the virus to the surrounding area. He did set aside a house in Chihuahua, however, to serve as a deposit of the fluid. Salcedo ordered the interns of the Hospital General and the barbers of the neighboring districts as well as those of the *presidios* in New Vizcaya to come to Chihuahua and observe the operation. They could bring children for vaccination and, after conveying the virus to their own villages, continue the operation. By October over 2,500 persons had been immunized in the province of New Vizcaya alone. Salcedo announced that a physician and a number of children would soon arrive in Chihuahua from New Mexico to obtain vaccine for the people of that distant province. He also reported that some cattle in Chihuahua were suffering from a disease which appeared to be cowpox. After further investigation he promised to submit a full account on the state of that malady.[76]

On June 1 Juan Antonio Riaño, intendant of Guanajuato, reported that José María Pérez had forwarded vaccine to Sebastián de Sorondo, a resident of that mining center, who had vaccinated his own two children. Riaño learned of the event some time later. Perhaps irritated because he was not immediately informed of Sorondo's actions, Riaño judged that such an "impudent action" merited the viceroy's attention.[77] Assuming a typical bureaucratic attitude, Iturrigaray

[68] *Ibid.*, f. 57.

[69] *Ibid.*, fs. 57v–58.

[70] *Ibid.*, fs. 58–58v.

[71] *Gaceta de México,* Suplemento al núm. 12, 26 Mayo 1804: pp. 93–108.

[72] José de Iturrigaray, "Circular," México. 8 Junio 1804, AGN, "Epidemias," v. **4**, exp. 1, f. 1.

[73] García Arboleya to Iturrigaray, México, 15 Agosto 1804, AGN, "Epidemias," v. **10**, exp. 12, fs. 27–28.

[74] Iturrigaray to Francisco Xavier Lizanza, México, 31 Julio 1804, AGN, "Epidemias," v. **12**, exp. 6, fs. 66–67v.

[75] Lizanza to Iturrigaray, México, 10 Agosto 1804, AGN, "Epidemias," v. **12**, exp. 6, fs. 69–69v.

[76] *Gaceta de México,* Suplemento al núm. 22, 6 Octubre 1804: pp. 181–183.

[77] Riaño to Iturrigaray, Guanajuato, 1 Junio 1804, AGN, "Epidemias," v. **4**, exp. 4, fs. 1–1v.

replied that Sorondo should not have vaccinated his children without previous authorization and called his action a "reprehensible liberty." He advised Riaño that no one was to vaccinate except under the closest scrutiny of the local magistrates.[78]

On June 6 Dr. Pedro Puglia, a resident of Mexico City, sent Christóval Corvalán, the royal treasurer of San Luis Potosí, instructions and a portion of the virus in vials.[79] When the lymph arrived on the afternoon of June 22, Corvalán immediately vaccinated four children in the presence of three local physicians. Although the virus had deteriorated slightly, it did produce favorable results in one little girl who later communicated it to thirty others.[80]

On August 1 Serrano, García Arboleya, and Pérez notified Iturrigaray that 479 persons, mostly young children, had been vaccinated in the capital. They pointed out that, although this figure seemed low, it represented only those vaccinations officially reported to the commission. Many physicians had performed unreported operations.[81]

Total vaccinations in the capital and its environs are impossible to determine. However, judging by the official figure of 479, which represented the work of at least three physicians for three months, it would appear that the numerous potential recipients in the capital were barely exploited.

V. THE ROYAL EXPEDITION IN NEW SPAIN

FROM HAVANA TO MEXICO CITY

Although Balmis was well satisfied with his accomplishments in Cuba, he anticipated an even greater achievement—the introduction of vaccination into New Spain. Mexico was Spain's richest and most important colony, and Mexico City, its capital, was the spiritual, political, and economic center of the vast viceroyalty. The expedition's fortunes in the capital would probably indicate its success in the entire viceroyalty. Balmis's task, however, went beyond the mere transportation of vaccine. He must establish throughout New Spain a network of vaccination centers which would perpetuate the virus through chain inoculations. To fulfill this assignment he must instruct an incipient Mexican medical community and secure the cooperation of phlegmatic colonial officials. Primarily, of course, he must persuade the populace to accept vaccination. The suc-

cess of the venture depended largely upon Balmis himself. The director needed determination, intelligence, bravery, and tact to surmount any physical, human, or bureaucratic obstacles which could frustrate his mission.

On June 10 Balmis had advised Iturrigaray from Havana that after stopping briefly in Campeche he would reach Veracruz toward the end of the month. He mentioned that the expedition would remain but a short time in Veracruz in order to avoid the prevalent diseases which infested that port during the summer season. He did promise, however, to vaccinate in Jalapa, Córdoba, Orizaba, and Puebla en route to the capital. He announced the expedition's division in La Guayra and submitted a list of the members in his party.[1]

Iturrigaray had initiated preparations to receive the expedition several months before he received Balmis's note. In December, 1803, he had received Soler's preliminary notification of August 4[2] and Cavallero's minute instructions of September 1, 1803.[3] Cavallero's orders clearly outlined the government's obligations. The Spanish minister recapitulated the expedition's itinerary and informed Iturrigaray that the Royal Treasury would absorb the entire cost of its transportation. It would also pay all expenses incurred by the boys who carried the virus, including their transportation, board, lodging, clothing, care, and compensation to their parents if they were known. In return for their services, the king promised to maintain and educate the children in institutions of public tutelage until they could support themselves. Members of the Royal Expedition, however, would pay all personal expenses from their salaries, which they would draw from the Royal Treasury in Mexico City. Cavallero emphasized, however, that the king would be greatly pleased if municipal governments would absorb the "slight expense" incurred by the expedition in Mexico, and therefore ease the strain on the Royal Treasury. He explained that when the expedition completed its mission in New Spain, the viceroy should furnish transportation and maintenance for all members going to the Philippine Islands. He closed by stressing the king's desire that all colonial officials give Balmis their full cooperation.[4]

On December 28, 1803, Iturrigaray communicated the royal instructions to the governor of Veracruz, the Royal Tribunal of Accounts, the Royal Protomedicato, and the ministers of the General Treasury—the individuals who were most immediately concerned with the expedition.[5] He then ordered Ambrosio Saparzurieta,

[78] Iturrigaray to Riaño, México, 8 Junio 1804, AGN, "Epidemias," v. 4, exp. 4, fs. 2–2v.

[79] Corvalán to Iturrigaray, San Luis Potosí, 14 Julio 1804, AGN, "Epidemias," v. 4, exp. 9, f. 6; Ayuntamiento de San Luis Potosí to Iturrigaray, San Luis Potosí, 21 Julio 1804, AGN, "Epidemias," v. 4, exp. 9, f. 4.

[80] Corvalán to Iturrigaray, San Luis Potosí, 14 Julio 1804, AGN, "Epidemias," v. 4, exp. 9, fs. 6–6v.

[81] Serrano, Pérez, and García Arboleya to Iturrigaray, México, 1 Agosto 1804, AGN, "Epidemias," v. 10, exp. 12, fs. 26–26v.

[1] Balmis to Iturrigaray, Havana, 10 Junio 1804, AGN, "Epidemias," v. 10, exp. 7, fs. 27–28.

[2] Iturrigaray to Soler, México, 27 Diciembre 1803, AGN, "Virreyes," v. 214, exp. 349, fs. 234–234v.

[3] Iturrigaray to Cavallero, México, 27 Diciembre 1803, AGN, "Virreyes," v. 214, exp. 122, f. 135.

[4] Cavallero to Iturrigaray, San Ildefonso, 1 Septiembre 1803, AGN, "Epidemias," v. 10, exp. 7, fs. 1–4v.

[5] Iturrigaray to Governador de Veracruz, Real Tribunal de Cuentas, Real Protomedicato, and Ministros de la Caja Gen-

fiscal de lo civil and Iturrigaray's chief consultant on civil matters, to coordinate the initial preparations. On January 31, 1804, Saparzurieta forwarded the royal orders to the fiscal of the Royal Exchequer, the General Treasury of the Army, the General Accounting Office, and the Royal Auditing Tribunal of the General Treasury. He ordered them to formulate a plan which would designate a method to finance and accommodate the expedition during its stay in New Spain.[6]

On February 22 the office of the General Treasury of the Army submitted a plan for the preliminary arrangements. The viceroy should instruct the governor of Veracruz to provide transportation for the expedition to Jalapa, since the coastal climate would probably not permit the initial operations in the port. A sufficient number of coaches furnished by the intendant of Puebla should be ready in Perote to conduct the expedition to Puebla or directly to the capital, depending upon Balmis's plans. The treasury officials also suggested that Balmis receive a sum adequate to maintain the children during the trip from Veracruz to the capital. In the meantime a residence for the expedition should be set aside in Mexico City. The viceroy and Balmis could later agree upon servants, a monthly allotment for the children, and any other expenses the expedition might incur.[7] Thus some procedure had been established long before the expedition arrived in New Spain. Balmis's letter of June 10 was the signal to put this plan into action.

The Royal Expedition cast anchor in Sisal on June 25 and immediately moved inland to the provincial capital. On June 29 Captain General Benito Pérez y Valdelomas cordially received Balmis in Mérida.[8] Pérez y Valdelomas had earlier directed Miguel José Monzón to submit a complete account of his activities in Campeche.[9] On June 30 he forwarded Monzón's report to the director.[10] When Balmis discovered that Monzón had been vaccinating since May, he resumed his choleric attitude of Puerto Rico. He charged that Monzón was disseminating vaccine that was prejudicial to public health. Balmis dispatched assistant Antonio Gutiérrez to examine Monzón's work, propagate fresh virus, and instruct local physicians. Gutiérrez accompanied Francisco Pastor, who was leading a subsidiary mission to

Guatemala, as far as Campeche. In a letter announcing the investigation, the captain general cautioned Monzón to receive the assistant with all the consideration his commission demanded.[11]

Monzón bitterly replied a week later that he could not understand why Balmis was so sure that his vaccine was spurious. Only Dr. Carlos Escofiet, who had been prosecuted for his slanderous remarks, had impugned the quality of Monzón's vaccine. Monzón claimed that further instruction in Campeche was unnecessary since all local physicians—and most barbers—had sufficient training to administer the lymph. He also noted the incompatibility between Balmis's claim that his vaccine was ineffectual and the fact that the director had sent four boys from Mérida to be vaccinated with that very vaccine. He sarcastically asked why Balmis had not utilized the "superior" vaccine he had brought from Spain.[12]

Gutiérrez duly approved Monzón's vaccine on July 9 during an inquiry held in the town council room. Together with the Ayuntamiento, local practitioners, and Monzón, Gutiérrez examined numerous vaccination lesions in various stages of development. He immediately classified the lymph "legitimate" and sanctioned its continued propagation. The assistant then vaccinated the four children he brought from Mérida to communicate the vaccine to the Presidio del Carmen and the surrounding region.[13]

On July 17 Monzón informed Pérez y Valdelomas that his commission had officially terminated when Gutiérrez arrived in Campeche. The Ayuntamiento, however, had convinced him to continue his work.[14] Monzón did remain in Campeche until at least July 24, by which time he had vaccinated 1,366 persons.[15]

Gutiérrez's approval of Monzón's vaccine evidently did not diminish Balmis's irritation. On July 14, when the five musicians who had accompanied Monzón to Campeche boarded the *María Pita* in Sisal to return to Veracruz, the director became enraged. He first quartered them in the bow of the vessel along with some cattle and sheep, then summarily ordered them ashore. Captain Pedro del Barco, who had a direct order from Pérez y Valdelomas to conduct the boys to Veracruz, protested Balmis's arbitrary action. But the director became so incensed that he struck one of the young musicians and forcibly removed all of them from the

eral, México, 28 Diciembre 1803, AGN, "Epidemias," v. 10, exp. 7, f. 8.

6 Fiscal de lo Civil to Fiscal de Real Hacienda, Tesorería General de Ejército, Mesa Primera de Cajas en la Contaduría Mayor de Cuentas, Real Tribunal Auditora de la Contaduría Mayor de Cuentas, México, 31 Enero 1804, AGN, "Epidemias," v. 10, exp. 7, fs. 13–15.

7 Tesorería General de Ejército y Real Hacienda to Viceroy, AGN, "Epidemias," v. 10, exp. 7, fs. 18v–20.

8 Pérez y Valdelomas to Viceroy, Mérida, 16 Junio 1804, AGN, "Epidemias," v. 4, exp. 11, fs. 1–1v.

9 Pérez y Valdelomas to Monzón, Mérida, 16 Junio 1804, AGN, "Epidemias," v. 4, exp. 10, f. 7.

10 Pérez y Valdelomas to Monzón, Mérida, 30 Junio 1804, AGN, "Epidemias," v. 4, exp. 10, f. 8.

11 Pérez y Valdelomas to Monzón, Mérida, 3 Julio 1804, AGN, "Epidemias," v. 4, exp. 10, f. 8.

12 Monzón to Pérez y Valdelomas, Campeche, 10 Julio 1804, AGN, "Epidemias," v. 4, exp. 10, fs. 8–8v.

13 Escribano de S.M. Público y del Cabildo de esta Ciudad, "Certificación," Campeche, 24 Julio 1804, AGN, "Epidemias," v. 4, exp. 10, fs. 12–13.

14 Monzón to Pérez y Valdelomas, Campeche, 17 Julio 1804, AGN, "Epidemias," v. 4, exp. 10, f. 9.

15 Miguel José Monzón, "Estado que manifesta . . . ," Campeche, 25 Julio 1804, AGN, "Epidemias," v. 4, exp. 10, fs. 10–11.

vessel. The boys returned to Campeche and later secured passage to Veracruz in a merchant ship.[16]

On Tuesday, July 24, after a debilitating ten-day trip from Sisal, the *María Pita* anchored in Veracruz. All members of the expedition were ill. The suffocating climate dampened their morale and dysentery sapped their strength. Balmis believed that he had contracted yellow fever during the voyage.[17] Governor García Dávila and two regidores met the expedition and immediately escorted the members to their accommodations. The governor gave Balmis a letter from Iturrigaray welcoming the expedition to New Spain. With the letter was a copy of the supplement to the May 26 issue of the *Gaceta de México* which described extension of the vaccine before the expedition's arrival.[18]

A visible lack of enthusiasm for vaccination in Veracruz further exacerbated Balmis's flagging morale. The vesicles of the children he had brought from Sisal were at their peak of maturity the day the expedition landed. The director wanted to begin inoculations immediately. Despite the fact that the vaccine had been lost more than a month before, regidores and physicians found no volunteers. Balmis's situation was critical. He explained to García Dávila that if he did not immediately communicate the virus, he was in "imminent danger of losing the treasure which had cost so many tribulations." The governor finally brought ten recruits from the garrison regiment whom Balmis inoculated on the twenty-fifth. The virus produced the desired effect in three of the soldiers, thus insuring Balmis's reservoir of vaccine. These ten conscripts were the only individuals the director was able to vaccinate in Veracruz.[19]

Poor health and apparent public apathy convinced Balmis to abbreviate his stay in Veracruz. Recurring fevers, aggravated by a severe case of dysentery, further weakened his failing health, and he bitterly realized there was "nothing to do" in the port. Balmis complained that the "indolent" populace had lost the vaccine from Havana, and they now refused to vaccinate their children. Local physicians were already fully instructed in the operation, and several copies of his *Tratado histórico* circulated throughout the city. He informed Iturrigaray of his intention to retire to the healthier climate of Jalapa, from where, after recuperating, he would proceed directly to the capital.[20] On July 28 Balmis dejectedly led the Royal Expedition to Jalapa, the first leg of the ninety-three league journey to Mexico City.[21]

Long after Balmis left Veracruz, Iturrigaray instructed the Ayuntamiento to answer the director's charges. He declared that Balmis's complaints of the apathy exhibited by the citizens of Veracruz greatly surprised him. The director's accusations were contrary to all previous descriptions of the response to the vaccine brought from Havana three months before.[22]

In its reply the Ayuntamiento reviewed the accomplishments of which it had so often boasted and told of its difficulty in preserving the lymph. The public had clamored to receive the vaccine from Havana. There had been no repugnance for it in Veracruz as Balmis charged; there simply was no one left to vaccinate. The Ayuntamiento could not understand the director's charges. Only the viceroy had done more to spread the new protective than the citizens of Veracruz. The Ayuntamiento suggested a number of possible reasons for Balmis's slanderous allegations: his extremely delicate health had distorted his judgment, the gossip of some foolish woman had misrepresented public sentiments, or perhaps the Ayuntamiento's success had aroused his jealousy.[23]

The Ayuntamiento was moved to level criticism of its own. It complained of Balmis's haughty attitude and reprehensible treatment of the boys in Campeche, and charged that his assistant had not communicated vaccine to the Presidio del Carmen as he had promised. Instead, Gutiérrez had immediately returned to Mérida, joined Balmis, and sailed to Veracruz where he employed the same lymph that he had "begged" in Campeche. The Ayuntamiento added, however, that its comments were not intended to "defame" the director, but rather to rectify his inexact account.[24]

Although Balmis's health improved in the temperate environs of Jalapa, his disposition did not.[25] Vaccine introduced earlier from Veracruz was still available in the city, but Balmis adamantly refused to utilize it. When he had to replenish his own reserve of lymph for the trip to the capital, Balmis sent for the three conscripts from Veracruz. Although numerous children still had not been immunized, the director declined to vaccinate in Jalapa.[26] On Sunday, August 5, the coaches from Puebla arrived in Perote, and the expedition moved on to Mexico City.[27]

[16] Miguel José Monzón, "Relación, circunstanciada," Campeche, 25 Julio 1804, AGN, "Epidemias," v. 4, exp. 10, fs. 15–15v.

[17] Balmis to Cavallero, Jalapa, 1 Agosto 1804, AGI, "Indif. Gen.," Leg. 1.558, I, f. 1.

[18] Balmis to Iturrigaray, Veracruz, 25 Julio 1804, AGN, "Epidemias," v. 10, exp. 7, f. 41.

[19] *Ibid.*, fs. 41–41v.

[20] *Ibid.*, fs. 41–42.

[21] García Dávila to Iturrigaray, Veracruz, 28 Julio 1804, AGN, "Epidemias," v. 10, exp. 7, f. 43.

[22] Iturrigaray to Ayuntamiento de Veracruz, México, 29 Agosto 1804, AGN, "Epidemias," v. 10, exp. 11, fs. 2–4.

[23] Ayuntamiento de Veracruz to Iturrigaray, Veracruz, 12 Septiembre 1804, AGN, "Epidemias," v. 10, exp. 11, fs. 2–4.

[24] *Ibid.*, fs. 4–6.

[25] Balmis to Cavallero, Jalapa, 1 Agosto 1804, AGI, "Indif. Gen.," Leg. 1.558, I, f. 1.

[26] Ayuntamiento de Veracruz to Iturrigaray, Veracruz, 12 Septiembre 1804, AGN, "Epidemias," v. 10, exp. 11, f. 6.

[27] Balmis to Iturrigaray, Jalapa, 2 Agosto 1804, AGN, "Epidemias," v. 10, exp. 7, fs. 46–46v.

MEXICO CITY: THE SECOND CONFRONTATION

On July 10 Iturrigaray had notified the Ayuntamiento of Mexico City of the expedition's impending arrival and ordered lodgings for its members. He also requested that the town council contribute to the maintenance of the children until their placement according to the king's instructions.[28] Antonio Méndez Prieto, *Regidor Decano* (Senior Councilor) of the Ayuntamineto, was commissioned to assist the expedition while it was in Mexico City. He was also instructed to secure a residence large enough to accommodate Balmis and his aides and to allow the director to exercise his duties.[29]

Balmis arrived in the capital much sooner than the viceroy had anticipated. Iturrigaray had not received Balmis's letter from Jalapa and believed that the expedition would first introduce the vaccine into Puebla before continuing on to the capital. The expedition, however, reached the Villa de Guadalupe, situated half a league from Mexico City, at 8 A.M. on August 8. Balmis advised Iturrigaray that after the children had rested, the mission would make its formal entrance into the city at dusk.[30]

Balmis encountered difficulties almost immediately. Iturrigaray had not received his letter from the Villa de Guadalupe, for Balmis had sent it by a courier who had left it on one of the desks in the secretariat of the chamber of the viceroy. Disregarding the protocol of awaiting an official reply, Balmis entered Mexico City at nightfall.[31] He was shocked when no welcoming party, public reception, or official delegation met the mission.[32] On the other hand, Iturrigaray's first news of the expedition's arrival came when Balmis personally presented himself in the viceroy's chamber that evening.[33]

The expedition was never officially received in Mexico City. Iturrigaray later explained that it was impossible to arrange a public welcome the night of Balmis's arrival because of the late hour. The annual festivities commemorating the conquest of Mexico made it impossible to organize a reception during the immediately succeeding days since all colonial officials, civil and religious corporations, and distinguished citizens of the capital were required to attend the celebration.[34]

Balmis's unexpected arrival also created confusion concerning the expedition's accommodations, for the residence selected for the delegation was not yet ready for occupancy. Méndez Prieto offered to find lodgings in a comfortable inn until the house was ready. Balmis, however, felt that a public house was inappropriate for an emissary of the king and insisted upon the official residence. Since the master carpenter in charge of preparing the house was unavailable that evening, it was necessary for Méndez Prieto to break into the dwelling, clean up scattered building materials, and hastily secure lights and furniture to make the house livable. In the midst of these frantic preparations, Balmis indignantly complained because the lamps were made of clay.[35] Although workmen made the dwelling as comfortable as possible under the circumstances, Balmis alleged that it was unsuitable and too far from the center of the city. Méndez Prieto and Cosme de Mier finally found him one of the finest homes in the capital—a new residence recently constructed for the Marquesa de Sierra Nevada—situated a few blocks from the Plaza de Armas.[36] Although the new location satisfied Balmis's sense of prerogative, the director's haughty disposition exasperated Méndez Prieto, who resigned his commission. Ignacio de la Peza, another member of the Ayuntamiento, replaced him.[37]

After this acrimonious beginning, Balmis's first preoccupation was to entrust the Spanish children to the viceroy's care. Here a short digression on the fate of the children does not seem inappropriate. The Royal Order of September 1, 1803, directed the viceroy to maintain and educate the boys at royal expense until they were able to support themselves. After conferring with Iturrigaray, Balmis delivered the children to Cosme de Mier, who was charged with their placement and care. Benito Vélez, the adopted son of Isabel Gómez y Cendala, however, remained with his foster mother.[38]

On August 13 Mier assigned the children to the Real Hospicio de Pobres and instructed the administrator, Juan Antonio de Araujo, to provide them with comfortable, independent quarters.[39] The older boys, separated by age groups, were placed in ordinary wards, while the younger children were taken to the Department of Women. Mier later inspected their accommodations and found everything satisfactory.[40]

The children remained in the asylum for the remainder of the year. On January 4, 1805, two weeks before his departure from Mexico City, Balmis complained to Cavallero of the selection of the Real Hospicio. He

[28] Iturrigaray to Ayuntamiento de México, México, 10 Julio 1804, AGN, "Epidemias," v. 10, exp. 7, fs. 34–34v.
[29] Iturrigaray to Méndez Prieto, México, 8 Agosto 1804, AGI, "Indif. Gen.," Leg. 1.558, I, f. 1.
[30] Balmis to Iturrigaray, Santuario de Guadalupe, 8 Agosto 1804, AGN, "Epidemias," v. 10, exp. 7, fs. 47–47v.
[31] Iturrigaray to Cavallero, México, 29 Mayo 1807, AGI, "Indif. Gen.," Leg. 1.558, I, fs. 1–3.
[32] Cavallero to Viceroy of New Spain, San Lorenzo, 15 Octubre 1805, AGI, "Indif. Gen.," Leg. 1.558, II, fs. 3–4.
[33] Iturrigaray to Cavallero, México, 29 Mayo 1805, AGI, "Indif. Gen.," Leg. 1.558, I, f. 3.
[34] *Ibid.*, fs. 4–5.

[35] *Ibid.*, fs. 5–6.
[36] Cosme de Mier to Iturrigaray, México, 14 Agosto 1804, AGN, "Epidemias," v. 10, exp. 13, f. 3.
[37] Iturrigaray to Cavallero, México, 29 Mayo 1804, AGI, "Indif. Gen.," Leg. 1.558, I, f. 9.
[38] Balmis to Iturrigaray, México, 11 Agosto 1804, AGN, "Epidemias," v. 10, exp. 7, f. 48v.
[39] Cosme de Mier to Iturrigaray, México, 14 Agosto 1804, AGN, "Epidemias," v. 10, exp. 13, fs. 2–2v.
[40] Cosme de Mier to Iturrigaray, México, 27 Agosto 1804, AGN, "Epidemias," v. 10, exp. 13, f. 6.

charged that the children were living on a paltry subsidy and were indiscriminately mixed with a "multitude of miserable, filthy urchins." He suggested that the boys be placed in one of Mexico City's many respectable boarding schools, preferably one administered by the Bethlehemite fathers. He also implored Cavallero to entrust them to the immediate care of the archbishop. The archbishop, he suggested, could place the older boys in seminaries. Since both the king and the archbishop granted numerous scholarships each year, the boys could be educated at no additional expense to the Royal Treasury. In this manner, he reasoned, they would become useful servants of both the State and the Church. The Spanish government, however, took no immediate action on Balmis's suggestions.[41]

In February, 1805, the ministers of the General Treasury informed Iturrigaray that they had allotted 120 pesos per month to support the twenty children in the Real Hospicio. Iturrigaray, however, felt that the expense would be wasted if the children did not take advantage of the opportunity and inquired whether their education in the asylum met the king's expectations.[42] Cosme de Mier then directed Juan Antonio de Araujo to submit a report on their progress.

Araujo's appraisal was highly uncomplimentary. The fourteen older boys, those six years old and over, were attending regular morning and afternoon classes. All were receiving religious instruction, since not one could even make the Sign of the Cross. He reported that five of the fourteen were industrious students; the other nine were "stupid." The six younger boys attended a special type of nursery school in the Department of Women. Araujo described the children's behavior as uniformly poor and related the instructors' difficulty in breaking them of the profanity they had learned from the sailors during the voyage to America.[43]

After Balmis's return to Spain in 1806, he again complained of the boys' plight in the Real Hospicio. In late 1806, therefore, the king ordered the archbishop of Mexico and the Audiencia to assume responsibility for the children and remove them from the asylum.[44] In the meantime, however, the boys had been placed in the Escuela Patriótica, a new institution adjacent to the Real Hospicio.[45] The school had been constructed from the generous endowment of a certain Captain Francisco Zúñiga, a wealthy mine owner who had bequeathed two hundred thousand pesos to provide vocational training

for orphans of both sexes.[46] Evidently the boys' transfer to the new school on July 1, 1806, had not been reported to the king.

The final official inquiry into the children's care and education was made in 1809. For some undisclosed reason Viceroy Pedro de Garibay was commanded to assume complete responsibility for the children and remove them from the Real Hospicio, "where his indifferent predecessor had placed them."[47] Garibay, therefore, instructed Ciriaco Gonzales Carvajal, president of the Mexico City Charity Board, to present a complete report on the children.[48]

Gonzales Carvajal explained that the boys had remained in the Real Hospicio only until completion of the Escuela Patriótica to which they were immediately transferred. The school, which had a separate administrator and board of directors, was completely independent of the Real Hospicio. The children were, therefore, well removed from the "beggars" who inhabited the Real Hospicio.[49]

At that time four of the boys, Vicente Ferrer, Pascual Aniceto, Martín, and Juan Francisco, still lived in the Escuela Patriótica. Tomás Metitón and Juan Antonio had died since their transfer to the school. By order of Colonel Ignacio Obregón, deputy of the Escuela Patriótica, the other boys had been remanded to the care of private citizens. José Jorge Nicolás de los Dolores was taken by Agustín Cepeda, surgeon of the Escuela Patriótica, in September, 1806. Antonio Veredia was entrusted to the rector of the Colegio de San Pedro in March, 1807. Pedro Marcos Gutiérrez, a Mexico City merchant, adopted Francisco Antonio, Clemente, and Manuel María in November, 1807. In July, 1808, José Manuel María and Domingo Naya were given to the rector of the Hospicio de San Nicolás. The rector of the Hospicio de San Jacinto took in José, Vicente María Sale y Vellido, and Francisco Florencio in July, 1808. In September, 1808, Andrés Naya was adopted by a priest, Juan José Simón de Haro, who later reported that the boy had run away. Manuel Domingo Paulín, a merchant from Ismiquilpan, adopted Cándido, Gerónimo María, and Jacinto in November, 1808. Although the king's instructions were never precisely carried out, the children's fate in Mexico was perhaps better than it would have been if they had never left Spain.[50]

[41] Balmis to Cavallero, México, 4 Enero 1804, AGI, "Indif. Gen.," Leg. 1.558, II, fs. 7–9.

[42] Iturrigaray to Cosme de Mier, México, 26 Febrero 1805, AGN, "Epidemias," v. 10, exp. 13, fs. 18–18v.

[43] Juan Antonio de Araujo to Cosme de Mier, México, 4 Marzo 1805, AGN, "Epidemias," v. 10, exp. 13, f. 21.

[44] Balmis to Gutiérrez, Madrid, 28 Diciembre 1806, AGN, "Epidemias," v. 17, exp. 8, fs. 95–99.

[45] Pascual Portillo, "Lista de los Niños que por Real Orden de S.M. vinieron de España con la Expedición de la Vacuna," México, 27 Junio 1809, AGN, "Filipinas," v. 53, exp. 15, f. 374.

[46] "Copia de las cláusulas 10 y 26 del Testamento del Capitán Dn. Francisco Zúñiga sobre la nueva ampliación, a espaldas de este Real Hospicio de Pobres para niños Huérfanos de Ambos sexos," AGN, "Epidemias," v. 10, exp. 13, fs. 19–19v.

[47] Benito de Hermida to Garibay, Real Alcazar de Sevilla, 17 Marzo 1809, AGN, "Reales Cédulas," v. 201, exp. 53, f. 103.

[48] Garibay to Gonzales Carvajal, México, 23 Junio 1809, AGN, "Filipinas," v. 53, exp. 15, f. 373.

[49] Gonzales Carvajal to Garibay, México, 23 Julio 1809, AGN, "Filipinas," v. 53, exp. 15, fs. 376–376v.

[50] Pascual Portillo, "Lista de los Niños . . . ," México, 27 Julio 1809, AGN, "Filipinas," v. 53, exp. 15, fs. 374–374v.

Despite Balmis's high expectations, he encountered an apathetic populace and an indifferent viceroy in Mexico City. General reluctance to accept the expedition leads one to suspect sabotage of the mission. Perhaps even Iturrigaray himself was involved. The viceroy's zeal to promote pre-expedition propagation of the vaccine and his visible lack of interest in Balmis's efforts lend credence to the hypothesis.[51]

When Balmis arrived in Mexico City he had been on the verge of losing the vaccine but was unable to find anyone to inoculate. The viceroy had merely offered to publish some posters announcing the arrival of the expedition, and he proudly sent Balmis seven folders summarizing pre-expedition accomplishments with the lymph from Havana. Finally, on August 10 an alcalde compelled twelve individuals to submit to inoculation.[52]

When the vesicles from these first operations matured, Balmis prepared for the first public inoculations. Popular resistance persisted. The director himself aptly described the scene at the initial vaccination sessions:

I would have lost the lymph from all those beautiful vesicles resulting from my twelve vaccinations on the tenth if the zealous alcalde had not dragged in twenty Indian women whose children were vaccinated only after a thousand entreaties. They then exclaimed loudly that they did not owe anyone anything. Others cried that if they did owe something, they could not pay. All the while they asked why they had been brought to this terrible place. Then every single one immediately went to the closest apothecary to get an antidote for the poison that had been introduced into their children's arms.[53]

Despite public announcements that gratuitous vaccination would continue in Balmis's quarters on August 27 and 28, public apathy continued.[54] On the first day only seven persons appeared; on the second, none at all. In view of this "inconsolable" indifference, Balmis once again feared the vaccine would be lost. He implored the viceroy to exert general pressure on the masses to take advantage of the new preservative. He also charged that after studying the reports that Iturrigaray had given him, he found that only 479 persons had been immunized before his arrival. He reasoned, therefore, that at least thirty thousand residents of the capital were still exposed to the disease.[55]

The viceroy replied by praising popular acceptance of the vaccine sent from Veracruz and stating that under no circumstances would he condone forcible vaccinations. He did not accept Balmis's claim that only 479 individuals had been previously vaccinated and declared that at least "thousands" had voluntarily submitted to

the operation. Recourse to coercion had been unnecessary. He concluded by reminding Balmis that in a previous letter the director had promised to submit a plan which would propose measures to perpetuate and propagate the vaccine. The viceroy believed that a solution to public indifference should come from this document.[56]

In the meantime Balmis suffered another reversal. In some unexplained manner, Iturrigaray learned that a number of boys recently vaccinated by Balmis in the Casa de Niños Expósitos had become ill with a disease diagnosed as dropsy. Several children had died from the ailment, and it was suspected that Balmis's vaccine was the cause. As a result Iturrigaray convoked a hearing in the Casa to investigate the fatalities. The inquiry was scheduled for 4:00 P.M. on August 17 with José Ignacio García Jove, president of the Royal Protomedicato, presiding. On the morning of August 17, Balmis received instructions to attend the meeting.[57] The director replied that he would be pleased to attend if his failing health permitted and suggested that Iturrigaray postpone the hearing until his health improved.[58]

The inquiry, however, began at four o'clock as scheduled. In addition to García Jove and Balmis, other members of the investigation were Antonio Serrano; Alejandro García Arboleya; Drs. Mariano Aznárez, Joachín Muro, and Luis Montaña, three eminent physicians appointed by García Jove; and Ignacio Segura, physician of the Casa de Niños Expósitos. After examining inmates of the Casa and discussing individual cases, each physician was instructed to submit a written report to the viceroy.[59]

After carefully considering the observations of the other practitioners and scrutinizing conditions in the Casa, Balmis easily diagnosed the causes of the disease. In general terms he blamed the illness on low, damp, poorly ventilated rooms, inadequate clothing, the uniformity of diet, a lack of maternal affection, and the children's chronically poor health. All inmates of the institution were suffering from cutaneous eruptions of various species.[60]

He then described what would happen to any child in these circumstances following exposure to a slight case of smallpox through inoculation:

Vaccination inhibits the full development of the cutaneous eruption, causing it to recede into the body . . . occasioning, among other maladies, sudden dropsy . . . which initially manifests itself in the form of swollen face and feet. It

[51] Cook, 1942: 12, 6: pp. 70–71.
[52] Balmis to Iturrigaray, México, 11 Agosto 1804, AGN, "Epidemias," v. 9, exp. 7, f. 48.
[53] Balmis to Iturrigaray, México, 24 Agosto 1804, AGN, "Epidemias," v. 10, exp. 7, f. 56.
[54] Aviso al Público, AGN, "Impresos Oficiales," v. 26, exp. 46, f. 149.
[55] Balmis to Iturrigaray, México, 29 Agosto 1804, AGN, "Epidemias," v. 10, exp. 7, fs. 63–64.

[56] Iturrigaray to Balmis, México, 30 Agosto 1804, AGN, "Epidemias," v. 10, exp. 7, fs. 65–66.
[57] Iturrigaray to Balmis, México, 17 Agosto 1804, AGN, "Epidemias," v. 10, exp. 15, f. 2.
[58] Balmis to Iturrigaray, México, 17 Agosto 1804, AGN, "Epidemias," v. 10, exp. 15, fs. 3–3v.
[59] Iturrigaray to García Jove, México, 17 Agosto 1804, AGN, "Epidemias," v. 10, exp. 15, fs. 1–1v.
[60] Balmis to Iturrigaray, México, 18 Agosto 1804, AGN, "Epidemias," v. 10, exp. 15, fs. 4–4v.

quickly rises to affect the stomach, and then to the chest, where it culminates in all the symptoms of sebaceous pneumonia which entirely impedes respiration. It ultimately passes to the brain in a state in which the compression of the humors precipates a true apoplexy of a type that kills quite suddenly on the same day.[61]

Although noticeably irritated at having to defend his precious vaccine, Balmis relished the opportunity to criticize the atrocious conditions which characterized mendicant asylums in the nineteenth century.

The other members of the inquiry reiterated Balmis's appraisal. Serrano, agreeing that the humid quarters were the main cause of the illness, declared that he had ordered the removal of the sick children to dryer upper floors a few days before the hearing. He affirmed that "in no way, not by any stretch of the imagination, could vaccination have caused the disease."[62] García Arboleya noted that a great many persons had been vaccinated in Mexico City without any ill effects. He also affirmed that more non-vaccinated children were ill than those who had been vaccinated.[63] Joachín Muro repeated that low, damp, poorly ventilated rooms, and a drainage ditch at the base of the structure created the perfect conditions to produce dropsy.[64] Mariano Aznárez noted that none of the girls, who lived in the upper level of the building, had been stricken although many had been vaccinated.[65] Luis Montaña,[66] Ignacio Segura,[67] and García Jove[68] presented similar reports. The inquiry completely vindicated the vaccine.

On September 6 Balmis gave Iturrigaray the instructions which he had earlier promised. Presented in two lengthy documents entitled "The Means for the Maintenance and Perpetuation of the Precious Vaccine in this, the Capital of Mexico," and "On the Establishment of a Public Vaccination Clinic," Balmis's proposals elucidated the most highly approved contemporary techniques of vaccine administration and preservation. The plan was similar to Balmis's earlier guidelines for the creation of vaccination boards and clinics in Caracas and Cuba. Based on Balmis's experience in Spain and the New World, the project was intended to be the principal instrument to continue the expedition's labors in America.

Balmis introduced the proposal with a short preface describing the expedition's dual objective of introducing the vaccine and creating machinery to assure its perpetuation for future generations. He affirmed that without the latter obligation, the former would be only a sterile gesture. Balmis's experience demonstrated the ephemeral existence of the vaccine when it was entrusted to the care of individual physicians. An effective administrative vehicle was necessary to insure perpetuation of the vaccine. Overt support of leading ecclesiastic and civil officials was the key to popular acceptance and ultimate success of the scheme.[69]

Balmis noted that the most indispensable step was the establishment of a central vaccination board in Mexico City. The board would include the *regidor decano* and the *procurador general* as permanent members, eight leading civil and religious figures, and six distinguished physicians. One member of the board would be elected to serve as its president.[70]

Two secretaries were required to keep a record of the organization's activities. One secretary would deal with routine aspects of the board's work—such as administration of the vaccine, correspondence with regional organizations, collection of funds to support the board's activities, and distribution of lymph to the provinces. The other secretary, a physician, would record scientific data concerning all aspects of vaccination.[71]

During its semi-monthly meetings, the board would review the number and results of operations performed during the previous two weeks. It would also discuss problems of the surrounding towns, dispatch vaccine to the provinces, and select qualified practitioners to transport the virus to afflicted areas.[72]

As was customary, board members would serve without salaries. The two secretaries, however, would receive a moderate allotment to cover expenses occasioned by their correspondence. Balmis designed an elaborate system of rotation by which one-half of the board was replaced annually, "thus dividing the work as well as the honor of serving."[73]

Only physicians licensed by the board could administer vaccine. The board would also endeavor to control the quality of the vaccine to prevent immune reactions or complications originating from inferior lymph. Each month the board would name two of its members to oversee public vaccinations which would be held every nine or ten days. Variolization (inoculation directly from a smallpox vesicle) was strictly prohibited.[74]

If an epidemic occurred in some area of the viceroyalty, the board would immediately dispatch a physician to propagate the vaccine and instruct the physicians

[61] *Ibid.*, fs. 5–5v.

[62] Serrano to Iturrigaray, México, 19 Agosto 1804, AGN, "Epidemias," v. 10, exp. 15, f. 8.

[63] García Arboleya to Iturrigaray, México, 20 Agosto 1804, AGN, "Epidemias," v. 10, exp. 15, fs. 11–12.

[64] Muro to Iturrigaray, México, 20 Agosto, AGN, "Epidemias," v. 10, exp. 15, f. 16.

[65] Aznárez to Iturrigaray, México, 20 Agosto 1804, AGN, "Epidemias," vol. 10, exp. 15, fs. 18–18v.

[66] Montaña to Iturrigaray, México, 18 Agosto 1804, AGN, "Epidemias," v. 10, exp. 15, fs. 14–15.

[67] Segura to Iturrigaray, México, 20 Agosto 1804, AGN, "Epidemias," v. 10, exp. 15, f. 13.

[68] García Jove to Iturrigaray, México, 23 Agosto 1804, AGN, "Epidemias," v. 10, exp. 15, fs. 20–21v.

[69] Balmis to Iturrigaray, México, 5 Septiembre 1804, AGN, "Epidemias," v. 10, exp. 7, fs. 72–75v.

[70] *Ibid.*, fs. 76–76v.

[71] *Ibid.*

[72] *Ibid.*, fs. 76v–77.

[73] *Ibid.*

[74] *Ibid.*, fs. 77v–78.

of the region. These emissaries would be paid by the local districts.[75]

The Mexico City board was obligated to name and maintain corresponding members in the various provinces. These provincial members would conduct searches for cowpox in their region and record all new cures attributed to the vaccine. In periodic reports to Mexico City they would discuss new discoveries and give credit to the physicians who made them. Balmis would eventually incorporate all this information into his general account of the expedition in America.[76]

Balmis praised the myriad benefits of vaccination. He claimed that it would successfully heal a variety of cutaneous eruptions, fortify sickly constitutions, as well as cure venereal disease, rickets, and many other common illnesses. He further suggested that the virus might be effective in the treatment of elephantiasis and St. Anthony's Fire and expressed hopes it would prevent *vómito prieto* and yellow fever. Perhaps Balmis actually believed that the vaccine would cure such diseases, but it most likely is that he was simply propagandizing.[77]

To insure against loss of the vaccine, Balmis recommended the creation of central vaccination boards, similar to the one proposed for Mexico City, in all principal cities of the viceroyalty. These provincial juntas, maintaining correspondence with each other and Mexico City, would exchange ideas and discuss new vaccination techniques.[78]

Revealing a prejudice common to Europeans at that time, and perhaps magnified by his unpleasant experiences in America, Balmis explained why it was essential to create an especially effective means to extend and preserve vaccine in the New World:

America is less enlightened [than Europe] and the character of its natives is commonly indolent. They look upon even the greatest benefit that outsiders propose for them with the greatest suspicion. They prefer to follow their erroneous ways and fall victims to deadly epidemics rather than accept the remedies which physicians commissioned by the leaders of the American dominions offer them. . . . America, I repeat, requires the closest study and care in order to propagate successfully this great gift, especially since it is difficult for natives to accept what their elders did not know. Therefore the Superior Government must rely upon the venerable parish priests, local officials, and physicians . . . to maintain the precious preservative in deposit and distribute it among these inhabitants.[79]

Balmis suggested that the Public Vaccination Clinic of Mexico City be established in a centrally located building whose clean, comfortable rooms would attract the public. His plan, however, strictly prohibited even temporary use of hospitals, mendicant asylums, or foundling homes as clinics. All vaccinations in the center would be performed free of charge. A doorman would maintain order while the center was open, provide lights for board meetings held in the clinic, and place posters outside the center announcing the next vaccination date. One board member would serve as treasurer to collect and administer funds required for rent of the clinic, utilities, and an occasional gratuity for the doorman.[80]

Members of the board and vaccinating physicians should oblige all recipients to return to the clinic in order to communicate the virus to others. They would receive a small monetary reward if they attended the following session. Balmis believed that this system would provide a simple, inexpensive, and attractive method to create general interest in vaccination.[81]

Iturrigaray completely disregarded the director's laudable recommendations. Two months passed before the viceroy even acknowledged receipt of the proposal. Iturrigaray then declared that he must reconcile Balmis's plan with the project Serrano, García Jove, and García Arboleya had submitted before the Royal Expedition arrived in New Spain. Another problem that he must resolve concerned a provision in the Royal Order of May 20, 1804, which required the creation of a vaccine deposit in "a room of the capital's principal hospital and one in each of the districts." This stipulation was, of course, contrary to one of Balmis's primary concerns. Although the viceroy promised to advise Balmis "opportunely" of his decision, he took no further action on the proposal while the expedition was in New Spain.[82]

On March 7, 1805, however, Iturrigaray instructed the director of the Real Hospicio de Pobres to establish a vaccine deposit in that institution according to the project which García Jove, Serrano, and García Arboleya had presented on May 24, 1804.[83] The following day he informed the three physicians of his decision to institute their plan and explained that the archbishop would provide funds to maintain the children. The director of the Real Hospicio would present four youngsters, six years and under, every nine days until all children in the institution had been vaccinated. Thereafter the alcaldes would provide children from their districts.[84] Iturrigaray then informed the Protomedicato[85] and the alcaldes of the eight cuarteles mayores[86] of the new arrangements.

[75] *Ibid.*

[76] *Ibid.*, fs. 78–78v.

[77] *Ibid.*, fs. 78v–79.

[78] *Ibid.*, fs. 79–80.

[79] *Ibid.*, fs. 81–81v.

[80] *Ibid.*, fs. 81v–82.

[81] *Ibid.*, fs. 82–83.

[82] Iturrigaray to Balmis, México, 6 Noviembre 1804, AGN, "Epidemias," vol. 10, exp. 7, f. 87.

[83] Iturrigaray to Director del Hospicio de Pobres, México, 7 Marzo 1805, AGN, "Epidemias," v. 12, exp. 6, fs. 89–89v.

[84] Iturrigaray to Serrano, García Jove, and García Arboleya, México, 8 Marzo 1805, AGN, "Epidemias," v. 12, exp. 6, fs. 87–88v.

[85] Iturrigaray to Real Tribunal del Protomedicato, México, 8 Marzo 1805, AGN, "Epidemias," v. 12, exp. 6, fs. 93–93v.

[86] Iturrigaray to Alcaldes de los Ocho Quarteles Mayores,

A few weeks later Serrano, García Jove, and García Arboleya reported that the section of their plan dealing with vaccine conservation required reform. Their suggested modifications reiterated many of Balmis's proposals for the same purpose. They also discouraged the deposit of vaccine in mendicant asylums and suggested the formation of an independent central vaccination board. The board would include García Jove, Serrano, García Arboleya, and Juan José Güereña, priest of the parish of San Miguel, who had actively encouraged vaccination. The rest of their scheme duplicated Balmis's project.[87]

Iturrigaray also refused to authorize this proposal. On August 16, 1806, he sent all three propositions to Juan José Güereña and explained that "none of them have been put into practice up to now because certain differences have not been reconciled." The viceroy believed that still another variation was needed and asked Güereña to formulate a new plan.[88]

On August 26, Güereña replied that Balmis's project was by far the most complete. Generally agreeing with the director's recommendations, Güereña suggested a few minor additions. He proposed offering half a real to each person who submitted to the operation, requiring alcaldes to bring one child each day for vaccination, and publishing a short guide for distribution to villages which had no physician.[89]

Evidently dissatisfied with Güereña's proposal, on January 13, 1807, Iturrigaray sent all previous proposals to the fiscal de lo civil for yet another opinion. Basically approving Balmis's instructions with Güereña's additions, Saparzurieta made important alterations of his own. These reforms, primarily of an administrative nature, rendered Balmis's main concerns virtually impotent. Saparzurieta stubbornly insisted upon adherence to the Royal Order of May 20, 1804. He stated that the most appropriate place to conserve the vaccine was the Real Hospicio de Pobres. A Charity Board, whose members included the viceroy as president and the *oidor decano* (senior judge) of the Audiencia as vice-president, governed the Hospicio. Other members of the board were leading ecclesiastical and civil figures who divided their duties among the Hospicio's four departments. The asylum could easily add a fifth department to administer the vaccine under rules established by Balmis and Güereña while complying with the Royal Order of May 20, 1804. In addition,

this board would be considered superior to similar organizations created throughout the viceroyalty.[90] As a result, Saparzurieta's proposal

vitiated, if it did not nullify completely, the independent status which Balmis regarded as essential to efficient operation of the Board, since it threw all control into the hands of the local political group who already were in power. In other words, the Fiscal managed very effiectively to kill the spirit of Balmis's enterprise, while conserving much of the form.[91]

The new plan ultimately went into operation. On June 7, 1807, Iturrigaray ordered the creation of the fifth department in the Real Hospicio de Pobres and instructed the Charity Board to obey the fiscal's directives.[92] On August 7, the *Diario de México* publicly announced the Charity Board's additional duties. The board's initial act was the creation of five vaccination centers conveniently distributed throughout the capital. The clinics were located in the parishes of San Sebastián, Santo Domingo, and San Miguel, the Escuela Patriótica, and the Royal University. Every week the thirty-two alcaldes would bring a non-immune child to any of the centers for vaccination. The districts of San Juan and Santiago would contribute four children every seven days. A physician and a surgeon would conduct operations at each center. Alejandro García Arboleya, Antonio Serrano, Jose Ignacio García Jove, Luis Montaña, Ignacio Acevedo, Rafael Sagaz, Francisco Giles, and José Mustilier were named consultants to witness the proceedings. In addition, the Charity Board appointed special representatives to each of the five clinics: the Marqués de Guardiola (Royal University), Don Gregorio Gonzales (San Sebastián), Dr. Fr. Domingo Arana (Santo Domingo), Mariscal de Castilla, Marqués de Ciria (Escuela Patriótica), and Juan José Güereña (San Miguel).[93]

Evidently the first operations under the new organization took place on Saturday, August 8. After some confusion during the initial sessions, the Charity Board took measures to simplify procedures of the new system. Each cuartel was assigned to a particular clinic. In addition, alcaldes would present two children every nine days at the center.[94] Although the new enterprise was definitely launched, no record of its activities remains.

THE ROYAL EXPEDITION IN PUEBLA

After presenting his proposals to Iturrigaray on September 5, Balmis judged that the expedition had

México, 8 Marzo 1805, AGN, "Epidemias," v. 12, exp. 6, fs. 90–91.

[87] Serrano, García Jove, García Arboleya, "Plan que manifiestan al Exmo. Sr. Virrey, los comisionados de la vacuna, para la segura conservación del fluído vacuno en esta capital," México, 1 Abril 1805, AGN, "Epidemias," v. 12, exp. 6, fs. 95–97.

[88] Iturrigaray to Güereña, México, 16 Agosto 1806, AGN, "Epidemias," v. 11, exp. 7, fs. 89–89v.

[89] Güereña to Iturrigaray, México, 26 Agosto 1806, AGN, "Epidemias," v. 10, exp. 7, fs. 91–94.

[90] Ambrosio Saparzurieta, "Auto," México, 31 Enero 1807, AGN, "Epidemias," v. 10, exp. 7, fs. 101–104.

[91] Cook, 1942: 12, 6: p. 79.

[92] Iturrigaray to Junta de Caridad del Hospicio de Pobres, México, 7 Junio 1807. AGN, "Epidemias," v. 10, exp. 7, fs. 110–110v.

[93] *Diario de México*, 7 Agosto 1807: pp. 393–396.

[94] *Ibid.*, 21 Septiembre 1807: pp. 81–83.

completed its duties in the capital. He then prepared to transport the vaccine to Puebla, a step which he had omitted on his hurried trip from Veracruz to Mexico City. Balmis requested a coach and two boys between ten and twelve years old to convey the vaccine to the southeastern city. He presented a list of persons vaccinated on September 5 and requested that Iturrigaray place them in the care of physicians until they communicated the virus.[95] A broadside announced that the next session would be held in Balmis's residence on September 14 and 15 and promised the poor one real for each child vaccinated.[96] Regidor Manual Gamboa, substituting for Ignacio de la Peza, was instructed to provide Balmis with two boys from the Real Hospicio de Pobres.[97] On September 13 Iturrigaray informed the intendant of Puebla of Balmis's impending departure for that city.[98]

Preceded by a troop escort, Balmis left Mexico City on September 18. Reaching Puebla two days later, the expedition received an uncommonly cordial reception. Intendant Manuel de Flon and Bishop Manuel Ignacio Gonzales del Campillo, along with the Ayuntamiento and distinguished citizens, met the expedition at the main entrance to the city. The bishop took the two young carriers into his coach, while Balmis joined the intendant. The impressive cavalcade proceeded to the cathedral where the *cabildo eclesiástico* had assembled for a thanksgiving mass. After a brief sermon in which the bishop paid homage to the king and praised the expedition, a solemn Te Deum closed the religious ceremonies. The whole group then accompanied the expedition to the residence which the Ayuntamiento had prepared.[99]

On September 22 the intendant published a proclamation announcing the arrival of the expedition, applauding the value and simplicity of vaccination, and exhorting all citizens to take advantage of the operation.[100] On the following morning Balmis immunized 230 children before exhausting his supply of lymph.[101] Subsequent response to vaccination in Puebla was astonishing. By October 11 Balmis had vaccinated 10,209 persons.[102]

A vaccination board—"La Junta Central Filantrópica de San Carlos de Puebla"—was created to perpetuate the vaccine in the capital and the surrounding province.

This organization, with slight modifications to meet local conditions, greatly resembled the board suggested by Balmis in Mexico City. The board's inauguration, attended by the Ayuntamiento, the ecclesiastical cabildo, all city priests, representatives from the regular religious orders, military officials, and distinguished citizens, was held on October 9. Speeches by the intendant and the bishop and a concert by the provincial regimental band highlighted the festivities.[103]

The vaccination board was composed of eighteen of Puebla's leading citizens. Ecclesiastics serving as members of the board included the bishop; the dean and precentor of the cathedral; Gaspar Mexía, provisional judge of testaments, chaplaincies, and pious works; Francisco Vásquez, secretary to the bishop; the eldest curate of the cathedral; and the priest of the parish of San José. Civil representatives included the intendant; Balmis; the *alguacil mayor* (chief constable); the *alférez real* (herald); José Alejo de Alegría, ex-secretary of the viceroyalty; Alcalde Francisco Xavier Gorospe; Juan Nepomuceno Quintero, fiscal of the Royal Audiencia; and Pedro de la Rosa, the royal printer. Drs. José Morales, Mariano Anzures, Mariano Rivillas, Antonio Naveda, José Gonzales, and Francisco La Madrid were appointed consulting physicians. Francisco Monroy was named secretary of the board.[104]

Although subordinate to the board established in Mexico City, the Puebla organization was preeminent in the province. Its duties included the promotion of dependent juntas in all regional centers within the intendancy.[105] The bishop of Puebla was the leading light of the organization. Besides furnishing rooms in the Episcopal Palace for board meetings and vaccine deposit, he provided the initial financial support.[106]

Financing the organization ultimately proved difficult. In a letter to Carlos IV on January 27, 1805, the board explained the difficulty of continuing its activities. Although board members served without compensation, it still required funds to finance the secretaries' correspondence, conserve the vaccine, remit lymph to remote districts of the intendancy, and periodically dispatch physicians to inoculate the residents of surrounding Indian villages. Contributions from wealthy citizens were insufficient to maintain the organization, and the bishop could not support the board indefinitely.[107]

The board, therefore, petitioned the king to authorize the appropriation of public revenues and community funds to spread the vaccine. Since these revenues were employed to stage national festivals, secure schoolmasters, and finance all types of public works, it seemed

[95] Balmis to Iturrigaray, México, 6 Septiembre 1804, AGN, "Epidemias," v. 10, exp. 7, fs. 85–86v.

[96] Aviso al Público, México, 1804, AGN, "Impresos Oficiales," v. 26, exp. 46, f. 150.

[97] Cosme de Mier to Iturrigaray, México, 12 Septiembre 1804, AGN, "Epidemias," v. 4, exp. 3, fs. 4–5.

[98] Iturrigaray to Intendente de Puebla, México, 13 Septiembre 1804, AGN, "Epidemias," v. 4, exp. 3, f. 2.

[99] *Gaceta de México,* 27 Octubre 1804: p. 193.

[100] Conde de Cadena, *Bando,* Puebla, 22 Septiembre 1804, AGN, "Epidemias," v. 4, exp. 3, fs. 18–20v.

[101] *Gaceta de México,* 27 Octubre 1804: p. 194.

[102] Balmis to Iturrigaray, México, 18 Octubre 1804, AGN, "Epidemias," v. 4, exp. 2, f. 1.

[103] *Gaceta de México,* 27 Octubre 1804: p. 194.

[104] "Estatuos," Puebla, 29 Octubre 1804, AGN, "Epidemias," v. 4, exp. 3, f. 26v.

[105] *Ibid.,* f. 29.

[106] *Gaceta de México,* 27 Octubre 1804: p. 194.

[107] Junta Central Filantrópica de San Carlos de Puebla to King, Puebla, 27 Enero 1805, AGN, v. 4, exp. 3, fs. 42v–44v.

only proper that such a noteworthy public benefit should also have access to these funds.[108]

In response to this request, the king ruled that any vaccination board established in New Spain could employ public rents and community funds to finance perpetuation of the vaccine. He stipulated, however, that such monies come from revenues and not from producing capital.[109] This measure, therefore, insured financial support of the organization for as long as it existed.

Enthusiasm for vaccination did not diminish after Balmis's departure from Puebla on about October 12. By December 14 the total number of vaccinations had risen to 11,996. If this figure represents a true estimate of total vaccinations, the major segment of the city's nearly fifty thousand inhabitants must have been rendered immune by the end of the year.[110] To maintain a reserve of active virus, parish priests alternately presented fifteen non-immune children every nine days for inoculation.[111] In recognition of Balmis's service to the city, the Ayuntamiento named him "perpetual honorary councilman."[112] On April 7, 1805, Carlos IV approved the appointment.[113]

In addition to Balmis's signal success in Puebla, he also discovered cowpox in the Valley of Atlixco near the city. For the first time a native source of vaccine was available in New Spain. Balmis commissioned Dr. Mariano Joaquín Anzures to conduct experiments with the virus. Anzures later reported many successful vaccinations with the indigenous vaccine.[114]

THE GARCÍA ARBOLEYA MISSION TO OAXACA

On September 6, 1804, Iturrigaray had informed Balmis that the vaccine sent from Veracruz to Oaxaca in May had deteriorated before its arrival.[115] Antonio María Izquierdo, the chief military officer, requested more lymph from the capital. The director replied that it was indispensable to dispatch vaccine to Oaxaca. Since no one in that region possessed sufficient training, a qualified physician should transport the preservative

"in vivo" and teach local practitioners to conserve it. Balmis added that despite his own failing health, he had promised to lead an expedition to Puebla. His only assistant and two male nurses were indisposed and unable to make the difficult journey south. He suggested, however, that Iturrigaray commission Alejandro García Arboleya, who was fully qualified for the assignment.[116]

Accepting Balmis's suggestion, on September 21 Iturrigaray notified García Arboleya of his new task and appointed him assistant of the Royal Expedition. Ignacio de la Peza was ordered to outfit the expedition. Cosme de Mier secured boys from the Real Hospicio de Pobres to transport the vaccine. Iturrigaray informed García Arboleya to obtain his final instructions from Balmis.[117] On that same day the viceroy commanded officials of all villages between Mexico City and Oaxaca to give the expedition their full cooperation. He also notified Izquierdo of García Arboleya's mission and requested that he finance the expedition through the municipal treasury.[118]

On September 26 García Arboleya acknowledged his appointment and informed Iturrigaray that he had completed all necessary arrangements in Mexico City. He would leave for Puebla as soon as the boys' vaccination vesicles were sufficiently mature. He notified the viceroy that he had met with Balmis, who had since departed for Puebla, and would receive complete instructions in Oaxaca.[119]

On October 1 García Arboleya and three boys left Mexico City. They made their first stop in Tehuacán de las Granadas four days later. Although García Arboleya intended to proceed directly to Oaxaca, he paused long enough in Tehuacán to vaccinate eighty children on October 2. He also instructed surgeons José Mariana de Castro and Bartolomé Castro, who would care for the children and continue immunization. On October 7, after leaving one of the boys from Mexico City with local authorities, García Arboleya departed. He took along several recently vaccinated boys from Tehuacán to preserve the vaccine during the remainder of the journey.[120]

The mission moved on to Teotitlán del Camino Real, where García Arboleya vaccinated 187 children on October 7, 8, and 9. He selected one child from each session to transmit the virus to Oaxaca. In Teotitlán he left the last two boys from Mexico City and made

[108] Ibid., fs. 46v–49v.
[109] Cavallero to Iturrigaray, San Lorenzo, 17 Diciembre 1805, AGI, "Indif. Gen.," Leg. 1.558, I, f. 1.
[110] Conde de Cadena, "Relación de los Individuos vacunados en este Ciudad de Puebla hasta el Día 14 de Diciembre de 1804," Puebla, 15 Diciembre 1804, AGN, "Epidemias," v. 4, exp. 3, f. 36.
[111] Junta Central Filantrópica de Vacunación Pública to King, Puebla, 29 Octubre 1804, AGI, "Indif. Gen.," Leg. 1.558, I, fs. 2–3.
[112] Ayuntamiento de Puebla to King, Puebla, 26 Noviembre 1804, AGI, "Indif. Gen.," Leg. 1.558, I, f. 5.
[113] King to Marqués de Bajamar, Aranjuez, 7 Abril 1805, AGI, "Indif. Gen.," Leg. 1.558, I, fs. 1–2.
[114] Balmis to Cavallero, Acapulco, 6 Febrero 1805, AGI, "Indif. Gen.," Leg. 1.558, I, f. 3.
[115] Iturrigaray to Balmis, México, 6 Septiembre 1804, AGN, "Epidemias," v. 4, exp. 6, f. 3.

[116] Balmis to Iturrigaray, México, 9 Septiembre 1804, AGN, "Epidemias," v. 4, exp. 6, fs. 9–9v.
[117] Iturrigaray to García Arboleya, México, 21 Septiembre 1804, AGN, "Epidemias," v. 4, exp. 6, fs. 9–9v.
[118] Iturrigaray to Izquierdo, México, 21 Septiembre 1804, AGN, "Epidemias," v. 4, exp. 6, fs. 6–6v.
[119] García Arboleya to Iturrigaray, México, 26 Septiembre 1804, AGN, "Epidemias," v. 4, exp. 6, fs. 11–12v.
[120] Necoechea to Iturrigaray, Tehuacán de las Granadas, 11 Octubre 1804, AGN, "Epidemias," v. 4, exp. 6, fs. 20–21.

arrangements to collect them on his return to the capital.[121]

On October 15 García Arboleya's party reached Oaxaca. Utilizing the lymph from the children he had brought from Teotitlán, the physician vaccinated during the next three days. In the first session he immunized 187 children from the city's principal families, including Izquierdo's infant son.[122] On November 5 García Arboleya completed his third vaccination session and considered his mission at an end. Besides instructing local physicians, he had given Izquierdo a proposal for the establishment of a vaccination board and clinic. Izquierdo, however, prevailed upon García Arboleya to remain in Oaxaca until the junta was formally constituted. He also convinced the physician to continue vaccinating in the neighboring Indian villages. In all, García Arboleya inoculated 541 children in Oaxaca and its environs.[123]

On November 10 the newly organized Central Vaccination Board of Oaxaca held its first meeting. The board, composed of sixteen leading ecclesiastical and lay citizens, was similar to the organization founded in Puebla. José María Izquierdo was chosen president and "protector" of the board. Diego de Villasante, regidor decano of the Ayuntamiento and member of the junta, donated the upper level of his own home as a temporary vaccination clinic.[124]

On November 15 García Arboleya began his return journey to the capital. The physician's ability and energy deeply impressed the local Ayuntamiento. As a demonstration of its esteem, the grateful town council voted him a reward of one thousand pesos.[125] García Arboleya refused the honor, however, declaring that he had gone to Oaxaca to serve humanity. He held the appreciation of the citizens of Oaxaca to be ultimately more satisfying than any pecuniary remuneration.[126] The Ayuntamiento did later request that Iturrigaray personally commend García Arboleya to the king.[127]

The enthusiasm of Oaxaca's leading citizens continued after García Arboleya's departure. On December 7 Bishop Antonio Bergosa y Jordán published a zealous pastoral letter praising vaccination and explaining its benefits. The prelate had secured a large number of vaccinating needles which he offered to distribute freely to all priests, vicars, and other persons interested in propagating the new preservative. He even offered a forty-day indulgence to anyone who presented himself for vaccination.[128]

In his eagerness to disseminate the vaccine, however, the prelate overstepped his authority and received a prompt, but extremely discreet reprimand from Cavallero. The Spanish minister noted that although the bishop's interest in spreading the vaccine greatly pleased the king, he suggested that the bishop follow the Ayuntamiento's regulations which limited the operation to trained personnel.[129]

On November 26 the recently formed vaccination board decided to send an expedition of its own to the Mixteca, a region comprising the western and northwestern part of the modern state of Oaxaca.[130] The Mixteca was an area of primitive hill country principally inhabited by pure Mixtec and Zapotec Indians. This mission was the only concentrated effort to distribute the vaccine to the poorer rural districts of New Spain. The Royal Expedition limited its activities mainly to viceregal or provincial centers.

Surgeon Santiago Coda was selected to lead the Mixteca expedition and was voted a generous allowance of three pesos per diem. Since the board had no funds, Manuel Lázaro Capitán, a local attorney, offered to absorb the initial expense to prevent any delay in the expedition's departure. Coda apparently set out for the Mixteca on November 29. When he returned over a year later, on January 3, 1806, he reported 16,983 inoculations—an astonishing average of over four hundred per day. His accomplishment is even more remarkable considering that he had to walk or travel by mule through hostile terrain and overcome the resistance of a suspicious Indian population which had learned by centuries of experience to distrust anything offered by white men. Coda's achievements in that desolate land mark him as a truly extraordinary physician.[131]

During Coda's absence the junta's financial plight had not improved, and there were no funds available to pay his accumulated salary. The board finally appealed to Iturrigaray and requested permission to finance its efforts by the appropriation of public funds. The board hesitated to initiate such a step without prior authorization.[132] Although the viceroy was later instructed to allow local vaccination boards to make use of public revenues, there is no record to indicate that the practice was followed in Oaxaca.

In November, 1806, Diego de Villasante complained that the junta was still struggling to support its activ-

[121] García Arboleya to Iturrigaray, Teotitlán del Camino Real, 10 Octubre 1804, AGN, "Epidemias," v. 4, exp. 6, fs. 15–18.

[122] Garcí Arboleya to Iturrigaray, Oaxaca, 19 Octubre 1804, AGN, "Epidemias," v. 4, exp. 6, fs. 28–30.

[123] García Arboleya to Iturrigaray, Oaxaca, 6 Noviembre 1804, AGN, "Epidemias," v. 4, exp. 6, fs. 35–36v.

[124] Junta Central de Oaxaca, "Auto," Oaxaca, 20 Noviembre 1804, AGN, "Epidemias," v. 4, exp. 6, fs. 52–55v.

[125] Izquierdo to García Arboleya, Oaxaca, 14 Noviembre 1804, AGN, "Epidemias," v. 4, exp. 6, f. 56.

[126] García Arboleya to Izquierdo, Oaxaca, 14 Noviembre 1804, AGN, "Epidemias," v. 4, exp. 6, fs. 57–57v.

[127] Ayuntamiento de Oaxaca, "Acuerdo," Oaxaca, 23 Noviembre 1804, AGN, "Epidemias," v. 4, exp. 6, fs. 59–59v.

[128] Bishop of Oaxaca, Bando, Etla, 7 Diciembre 1804, AGI, "Indif. Gen.," Leg. 1.558, I, 15 fs.

[129] Cavallero to Bishop of Oaxaca, Madrid, 12 Julio 1805, AGI, "Indif. Gen.," Leg. 1.558, I, 2 fs.

[130] Izquierdo to Iturrigaray, Oaxaca, 11 Enero 1805, AGN, "Epidemias," v. 4, exp. 6, f. 62.

[131] Ibid., f. 62v.

[132] Ibid., fs. 62v–63.

ities. It had no money to finance distribution of lymph to provincial centers or even to pay the janitor of the vaccination clinic. He also reported that either because most Oaxacans believed that the chances of a new epidemic were remote or because the novelty had worn off, very few persons appeared for vaccination. He added that the viceroy had not yet replied to their letter requesting employment of public funds.[133] The junta's initial zeal eventually waned, and it is doubtful that the Central Vaccination Board of Oaxaca enjoyed either a long or effective existence.

THE BALMIS EXPEDITION TO GUANAJUATO, ZACATECAS, AND DURANGO

After Balmis returned to Mexico City from Puebla in mid-October, he announced plans for an extensive expedition to provinces north and northwest of the capital. In addition to propagating the virus in these areas, Balmis intended to collect the carriers he needed to convey vaccine to the Philippine Islands. He asked the viceroy to provide him with a coach and two young boys. He also requested that Iturrigaray instruct authorities of these districts to help him secure non-immune boys from local mendicant asylums or from parents willing to allow their sons to make the journey to Manila.[134] The viceroy and the archbishop sent a series of communications exhorting secular and ecclesiastical officials to give Balmis their complete support.

The expedition departed from Mexico City on November 7. On November 13 the mission paused in Querétaro to introduce vaccination. Balmis moved on two days later, after inoculating approximately two hundred children, instructing local physicians, and presenting two copies of his *Tratado histórico* as a guide for future vaccinations. Miguel Domínguez, the provincial administrator, provided three boys—José Marcelino Ferroz, Juan Nepomuceno Marnz, and José Luiz Gonzaga—to transmit the lymph to Valladolid (Morelia) and Guanajuato. Domínguez paid fifteen pesos to the parents of two of the boys and sixteen pesos to the others in return for their children's services.[135]

Reaching Celaya on November 16, the expedition was met by a small, but enthusiastic, welcoming party composed of the Ayuntamiento and the local parish priest. The entrance into the city, lightened by music from the provincial regiment band, was followed by a banquet attended by representatives of all regular and secular religious corporations, military officials, and public figures. Shortly thereafter, Balmis vaccinated 140 children and explained several techniques for propagating the vaccine to Juan Ignacio Gómez, surgeon of the pro-

vincial regiment, and other interested persons. After gathering in the council hall on the following day, all city officials accompanied Balmis to the parish church where a Te Deum was offered in thanksgiving.[136]

Before leaving the city on November 17, Balmis divided the expedition. The director, two aides, and three young carriers continued on to Guanajuato, while Antonio Gutiérrez and two boys set out for Valladolid and Guadalajara.[137] Balmis instructed Gutiérrez to propagate the vaccine, promote the formation of vaccination boards and clinics, and instruct local physicians in each of the two cities. The assistant was to vaccinate only two days in each place and then rejoin Balmis in Guanajuato. Gutiérrez also carried specific orders to seek cowpox and secure at least three children in each city to serve as carriers for the Philippine expedition. Balmis authorized his assistant to offer as much as one hundred pesos or more to parents who allowed their children to make the trip, but cautioned him to institute this procedure only if local authorities agreed to the arrangement.[138]

Balmis was encountering a great deal of resistance in his attempt to gather children for the trip to the Far East. He had informed Iturrigaray from Celaya that "experience has taught me in Querétaro as well as in this city, that the suspicious and stupid character of these natives makes them prefer a single, immediate pecuniary reward to the great promises the king has made in return for voluntarily offering their children for the trip." He requested, therefore, that the viceroy authorize this modification of the royal instructions to insure the acquisition of a sufficient number of carriers. He pointed out that the new procedure would ultimately be much less expensive for the Royal Treasury although far less advantageous to the children.[139] The viceroy, however, refused to institute any innovation in the royal orders.[140]

On November 20 Balmis was met by the president of the Ayuntamiento, regidores, chief religious officials, representatives of the Royal Treasury, ranking military officers, and distinguished citizens at the Real de Marfil, half a league outside Guanajuato. After the usual preliminaries of a public reception, laudatory speeches, and a solemn Te Deum, the expedition retired to its quarters. Later that afternoon Balmis submitted to the Ayuntamiento his proposals for the establishment of a vaccination board and clinic.[141] Three days later, when

[133] Villasante to Mora y Peysal, Oaxaca, 8 Noviembre 1805, AGN, 'Epidemias,' v. 4, exp. 6, fs. 68–69.

[134] Balmis to Iturrigaray, México, 18 Octubre 1804, AGN, "Epidemias," v. 4, exp. 2, fs. 1–2.

[135] "Recibos," Querétaro, 25 Diciembre 1805, AGN, "Epidemias," v. 4, exp. 2, fs. 17–19.

[136] Ayuntamiento de Celaya to Cavallero, Celaya, 29 Noviembre 1804, AGI, "Indif. Gen.," Leg. 1.558, I, fs. 1–5.

[137] *Ibid.*, f. 6.

[138] Balmis to Gutiérrez, Querétaro, 14 Noviembre 1804, AGI, "Indif. Gen.," Leg. 1.558, I, fs. 6–8.

[139] Balmis to Iturrigaray, Celaya, 16 Noviembre 1804, AGN, "Epidemias," v. 14, exp. 13, f. 12.

[140] Iturrigaray to Balmis, México, 19 Diciembre 1804, AGN, "Epidemias," v. 4, exp. 7, fs. 14–14v.

[141] Ayuntamiento de Guanajuato, "Acuerdo," Guanajuato, 26 Noviembre 1804, AGN, "Epidemias," v. 4, exp. 4, f. 21.

the children's vesicles had fully matured, Balmis vaccinated 520 children from the city's principal families. He delivered his supply of lymph to the Ayuntamiento with instructions to resume vaccinations on the following day. On November 24 the expedition, accompanied by two boys provided by Intendant Juan Antonio Riaño, left Guanajuato.[142]

Although 275 more children were vaccinated soon after Balmis's departure, officials in Guanajuato displayed a remarkable lack of initiative. They refused to implement Balmis's plan for the creation of a vaccination board and clinic until they had received permission from the viceroy.[143] In the interim they entrusted the vaccine to individual practitioners until the viceregal government authorized a more formal procedure. Apparently the vaccination board and clinic were never established. Vaccine did reach the surrounding areas of Irapuato, Valle de Santiago, Silao, Chamacuero (Dr. Mora), Acámbaro, San Francisco del Rincón, Apaseo, and San Luis de la Paz as representatives from these towns secured the virus in Celaya or the provincial capital.

The new protective met varied public reaction in the intendancy. Inhabitants of Silao "were indifferent" toward the operation, while in Salamanca and Valle de Santiago citizens regarded it with "absolute contempt."[144] In Salvatierra, even before a delegation sent to Celaya returned with the vaccine, parents were hiding their children in the hills.[145] Certainly the vacillation of provincial leaders heightened popular resistance to vaccination in Guanajuato.

Passing through León, Villa de Lagos (Lagos de Moreno), and Aguascalientes, although not stopping to vaccinate, Balmis reached "Guadalupe post," approximately one league from Zacatecas, on Thursday, November 29. The expedition spent the night outside the city before making its entrance the following morning. On November 30 Intendant Felipe Díaz de Ortega, the Ayuntamiento, local bureaucrats, and representatives of the mining and commercial corporations jubilantly welcomed the expedition. The parish priest took the children into his coach, while Balmis and his aides joined the intendant. The entire group went to the parochial church where representatives of the religious orders awaited them. Bachiller José María Semper delivered an enthusiastic sermon and offered the customary Te Deum. That evening the Ayuntamiento sponsored a gala banquet in honor of the expedition. On December 1 and 2 Balmis vaccinated 1,076 children. Local physicians attended the sessions as a body to

receive practical instruction in the operation from the director.[146]

On Monday, December 3, Balmis moved on to Durango, the northernmost point reached by the expedition proper. He took two young boys from Zacatecas to convey the vaccine. Before his departure from Zacatecas, Balmis presented the Ayuntamiento with regulations for the conservation and propagation of the virus. A central vaccination board composed of leading civil and ecclesiastical officials was created.[147]

The board's immediate concern was the next series of vaccinations, which would take place as soon as the vesicles of the children inoculated on December 1 and 2 had matured. Since the board had not yet created a vaccination clinic, José Fernández Moreno, director of the royal customhouse, offered a room in his home until a formal center was established. Enthusiasm created by the arrival of the expedition moved private citizens to contribute ample funds to support the board's activities. On December 9 a proclamation announced that public vaccinations would take place in the main room of the customhouse during the next two days.[148] Despite the board's enthusiasm and energy, however, only forty-four children appeared for vaccination.[149]

On December 15 Balmis returned from his trip to Durango. On his journey to the northern capital he had vaccinated in Fresnillo and Sombrerete. He had previously notified Governor Bernardo Bonvía that the mission would arrive in Durango on December 8 but could stay only twenty-four hours. A deputation from the Ayuntamiento awaited the expedition when it arrived on the scheduled date. After resting briefly in the home of the royal treasurer, Rafael Ahumado, Balmis joined Bonvía for dinner.[150] The following morning an edict notified the public of the expedition's arrival and announced that the first operations would be performed in the governor's home at eleven o'clock that morning. The session was given an added air of festivity since December 9 was also the birthday of Queen María Luisa.[151] There is no record of how many vaccinations Balmis performed in Durango, but during his short stay he did have the good fortune to

[142] Riaño to Iturrigaray, Guanajuato, 26 Noviembre 1804, AGN, "Epidemias," v. 4, exp. 4, f. 8.

[143] Ibid., fs. 8–8v.

[144] Riaño to Iturrigaray, Guanajuato, 3 Mayo 1805, AGN, "Epidemias," v. 4, exp. 4, f. 27.

[145] Domingo Gómez to Riaño, Salvatierra, 23 Marzo 1805, AGN, "Epidemias," v. 4, exp. 15, f. 47.

[146] Ayuntamiento de Zacatecas to Viceroy, "Noticia circunstanciada del recibimiento que se ha hecho en la Ciudad de Nuestra Señora de los Zacatecas a la Real Expedición de la Vacuna," Zacatecas, 26 Febrero 1805, AGN, "Epidemias," v. 9, exp. 4, fs. 10v–13v.

[147] Ibid., fs. 14–14v.

[148] Ibid., f. 15v.

[149] José Fernández Moreno, "Razón del número de niños de ambos sexos, a quienes se les ha ministrado, el fluído vacuno, desde el Día 1° de Diciembre de 1804 hasta el 17 de Febrero 1805," Zacatecas, 27 Febrero 1805, AGN, "Epidemias," v. 9, exp. 4, f. 32.

[150] Bonvía to Gaceta de México, Durango, 14 Diciembre 1804, AGI, "Indif. Gen.," Leg. 1.558, I, f. 1.

[151] Bernardo de Bonvía, "Circular," Durango, 9 Diciembre 1804, AGI, "Indif. Gen.," Leg. 1.558, I, f. 2.

discover cowpox after a brief examination of cattle on the outlying ranches.[152]

The expedition departed from Durango on Sunday morning, December 9. On his return to Zacatecas, Balmis stopped in Sombrerete to collect Buenaventura Safiro and José Teodoro Olivas, who would accompany the expedition to Manila. Five more boys—José Dolores Moreno, Juan Amador Castañeda, José Felipe Osorio Moreno, José Francisco, and José Catalino Rivera—were acquired in Fresnillo.

Reaching Zacatecas on December 15, members of the expedition rested three days before beginning their return trip to Mexico City. The Ayuntamiento of Zacatecas presented Balmis with six children—Teófilo Romero, Félix Barraza, José Manuel Portillo, Martín Márquez, José Antonio Salazar, and Pedro Nolasco Mesa—to join the expedition to the Philippines. When Balmis left the city on December 18, his ranks were swelled by the additional children for the journey to Manila plus another child from Zacatecas to convey the virus to Aguascalientes and León. The boys wore gala uniforms which had been provided by their respective ayuntamientos. Each uniform bore the royal crest and the inscription "Dedicated to María Luisa, Queen of Spain and the Indies." When Balmis later stopped in León, the parish priest, Don Tiburcio Camina, presented him with five-year old Guillermo Toledo y Pino to help transport the vaccine to Manila.[153]

The Central Vaccination Board of Zacatecas was active for at least a year after Balmis's departure. By December 31, 1805, working every eleventh day, the junta had vaccinated 2,448 young persons in the capital alone. The board was able to function solely on funds donated by private citizens. Most contributors, however, were members of the board itself.[154]

Balmis's party reached Querétaro on Christmas Eve. After pausing to enjoy the holiday celebrations, the expedition left for Mexico City on December 27.[155] In Querétaro, Balmis collected the six boys whom Antonio Gutiérrez had sent from Vallodolid, along with José María Ursula, who was presented by the city of Querétaro. The expedition reached Mexico City on December 30 after a breathtaking fifty-three-day tour of the northcentral provinces.[156]

THE GUTIÉRREZ MISSION TO VALLADOLID, GUADALAJARA, AND SAN LUIS POTOSÍ

Antonio Gutiérrez, who had separated from the main portion of the expedition in Celaya on November 17, reached Valladolid toward the end of the month. Little information is available on his sojourn in Valladolid. Shortly before his arrival the city had suffered a smallpox epidemic during which many citizens had been immunized by variolization and vaccination.[157] Documents, however, do not reveal the source of the vaccine. Soon after his arrival in Valladolid, Guitérrez made a brief examination of some cattle on the city commons and discovered cowpox. This was the third and final source of the virus found by the expedition in New Spain. Later, 205 persons received immunization from this local virus.[158]

According to Balmis's instructions, Gutiérrez immediately organized a vaccination board. Board members assessed themselves fifty pesos each to finance its operation. Despite the limited number of non-immune persons in Valladolid, the junta actively promoted vaccination after Gutiérrez's departure. Three sessions each week were held when the virus was available. By January 16 a total of 1,236 persons had submitted to vaccination. Moreover the board reported that the vaccine effectively treated intense fever and a variety of eye afflictions.[159]

Besides providing José Antonio Lagunas and José Ricardo Vello to transport the vaccine to Guadalajara, the Central Vaccination Board of Valladolid generously paid 1,300 pesos to the parents of Juan Nepomuceno Torrescano, Juan José Santa María, José Antonio Marmolejo, José Silverio Ortiz, Laureano Reyes, and José María Zarcehaga, the young boys who would accompany the expedition to the Philippines.[160]

On Monday, December 3, Gutiérrez left Valladolid and reached the outskirts of Guadalajara four days later. He encountered difficulties from the outset. On December 7 Gutiérrez advised the Audiencia from a place called San Lorenzo that he planned to enter the city at 10:30 that morning.[161] But he imprudently sent the communication with an Indian woman on her way to market. The message did not reach its destination until

152 Balmis to Cavallero, México, 4 Enero 1805, AGI, "Indif. Gen.," Leg. 1.558, II, f. 5.

153 Ibid., f. 9.

154 Junta Central de Vacuna to Iturrigaray, Zacatecas, 28 Enero 1806, AGN, "Epidemias," v. 9, exp. 4, f. 35.

155 Miguel Domínguez, "Cuenta de los gastos que se han suplido a la Real Expedición de la Vacuna," Querétaro, 19 Enero 1805, AGN, "Epidemias," v. 4, exp. 2, fs. 13–14.

156 Balmis to Iturrigaray, México, 30 Diciembre 1804, AGN, "Epidemias," v. 18, exp. 13, f. 17.

157 Díaz de Ortega to Iturrigaray, Valladolid, 2 Noviembre 1804, AGN, "Epidemias," v. 4, exp. 5, fs. 1–1v.

158 Díaz de Ortega to Iturrigaray, Valladolid, 18 Enero 1805, AGN, "Epidemias," v. 4, exp. 5, f. 4v.

159 Díaz de Ortega to Balmis, Valladolid, 16 Enero 1804, AGI, "Indif. Gen.," Leg. 1.558, I, fs. 1–4.

160 José Vicente Montano, "Cuenta de Gastos," Valladolid, 26 Marzo 1805, AGN, "Epidemias," v. 4, exp. 15, f. 5.

161 Gutiérrez to Real Audiencia de Guadalajara, San Lorenzo, 7 Diciembre 1804, AGI, "Indif. Gen.," Leg. 1.558, I, f. 1.

nearly noon.[162] Since an earlier letter announcing the expedition's trip to Guadalajara had not yet reached the city, the errant note was the Audiencia's first notice that Balmis was in the vicinity. In fact no official communiqué concerning the mission had ever reached Guadalajara. The local officials' only authoritative indication of the expedition's formation was a copy of the Royal Order of May 20, 1804, which briefly mentioned the mission.

When Pedro Catani, regent of the Audiencia, received Gutiérrez's note, he immediately ordered Fernando Cambres, the official notary, to accompany him to the customary entry point from Mexico City to meet the assistant. They could not find Gutiérrez, however, and a search of the local villages of San Pedro and San Lorenzo was fruitless. Gutiérrez had already entered the city by another route.[163]

Catani returned to the city and convoked an informal meeting of the Audiencia to discuss a public reception for the expedition. At that point Gutiérrez entered the council room and announced that after waiting from 10:00 A.M. until 1:00 P.M. at the entry point of Mexicaltzingo, he had proceeded to the home of the fiscal de lo civil.

After Catani had explained the Audiencia's failure to provide a welcoming delegation, it was decided to stage an official entrance at 4:30 P.M. on December 9.[164] The Ayuntamiento furnished a residence for the expedition "on one of the principal streets of the city," including complete facilities and a servant to care for the children.[165] Gutiérrez, however, abandoned the house a few days later and occupied quarters proffered by Bishop Juan Cruz in the Clerical Correctional Academy.[166] Gutiérrez later explained that the academy presented superior facilities, and he could conduct vaccinations in the same quarters. The Ayuntamiento gracefully accepted the change.[167]

The expedition's official entry into Guadalajara took place on the afternoon of December 9 as planned. Gutiérrez, Catani, and the two boys from Valladolid went out to the village of San Pedro that morning. In the afternoon they moved to the main entry point and joined the Audiencia and the Ayuntamiento. The oidor decano took one of the boys into his coach; the Ayuntamiento took the other. Gutiérrez joined Catani and the fiscal de lo civil. The impressive caravan withdrew to the cathedral, while the provincial infantry battalion band intoned a solemn overture. After the customary Te Deum, Gutiérrez and the boys retired to their quarters.[168]

On December 11 Gutiérrez presented to the Audiencia a copy of the Royal Order of September 1, 1803, Balmis's instructions for the creation of a vaccination board and clinic, and four copies of the director's *Tratado histórico*. The assistant requested the Ayuntamiento's aid in securing six boys between three and five years old to take to Manila. He expressed a desire that the children be ready to travel by his projected departure on December 21.[169]

Evidently vaccinations commenced that same morning. An edict published by the Audiencia announced that vaccinations would begin on December 11 at 9:00 A.M. in the municipal council room.[170] Surprisingly, however, none of the numerous documents in Mexican or Spanish archives mentions the number of inoculations performed in Guadalajara.

Local physicians were evidently unimpressed by the expedition and ignored Catani's order to attend the initial session. The regent therefore instructed Dr. Mariano García de la Torre to direct all practitioners to attend the afternoon session. Catani promised that the physicians would incur serious sanctions if their indifference toward superior orders persisted.[171]

An acrimonious dispute over finances accentuated Gutiérrez's difficulties in Guadalajara. The Royal Order of September 1, 1803, clearly indicated that the Royal Exchequer was responsible for the expedition's expenses. Normally the Audiencia of Guadalajara would absorb the cost, since it was the king's direct representative in western and northwestern New Spain. When Catani discovered the financial obligations incumbent upon that body, however, he stated that the Royal Treasury's funds were insufficient and appealed to the Ayuntamiento.[172] Although uncommonly high expenditures that year had left only 2,030 pesos in the city treasury, the municipal council generously contributed five hundred pesos to assist the expedition.[173]

The Audiencia was completely unprepared when Gutiérrez announced on December 21 that he was leaving Guadalajara on the twenty-fourth and presented a bill of 1,478 pesos for "extraordinary expenses." He requested that the Audiencia discharge this debt from the Royal Treasury.[174] The bill included rent of a coach

[162] Fernando Cambres, "Certificación de Decreto," Guadalajara, 7 Diciembre 1804, AGI, "Indif. Gen.," Leg. 1.558, I, fs. 14–14v.

[163] *Ibid.*, fs. 15v–18.

[164] *Ibid.*, fs. 18–21.

[165] Ayuntamiento de Guadalajara, "Acta," Guadalajara, 7 Diciembre 1804, AGN, "Epidemias," v. 4, exp. 8, fs. 9–9v.

[166] Ayuntamiento de Guadalajara, "Acta," Guadalajara, 10 Diciembre 1804, AGN, "Epidemias," v. 4, exp. 8, f. 13.

[167] Gutiérrez to Audiencia de Guadalajara, Guadalajara, 10 Diciembre 1804, AGI, "Indif. Gen.," Leg. 1.558, I, f. 1.

[168] Fernando Cambres, "Certificación," Guadalajara, 9 Diciembre 1804, AGI, "Indif. Gen.," Leg. 1.558, I, fs. 24–26.

[169] Gutiérrez to Audiencia de Guadalajara, Guadalajara, 11 Diciembre 1804, AGI, "Indif. Gen.," Leg. 1.558, I, fs. 15v–17v.

[170] Audiencia de Guadalajara, *Bando,* Guadalajara, 11 Diciembre 1804, AGI, "Indif. Gen.," Leg. 1.558, I, fs. 2–3v.

[171] Catani to Mariano García de la Torre, Guadalajara, 11 Diciembre 1804, AGI, "Indif. Gen.," Leg. 1.558, I, fs. 3v–4.

[172] Catani to Ayuntamiento de Guadalajara, Guadalajara, 13 Diciembre 1804, AGN, "Epidemias," v. 4, exp. 8, f. 20.

[173] Ayuntamiento de Guadalajara, "Acta," Guadalajara, 13 Diciembre 1804, AGN, "Epidemias," v. 4, exp. 8, fs. 21v–22v.

[174] Gutiérrez to Audiencia de Guadalajara, Guadalajara, 21 Diciembre 1804, AGN, "Epidemias," v. 4, exp. 7, f. 3v.

and three saddled horses, estimated travel costs, outfits and personal items for six children from Guadalajara who would accompany him to Manila, and miscellaneous expenses. It also included the astonishing total of nine hundred pesos which Gutiérrez had promised the parents who allowed their sons accompany the expedition to the Philippines.[175] It will be remembered that as compensation for their services, the king had promised to maintain and educate all children who took part in the expedition. Balmis, however, discovered during his northern trip that parents consistently rejected promises of deferred benefits but eagerly accepted cash. Parents in Guadalajara also preferred money in hand.

The Audiencia discreetly forwarded Gutiérrez's letter, bills, and the Royal Order of September 1, 1803, to Intendant José Ignacio Oritz de Salinas.[176] Ortiz de Salinas also refused to pay. He pointed out that the Ayuntamiento had already provided a sum sufficient to pay the expedition's ordinary expenses. The nine-hundred-peso bill for securing the children was a complete surprise. He agreed that the carriers were vital but noted that the royal instructions authorized their acquisition only through promises of future maintenance and education. He had no instructions from the viceroy to depart from the royal orders. He also explained that the royal instructions clearly stated that extraordinary expenses incurred by the expedition would be honored only after presentation and approbation of an itemized bill. The assistant had ignored this latter provision.[177] Ortiz de Salinas and Catani, therefore, requested that Gutiérrez justify his expenditures.

In a letter to Catani, Gutiérrez retorted that it was "difficult" to account for every item and alleged that he was not required to justify his expenses. His sole obligation was the presentation of his director's instructions, which directed him to secure the children and offer money if necessary. At this point it must be recalled that Balmis merely suggested this procedure only after local authorities had given their approval. Gutiérrez continued that he had enclosed the bill, not to become involved in "mechanics which do not concern me nor are part of my commission," but rather to guide the Audiencia. He had already submitted a copy of Balmis's instructions from which he could not depart a whit. He suggested that Catani attend to the matter and communicate his decision to the intendant. The expedition, he concluded, was already behind its scheduled departure.[178] Gutiérrez replied to Ortiz de Salinas in a

similar tone. He reiterated his intention to leave on the twenty-fourth and stated that "as for legalizing, justifying, and arranging payment of the expenses, you may decide what you please since it is not my concern." [179] A flurry of correspondence quickly developed between the intendant and the regent. Each official protested that he commanded no resources to cover the expenses. During the exchange, Gutiérrez, José Agapito Illán, José Feliciano Gómez, José Lino Velázquez, José Mauricio Macías, Ignacio Nájera, and Crisanto Caballero left Guadalajara to join Balmis in Guanajuato.

Ortiz de Salinas subsequently sent the entire file to the viceroy and asked him to resolve the conflict.[180] Iturrigaray referred the case to the fiscal de lo civil. The fiscal merely approved the Ayuntamiento's five-hundred-peso allotment of public funds but made no recommendations concerning the nine hundred-peso payment to the children's parents. The viceregal government had never authorized the substitution of a pecuniary reward for the king's promises. The fiscal, therefore, returned the problem to the Audiencia and intendant of Guadalajara.[181]

When Balmis was apprised of the financial controversy in Guadalajara on January 11, he could only express his surprise. He explained that Gutiérrez had informed him from Querétaro on January 1 that "all expenses of the Royal Expedition, or at least the greater part of them—gratuities for parents of the six boys I am bringing from Guadalajara, their apparel, and so forth, have been paid by that Illustrious Bishop." Balmis apologized for Gutiérrez's tactless impetuosity and ascribed his assistant's action to his excessive zeal to spread the vaccine.[182]

An undated report written by Fernando Cambres substantiates Gutiérrez's claim that the bishop of Guadalajara had paid the expedition's expenses. The document repeats Catani's affirmation that the bishop was paying the debt occasioned by the expedition.[183] Oritz de Salinas, however, was evidently unaware of the bishop's action. In March, 1805, he reported that as far as he knew, the problem had not been settled.[184]

When Gutiérrez reached Guanajuato and learned that Balmis had already departed for Mexico City, he too began his return to the capital. When he arrived in Querétaro on December 31, however, Gutiérrez found instructions from Balmis to transport the vaccine to San

[175] Antonio Gutiérrez y Robredo, "Noticia de los costos que causa el vestuario, conducción y manutención de los niños que con escala en Guanajuato marcharon de esta ciudad a Filipinas y Gratificaciones a sus Padres," Guadalajara, 21 Diciembre 1804, AGN, "Epidemias," v. 4, exp. 7, f. 4.
[176] Catani to Intendente Interino de Guadalajara, Guadalajara, 21 Diciembre 1804, AGN, "Epidemias," v. 4, exp. 7, f. 4.
[177] José Ignacio Ortiz de Salinas to Catani, Guadalajara, 21 Diciembre 1840, AGN, "Epidemias," v. 4, exp. 7, fs. 4v–5v.
[178] Gutiérrez to Catani, Guadalajara, 22 Diciembre 1804, AGI, "Indif. Gen.," Leg. 1.558, I, fs. 8–11v.

[179] Gutiérrez to Ortiz de Salinas, Guadalajara, 22 Diciembre 1804, AGN, "Epidemias," v. 4, exp. 7, fs. 5–6.
[180] Ortiz de Salinas to Iturrigaray, Guadalajara, 25 Diciembre 1804, AGN, "Epidemias," v. 4, exp. 7, fs. 13–13v.
[181] Saparzurieta, "Auto," México, 31 Enero 1805, AGN, "Epidemias," v. 4, exp. 8, fs. 30–32v.
[182] Balmis to Iturrigaray, México, 12 Enero 1805, AGN, "Epidemias," v. 4, exp. 7, fs. 15–16.
[183] Fernando Cambres, "Diligencia," Guadalajara, n.d., AGI, "Indif. Gen.," Leg. 1.558, I, fs. 15–16.
[184] Ortiz de Salinas to Viceroy, Guadalajara, 23 Marzo 1805, AGN, "Epidemias," v. 4, exp. 7, fs. 18–18v.

Luis Potosí. The assistant left the six boys from Guadalajara in the care of Miguel Domínguez, and after securing the services of Francisco Antonio Pablo Isguerra to convey the vaccine, set out for San Luis Potosí.[185]

Arriving in San Luis Potosí on January 5, Gutiérrez was received with the usual amenities. A proclamation announced that Gutiérrez's only vaccination session would be held on Monday, January 7. All parochial priests were exhorted to dedicate their Sunday sermons to the advantages of the operation. On January 7 Gutiérrez vaccinated 391 *potosinos* and fostered the creation of a vaccination board and clinic.[186] He returned to Querétaro on January 11. One of the boys from Guadalajara, Crisanto Caballero, had become ill and was unable to accompany the expedition.[187] Gutiérrez gathered the rest of the boys and on January 14 departed for Mexico City, where he rejoined Balmis three days later.

THE DEPARTURE FROM NEW SPAIN

After completing his tour of the northcentral provinces, Balmis prepared for the next step ordered by Carlos IV—the trip to the Philippines. Perhaps no other aspect of the expedition better illustrates the strained relations existing between Balmis and Iturrigaray. Balmis had been planning the voyage to Manila ever since his arrival in New Spain. In fact, it often appears from his correspondence that the director considered Mexico merely an interlude during his trip to the Far East. In his letter from Veracruz on July 25, 1804, Balmis declared that after entrusting the Spanish children to Iturrigaray's care, he would attend to his duties in New Spain until he could embark for Manila.[188] A week later he wrote from Jalapa that "since the China Ship has already arrived, I will arrange for my trip to that part of the world."[189] Soon after his arrival in Mexico City Balmis requested that Iturrigaray order the commander of the next Manila Galleon to furnish accommodations for between forty and forty-eight persons. Balmis also asked to be informed when the ship would depart so that he could make all arrangements well beforehand.[190]

Quite understandably, Iturrigaray insisted that Balmis complete his assignment in the capital and provincial centers of New Spain before rushing off to the Far East. The viceroy also noted that special preference on the Manila Galleon must be given to the transportation of a large number of troops who were required to reinforce island garrisons. In addition, there were many Dominican, Carmelite, and Augustinian monks from Spain who had postponed their trip on the last vessel to make way for military personnel. Although the viceroy promised to deal "opportunely" with Balmis's request, he warned that "you ought to know now, for your own plans, that if another ship does not present itself, it will be impossible to send the expedition in the present one."[191]

Barely disguising his irritation, Balmis resigned himself to comply: "Since you are the viceroy and the person whom I must obey under the circumstances, I submit to your decision." But he could not resist expressing his surprise at the viceroy's relegation of the expedition to a tertiary position. Although granting that additional military and religious personnel were needed in the islands, Balmis stated that he was "intimately aware of His Majesty's desire that the serum be sent flying if possible . . . to his beloved vassals, without sparing expense or effort." The viceroy remained adamant, nevertheless, and Balmis promised to meet his obligations in New Spain. He did remind the viceroy to send him prompt notification of the next ship's departure, which he estimated would be sometime during the following January.[192]

When Balmis returned from Puebla in mid-October, 1804, he contacted the commander of the *Magallanes,* Angel Crespo, who would command the next vessel to Manila. Crespo assured Balmis that despite the large number of passengers already signed on for the upcoming trip, there would be space on the ship for the expedition.[193] On October 26 Iturrigaray authorized Balmis to initiate arrangements with Crespo in accordance with the royal instructions. The viceroy stipulated, however, that if "news arrives that the vaccine has been introduced into those islands . . . the Royal Exchequer should excuse itself . . . from expenses which would be uselessly discharged in sending the expedition there."[194] Balmis communicated the viceroy's decision to Crespo and ordered cabins and special foods.[195] Iturrigaray's reservations, however, compelled Crespo to reply that since it was not yet certain that the expedition would even sail, he could not compromise himself by making any special arrangements on

[185] Gutiérrez to Domínguez, Querétaro, 1 Enero 1805, AGN, "Epidemias," v. 4, exp. 2, fs. 25–25v.

[186] José Ignacio Vélez to Iturrigaray, San Luis Potosí, 9 Enero 1805, AGN, "Epidemias," v. 4, exp. 9, fs. 13–13v.

[187] Miguel Domínguez, "Cuenta de los gastos," Querétaro, 19 Enero 1805, AGN, "Epidemias," v. 4, exp. 2, fs. 14–14v.

[188] Balmis to Iturrigaray, Veracruz, 25 Julio 1804, AGN, "Epidemias," v. 10, exp. 7, f. 42.

[189] Balmis to Iturrigaray, Jalapa, 1 Agosto 1804, AGI, "Indif. Gen.," Leg. 1.558, I, f. 2.

[190] Balmis to Iturrigaray, México, 11 Agosto 1804, AGN, "Epidemias," v. 10, exp. 7, fs. 48–48v.

[191] Iturrigaray to Balmis, México, 14 Agosto 1804, AGN, "Epidemias," v. 10, exp. 7, fs. 50–51v.

[192] Balmis to Iturrigaray, México, 24 Agosto 1804, AGN, "Epidemias," v. 19, exp. 7, fs. 53–54v.

[193] Balmis to Iturrigaray, México, 18 Octubre 1804, AGN, "Epidemias," v. 4, exp. 2, f. 2.

[194] Iturrigaray to Balmis, México, 26 Octubre 1804, AGN, "Epidemias," v. 4, exp. 2, f. 3v.

[195] Balmis to Crespo, México, 29 Octubre 1804, AGN, "Epidemias," v. 4, exp. 13, fs. 3–3v.

its behalf. He would be pleased to initiate preparations when the viceroy gave him direct authorization.[196]

In the face of this new obstacle, Balmis informed Iturrigaray that he could do nothing until the viceroy gave his unqualified permission to proceed. The director stated that he would have to make all arrangements well in advance in order to avoid any possibility of being unprepared when the ship was ready to sail. If the expedition did not leave Mexico in January, it would be six months or a year before another vessel departed for the Philippines. He also explained that even if the vaccine had already reached the islands, the expedition was still required to instruct physicians and create vaccination boards and clinics according to the king's instructions.[197]

Although Iturrigaray finally directed Crespo to receive the expedition,[198] he instructed Benito Vívero y Escaño, commandant of San Blas, to investigate possible prior introduction of the vaccine in the islands.[199] On January 10, 1805, Vívero y Escaño replied that the commander of the frigate *Concepción,* just in from Manila, had assured him that the vaccine had not yet reached the islands.

That was the final word Iturrigaray needed. On January 10 he gave Balmis permission to proceed with his preparations for the voyage.[200] Iturrigaray then notified the governor of Acapulco of the expedition's imminent departure for that western port and explained his obligations.[201] The viceroy also advised the ministers of the Royal Treasury in Mexico City to provide Balmis with funds for the trip to Acapulco, outfits for all the children, the passage to Manila, and three months' salary in advance to each member of the expedition. Iturrigaray then washed his hands of the entire affair. He informed the treasury officials that they were to superintend all subsequent arrangements concerning the expedition "since I can no longer dedicate this office to that object . . . you will inform me only of that which indispensably needs my authorization."[202]

Balmis immediately began preparations for his departure from Mexico City. Francisco Pastor had returned from Guatemala on January 3, and Antonio Gutiérrez

arrived from San Luis Potosí two weeks later. His truncated staff, however, was insufficient to provide adequate care for the children. In addition, the arduous journey through the interior had wrought great physical hardship on all members of the expedition. Another aide was absolutely necessary. Balmis requested that Iturrigaray appoint Angel Crespo, who had gratuitously helped during the greater part of the expedition, as an additional male nurse. He had earlier petitioned Cavallero to approve Crespo's nomination, but as yet had received no reply.[203] Although several months earlier Iturrigaray had commissioned Alejandro García Arboleya as an assistant for the expedition to Oaxaca, the viceroy stated that he had no authority to appoint Crespo. Crespo, however, did accompany the mission to Manila, and in November, 1805, Iturrigaray was ordered to recognize the commission and pay his salary retroactive to May, 1804.[204]

Balmis led the expedition out of the Mexican capital on January 18 after a flurry of last minute preparations. A child had been obtained from the Real Hospicio to transport the vaccine to Acapulco.[205] Reaching Chilpancingo on January 24, Balmis vaccinated sixty-five children and selected Dr. José Fuentes to propagate the lymph throughout the area. He also acquired Francisco Tapia to convey the vaccine to Acapulco.[206]

The expedition reached Acapulco on January 27, over a week before the ship's eventual departure. In the interim Balmis introduced the vaccine into the western port. When Francisco Tapia's vesicles matured on February 1, Balmis inoculated 377 children and instructed Juan de Molina, physician of the Hospital Real, in the procedure. On Fabruary 5 Balmis presented a plan to Governor José Barriero y Quijano for the formation of a vaccination clinic.[207]

Shortly before the *Magallanes's* departure, the director received one final message from Iturrigaray. The viceroy announced that he was sending a letter commending the expedition to the governor of the Philippines and then abruptly concluded:

Thus, with this, there is no other order I must give concerning the expedition. Therefore I must announce . . . that you should take all the expedition's equipment with you in order to return to Europe directly from the islands . . . since the Royal Exchequer in these dominions is in no condition to cover the expenses that your return to Mexico would cause. You should avoid (since it is in no way necessary to your mission) returning here. If you decide

[196] Crespo to Balmis, México, 29 Octubre 1804, AGN, "Epidemias," v. 4, exp. 13, fs. 4–4v.

[197] Balmis to Iturrigaray, México, 30 Octubre 1804, AGN, "Epidemias," v. 4, exp. 13, fs. 5–6.

[198] Iturrigaray to Crespo, México, 6 Noviembre 1804, AGN, "Epidemias," v. 4, exp. 13, f. 11.

[199] Iturrigaray to Vívero y Escaño, México, 28 Noviembre 1804, AGN, "Epidemias," v. 4, exp. 13, f. 14.

[200] Iturrigaray to Balmis, México, 10 Enero 1805, AGN, "Epidemias," v. 4, exp. 13, fs. 19–19v.

[201] Iturrigaray to Governador y Ministros de la Hacienda Real de Acapulco, México, 10 Enero 1805, AGN, "Epidemias." v. 4, exp. 13, f. 22.

[202] Iturrigaray to Ministros de Ejército y Real Hacienda, México, 10 Enero 1804, AGN, "Epidemias," v. 4, exp. 13, fs. 20–21v.

[203] Balmis to Iturrigaray, México, 14 Enero 1805, AGN, "Epidemias," v. 4, exp. 13, fs. 30–31v.

[204] Soler to Iturrigaray, San Lorenzo, 10 Noviembre 1805, AGN, "Reales Cédulas," v. 97, exp. 237, fs. 338–339.

[205] Iturrigaray to Cosme de Mier, México, 14 Enero 1804, AGN, "Epidemias," v. 4, exp. 13, f. 28.

[206] Antonio García de Cassal to Iturrigaray, Tixtla, 30 Enero 1805, AGN, "Epidemias," v. 4, exp. 13, fs. 42–42v.

[207] Barriero y Quijano to Iturrigaray, Acapulco, 16 Febrero 1805, AGI, "Indif. Gen.," Leg. 1.558, II, fs. 1–2.

to the contrary despite these reflections, you will do so at your own expense.[208]

Thus, with no parting farewell and no visible sign of appreciation, the viceroy summarily commanded Balmis to leave the country and not return.

The *Magallanes* was to weigh anchor on February 7, but insufficient winds delayed its sailing until the following morning. On the eve of his departure Balmis requested that the king grant him the Cross of Carlos III or the honors of the Council of the Indies in recognition of his work in America. He preferred the first award because it was more "public" and therefore would better advertise the success of the venture throughout Europe.[209] There is no record that this request was ever granted. On February 8 the *Magallanes* sailed for Manila. The Royal Expedition included Balmis; Antonio Gutiérrez y Robredo as assistant; Francisco Pastor as practitioner; Pedro Ortega, Antonio Pastor, Isabel Gómez y Cendala, and Angel Crespo as nurses; and the twenty-six boys who would preserve the lymph by arm-to-arm vaccination.

Despite his differences with the viceroy, Balmis could be proud of the expedition's achievements in New Spain. In a little over seven months the director or his aides visited all major cities and many small villages of the viceroyalty. They had created a networks of free vaccination clinics under the direction of carefully trained local administrators and physicians. This program of intercommunicating local organizations assured a continual availability of vaccine in preserved lymph and living carriers, while the discoveries of cowpox in Puebla, Durango, and Valladolid promised a domestic source of the virus. The Mexican medical profession and numerous laymen had received instruction in the latest vaccination and vaccine preservation techniques.

It is impossible to determine the exact number of vaccinations performed by the expedition since complete information is unavailable. Perhaps one hundred thousand is not an overestimation for the period between July, 1804, and February, 1805. This figure represents approximately two per cent of the population of New Spain at that time. While this may seem a rather insignificant figure, it must be recognized that the expedition neglected vast areas of the viceroyalty, including all the far northwestern, northern, and northeastern provinces. Moreover, vaccination was largely limited to children because the epidemics of 1779 and 1797 had exposed most of the adult population.

Utilizing Sherburn F. Cook's calculations, the expedition reached approximately one-half the population by area. Since perhaps only twenty per cent of the inhabitants were non-immune, Balmis and his staff did treat roughly twenty per cent of those reached who might

have benefited from vaccination. Considering that the expedition was of an introductory and propagandizing variety led by outsiders, the total of one hundred thousand represents a sizable achievement. In all respects the Royal Expedition was a resounding success.

VI. THE HISTORY OF VACCINATION IN GUATEMALA

THE INTRODUCTION OF SMALLPOX VACCINE INTO GUATEMALA

Perhaps no other area of Spanish America so eagerly sought or rapidly disseminated the vaccine as Guatemala. For two decades the unmerciful ravages of the epidemic of 1780 remained a vivid reality to its survivors. During the latter 1780's and 1790's the threat of another attack lurked in the minor infections which intermittently struck the captaincy general. Dr. José Felipe de Flores's success with variolization in 1780 erased most prejudices against prophylactic inoculation, and reports of Jenner's vaccination promised the eventual eradication of the deadly disease.

By the spring of 1802, however, all factors signaled the advent of another smallpox epidemic. In June reports from the northern province of Petén described a new attack far more serious than the mild infections which had struck most areas of Guatemala in recent years. District Commander Nicolás de la Barra announced that the disease had been extant in the pueblo of San Miguel since mid-April. Twenty-four of the eighty-four villagers who contracted the disease had perished. Smallpox was also present in the districts of Totonicapan and Quetzaltenango.[1] Most ominous, however, were the small-scale infections which menaced the capital from several adjacent provinces.[2]

Leading citizens of the captaincy general began a frantic search for smallpox vaccine. They requested the virus from Spain, Mexico, Cuba, and the United States, and sought cowpox throughout Guatemala. Principal figures in the quest for the protective included Captain General Antonio Gonzales Saravia, Oidor Jacobo de Villa Urrutia, Protomédico José Antonio de Córdoba, and Dr. Narciso Esparragosa y Gallardo, a protégé of José Felipe de Flores and perhaps the outstanding figure of Guatemalan medicine. Until the vaccine could be obtained, however, the government advised district officials to employ variolization, which had been so effective in 1780.[3]

Even before warnings of the new danger reached the capital, several attempts had been made to secure the virus. In April, 1802, Dr. José Antonio de Córdoba and Dr. Narciso Esparragosa y Gallardo promoted a

[208] Iturrigaray to Balmis, México, 22 Enero 1805, AGN, "Epidemias," v. **4**, exp. 13, fs. 35–35v.

[209] Balmis to Cavallero, Acapulco, 7 Febrero 1805, AGI, "Indif. Gen.," Leg. 1.558, I, f. 1.

[1] *Gazeta de Guatemala,* 21 Junio 1802: p. 151.

[2] *Ibid.,* 7 Junio 1802: p. 135.

[3] *Ibid.,* 21 Junio 1802: p. 150.

subscription to finance a vaccine-seeking mission to Mexico. Thirty-four citizens responded with contributions totaling 610 pesos. On April 25 the delegation expectantly sailed for Veracruz in the frigate *Argonaut,* but returned on June 1 empty-handed. The lymph had reached New Spain but was inert at the time of its arrival. The governor of Veracruz, however, promised to send active virus as soon as he acquired it.[4]

The mission did obtain two recent treatises concerning vaccination. One, an extensive manuscript by the noted naturalist José Mariano Moziño, included the translation of a report published by the Medical Society of Paris. This excellent guide served to rectify much erroneous information which Guatemalan physicians had encountered in previous instructions.[5]

On July 3 Don Tomás Urdiroz, from the port city of Trujillo, notified the *Gazeta de Guatemala* that he had solicited the vaccine in Havana, Mexico, and the Caribbean Islands. Dr. José Ledesma, a Guatemalan doctor visiting Havana, had replied that a small amount of lymph in glass slides had been taken to Havana from Spain, but had deteriorated during the voyage. Ledesma did promise to send a "good portion" of the vaccine to Guatemala when it reached Cuba. Urdiroz also announced that several Mexican physicians were seeking the vaccine in Spain, Havana, and the United States, and they promised to send him some when it arrived from any source.[6]

On August 17, 1802, excitement filled Guatemala City. Smallpox vaccine had just arrived in the capital. Don Ignacio Pavón y Muñoz had sent his brothers a small portion of the lymph by mail from Veracruz. Pavón y Muñoz had obtained the vaccine from New Orleans, where it had recently been introduced from the United States. The lymph, encrusted on a small thread enclosed in a vial and between glass slides, was entrusted to Dr. Narciso Esparragosa y Gallardo. He immediately inoculated five children, but the vaccine produced only immune reactions.[7]

Undaunted by this initial disappointment, Guatemalan physicians continued their requests for vaccine in Europe and America and intensified their search for cowpox in Guatemala. Dr. José Antonio de Córdoba even inoculated sheep with smallpox virus in an effort to induce cowpox or a similar disease.[8]

On December 16 another portion of lymph reached Guatemala City in the monthly mail from Oaxaca. An unnamed person in Madrid had sent the vaccine to Oidor Jacobo de Villa Urrutia. Villa Urrutia gave the fluid to Esparragosa y Gallardo, who inoculated the three children of Don Tomás Wading, the royal

accountant, and several other youngsters. Once again the virus had deteriorated en route to Guatemala.[9]

While all attempts to secure active vaccine failed, the *Gazeta de Guatemala* constantly publicized the new method. Dr. Esparragosa y Gallardo, who served as scientific editor of the paper, promptly conveyed any reports concerning the disease or vaccine to the public. The journal detailed the attempts of Guatemalans to obtain the virus abroad and their futile search for cowpox at home. The *Gazeta* reprinted excerpts from the outstanding French, English, and Spanish studies of vaccination, and each issue discussed the history of the operation, its spread throughout the world, or new uses attributed to the vaccine. The *Gazeta* also provided readers with much practical information concerning the recognition of cowpox, new inoculation techniques, development of a vaccination lesion and its effects, recognition of immune reactions, and the various methods of vaccine transportation. The paper also propagandized many questionable claims concerning the vaccine's powers such as making dull children intelligent, curing epilepsy, and moderating yellow fever.[10]

On July 3, 1803, after receiving news of a serious epidemic in the northern region around Ciudad Real de Chiapas, Captain General Antonio Gonzales Saravia appealed to the Spanish government for help. Gonzales Saravia explained that since the last general epidemic had occurred in 1780, an entire generation was exposed to the ravages of smallpox. A new infection could decimate one-third of Guatemala's population. He described the unsuccessful attempts to secure the vaccine abroad and the futile quest for cowpox in Guatemala. At the suggestion of leading Guatemalan physicians, he proposed that the Spanish government dispatch a maritime vaccination expedition to the New World. The vaccine could be preserved by successively inoculating young, non-immune boys during the voyage. Since the mission was too important to be placed in the hands of private citizens, he suggested that the Supreme Council for Surgery and Medicine in Madrid assume responsibility for organizing the expedition. In the meantime, he recommended that all ships sailing from Spanish ports carry a physician and several boys to transport the virus. He also suggested that vaccine be dispatched to the Protomedicato of Guatemala on the first vessel sailing from Cádiz to Honduras. Guatemalans themselves would pay all expenses of the mission. To finance the formal expedition, he suggested utilizing the municipal revenues of those communities which benefited from vaccination.[11]

By the time Gonzales Saravia's missive reached Spain, the Royal Expedition was en route to America. On December 16, 1803, Cavallero informed the captain

[4] *Ibid.,* 7 Junio 1802: pp. 135–137.
[5] *Ibid.*
[6] *Ibid.,* 26 Julio 1802: p. 188.
[7] *Ibid.,* 30 Agosto 1802: p. 212.
[8] Lanning, 1953: p. 47.

[9] *Gazeta de Guatemala,* 31 Enero 1802: p. 5.
[10] See *ibid.,* nos. 264–290, 21 Junio 1802 to 7 Febrero 1803.
[11] "Extracto," fs. 136–138v.

general that he would soon receive notification of and complete instructions concerning the Royal Expedition. Gonzales Saravia would be pleased to know, he added, that the expedition was transporting the vaccine in precisely the manner the captain general had suggested. Cavallero commended Gonzales Saravia's admirable concern for the welfare of the king's subjects and instructed him to send a physician and several young boys to any of the scheduled stops on the expedition's itinerary. The director would vaccinate the children and train the physician to communicate and preserve the vaccine.[12]

At the same time Cavallero notified Balmis, who was in the Canary Islands, of Gonzales Saravia's request. He ordered Balmis to complete his voyage as quickly as possible in order to deliver the virus to America without delay. He instructed the director to send fresh vaccine to the captaincy general either by means of one of his own aides or the physician commissioned by Gonzales Saravia.[13]

In mid-January, 1804, the Royal Order of September 1, 1803, finally arrived in Guatemala City. The captain general issued a decree ordering all local officials to comply with the royal instructions if the expedition or any part of it entered their jurisdiction. They should promptly notify him of the expedition's arrival, aid given to the director, the number of vaccinations and their results, and anything else worthy of mention. The Royal Treasury would pay all expenses incurred by the expedition upon presentation and justification of a certified bill. The decree and the royal order were subsequently printed in the *Gazeta de Guatemala* on March 12, 1804.[14]

In the meantime the search for the virus continued. On March 22 José Antonio de Córdoba, presuming that the Royal Expedition had already arrived in Cuba, requested that the governor of Havana send the vaccine to any port in the captaincy general. Weeks passed without results. Impatient with the delay, Dr. Córdoba appointed a delegation which would go to the island and secure the vaccine. He commissioned Dr. Vicente Carranza and Ramón Portillo, practicante mayor of the Real Hospital, to take six non-immune boys to Havana and then convey the virus to Guatemala by arm to arm inoculations. The commission would depart from Trujillo on the first ship sailing to Havana.[15]

Just as the mission was ready to leave Guatemala City on May 16, a special courier arrived from Veracruz. He brought Cavallero's letter of December 16,

1803, and another portion of vaccine from Don Ignacio Pavón y Muñoz. Pavón y Muñoz, a native of Guatemala City residing in Veracruz, had obtained the virus soon after its introduction into the Mexican port. Fearing that the lymph would deteriorate if he waited for the regular mail delivery, Pavón y Muñoz personally paid for the dispatch of the special courier. On April 22 he had carefully sealed the lymph between glass slides and sent it to his brothers, Cayetano and Manuel Pavón y Muñoz, in the Guatemalan capital. His shipment also included a new vaccination manual and several vaccinating needles.[16]

When the packet reached Guatemala City twenty days later, the Pavón y Muñoz brothers immediately entrusted it to Esparragosa y Gallardo. The physician deliberately unsealed the slides and extracted the lymph. The vaccine, "a little speckle the size of a fly's wing resting on a small piece of lint," was diluted and prepared for use.[17]

Esparragosa y Gallardo carefully recorded in his personal diary the development of these first vaccination vesicles. Assisted by José Antonio de Córdoba, he inoculated six children by pricking the upper portion of their arm four times with the point of the vaccinating needle. The children in the order of inoculation were: Alfonso Wading, son of Don Tomás Wading; Elogio de Villa Urrutia, son of Oidor Jacobo de Villa Urrutia; Magdalena Sosa, daughter of Don Francisco Sosa; Francisco Rivera, son of the general administrator of alcabalas; Dolores Valenzuela, daughter of Don Pedro José Valenzuela; and Vicente Salazar, son of Don Juan Nepomuceno Salazar.[18]

During the first few days, the vaccination lesions exhibited no signs of normal development. Perhaps, some thought, the vaccine had deteriorated during the three-week journey from Veracruz. Yet Esparragosa y Gallardo did not lose hope. Then on the seventh day, one small vesicle appeared on Alfonso Wading's right arm. In order to observe its development more closely, Esparragosa y Gallardo moved into the Wading home and kept the boy under constant observation. Maturation of the vesicles was carefully recorded in Esparragosa y Gallardo's diary.

Twenty-third day: . . . The vesicle is beginning to form. The scab is developing and he experiences sharp pains under the arm.

Twenty-fourth day: . . . This morning the vesicle was found burst at one edge, and almost drying up. . . . This occurrence leads to the suspicion that our hopes have ended unfortunately.

Twenty-fifth day: The vesicle is fuller and larger than in previous days; the areola has extended considerably. His arm is slightly swollen all around the lesion. I can see the depression quite well.[19]

[12] Cavallero to Gonzales Saravia, San Lorenzo, 16 Diciembre 1803; reprinted in *Reglamento para la Propagación y Estabilidad de la Vacuna en el Reyno de Guatemala*, Nueva Guatemala, 1805, AGI, "Indif. Gen.," Leg. 1.558, II, fs. 1–2.
[13] "Extracto," fs. 139–139v.
[14] Antonio Gonzales Saravia, *Decreto*, Real Palacio, 25 Enero 1804; reprinted in *Gazeta de Guatemala*, 12 Marzo 1804: p. 6.
[15] *Ibid.*, 25 Julio 1804: pp. 337–338.

[16] *Ibid.*, pp. 338–339.
[17] *Ibid.*, pp. 339–340.
[18] *Ibid.*
[19] *Ibid.*

Esparragosa y Gallardo would not be convinced that the operation had been successful until he had lanced the vesicle and examined the base of the lesion. This he did, assisted by José Antonio de Córdoba, on May 25. As soon as he removed the thin layer of skin covering the vesicle, Esparragosa y Gallardo observed "a small amount of very clear, transparent fluid . . . as the white of an egg" slowly emerging from the base of the lesion. Before probing the source of the fluid, he inoculated twenty more children. He then scrutinized the lesion with a magnifying glass. Examination revealed that Wading, indeed, had a true vaccination.[20]

On May 28 the vesicle partially filled again with the precious lymph and Esparragosa y Gallardo vaccinated seven more children.[21] Three of these seven inoculations proved effective.[22] On the same day the *Gazeta de Guatemala* reported that all twenty children vaccinated on the twenty-fifth were progressing satisfactorily.[23] These successful operations assured the captaincy general of an adequate source of vaccine.

Of the initial six children inoculated, only Alfonso Wading was able to transmit the virus. Magdalena Sosa's single vesicle contained too little lymph for further inoculations.[24]

Although the shipment of vaccine from Ignacio Pavón y Muñoz had provided a sufficient reserve for Guatemala, other deliveries soon followed. Don Venturo Batres, a native Guatemalan living in Mexico City, sent the vaccine to Ignacio Pavón y Muñoz in Veracruz. Pavón y Muñoz then forwarded the lymph by special courier to his two brothers in Guatemala City, where it arrived during the first week of June. Don Vicente Cervantes, professor of botany in Mexico City, sent a portion of vaccine to Don Alejandro Ramírez, secretary of the captaincy general, in the same shipment. Cervantes had taken the precaution of impregnating part of the lymph into threads and sealing them between slides. He deposited the remainder of the fluid in the hollow shank of a chicken feather. He then wrapped both receptacles in black paper to protect them from the light, for it was believed that the rays of the sun would vitiate the virus.[25]

By June 3 the Royal Order of December 16, 1803, finally reached Guatemala. In his reply, the captain general announced the felicitous introduction of the vaccine a few weeks previously and described its extension throughout the capital. He therefore excused himself from dispatching a physician to receive the lymph and instructions from Balmis.[26]

With vaccine now available in the capital, measures were taken to accelerate its propagation. In private and public instruction sessions, Dr. Narciso Esparragosa y Gallardo and Dr. José Antonio de Córdoba trained physicians, professors, students, and many non-professionals to vaccinate. On May 7 José Antonio de Córdoba had composed a guide summarizing the many vaccinating manuals he had received from Europe. The instructions were published and distributed to the several provinces.[27]

The vaccine spread rapidly throughout the capital. Inoculations were held every nine to eleven days when lymph was available. By June 23 an estimated four thousand persons had been vaccinated in Guatemala City and its immediate dependencies.[28] Dr. Narciso Esparragosa y Gallardo personally vaccinated 1,132 during the first month.[29]

Second only to Esparragosa y Gallardo in his zeal to disseminate the vaccine was Protomédico José Antonio de Córdoba. On May 28 his three sons had been vaccinated. As soon as their vesicles matured, he ordered all the leaders of religious communities and school administrators to present one or two non-immune individuals in the Tribunal of the Royal Protomedicato for vaccination. He then invited all local physicians, surgeons, practitioners, and their assistants to observe the proceedings, perform inoculations themselves, and continue the operation throughout the city. On July 2 the entire group gathered in the tribunal. Córdoba and Esparragosa y Gallardo inoculated 480 persons and instructed the assembled physicians.[30]

Eleven days later Dr. Córdoba took his recently vaccinated seven-year-old daughter to each convent and monastery in the capital. Utilizing the lymph from her mature vesicles, he inoculated several individuals in each place and trained the nuns and monks who had been selected to perform the operation within their respective religious communities. Within a few weeks, Dr. Córdoba personally vaccinated nearly eight hundred individuals and trained scores more.[31]

On June 17 the Ayuntamiento sponsored a special ceremony in the National Cathedral to give thanks for the introduction of the vaccine. The captain general, the archbishop, the faculty of the Royal University, the Royal Audiencia, civil and religious corporations, and prominent citizens attended the festive mass. Dr. Mariano García, priest of the Parroquia de los Remedios, offered a solemn Te Deum and delivered the thanksgiving sermon.[32]

The *Gazeta de Guatemala* continued to propagandize vaccination by printing interesting excerpts from Dr. Narciso Esparragosa y Gallardo's medical journal.

[20] *Ibid.*, pp. 342–343.
[21] *Ibid.*, p. 344.
[22] *Ibid.*, 2 Julio 1804: p. 349.
[23] *Ibid.*, 28 Mayo 1804: p. 112.
[24] *Ibid.*, 2 Julio 1804: p. 345.
[25] *Ibid.*, 25 Julio 1804: p. 339.
[26] "Extracto," fs. 139–140.

[27] *Gazeta de Guatemala*, 4 Junio 1804: pp. 113–115.
[28] *Ibid.*, 2 Julio 1804: p. 346.
[29] Esparragosa to Junta Central, Guatemala, 15 Noviembre 1806, AGI, "Indif. Gen.," Leg. 1.558, II, f. 3.
[30] *Gazeta de Guatemala*, 2 Julio 1804: p. 346.
[31] *Ibid.*
[32] *Ibid.*, p. 345.

Many articles recounted his unusual experiences with vaccination. The physician reported that he had asked a barber to sharpen one of his vaccinating needles. To test its point, the barber stuck the base of his thumb in much the same way that he often checked the cutting edge of his razors. Although Esparragosa y Gallardo had cleaned the needle twice, some lymph remained on its point. A few days later, a perfectly developed vesicle appeared on the barber's thumb. Esparragosa y Gallardo was able to utilize the unexpected vaccine in subsequent inoculations. He also related the case of a recently vaccinated young boy, who, after sleeping with his arm resting across his chest, later found a vesicle forming on his left nipple. Another vesicle developed on his back after he lay upon a piece of taffeta which had been used to cover the lesion.[33]

By the initiative of private individuals, vaccine soon reached the provinces. Don Gregorio Castriciones, a resident of San Salvador, was visiting Guatemala City when the lymph arrived from Veracruz. He obtained a portion of the vaccine and had several boys from the capital vaccinated. With the proper precautions he escorted the carriers to San Salvador. In the provincial capital, Dr. Nicolás Monteros took charge of the boys and in a short time vaccinated 9,220 persons. Don Benito Gonzales Patiño ably assisted Monteros by providing funds and a room in his home to conduct further vaccinations.[34]

In June Esparragosa y Gallardo dispatched the vaccine to Dr. Francisco Quiñones in León (Nicaragua). The lymph, however, arrived inert. A second remittance by Esparragosa y Gallardo and several subsequent shipments from Don Basilio Barrutia and Don Juan Pedro Oyarzábal were equally futile. Finally, the captain general personally sent fresh virus sealed between glass slides to the intendant of the province. The intendant gave the lymph to Dr. Quiñones, who immediately vaccinated twenty-seven children. The operations produced the desired effect, and from this reserve Quiñones, Dr. Juan Gómez, and Lic. Manuel del Sol spread vaccine throughout the capital and many surrounding Indian villages. Quiñones also dispatched lymph to Costa Rica, where it was later successfully propagated.[35]

After the vaccine had been thoroughly distributed throughout the capital and numerous physicians had been trained to perform the operation, Esparragosa y Gallardo led a private expedition to Antigua Guatemala, the old capital of the captaincy general. On June 25 he and an assistant reached the city and presented a letter from the captain general ordering local officials to provide their complete cooperation. With the aid of the alcalde mayor, Esparragosa y Gallardo imme-

diately organized distribution of the virus. He divided the city of thirteen thousand inhabitants into wards, compiled a list of all non-immune residents in each section, and designated a house in each area as a vaccination center. In less than a week Esparragosa y Gallardo vaccinated all susceptible citizens in the city except nursing babies and the infirm.[36] He also trained Drs. Mariano Fernández and Santos Alesio Coseros to vaccinate periodically in the capital and throughout the province.[37]

After completing his task in the city, Esparragosa y Gallardo moved on to the numerous neighboring Indian villages. Within a short time he distributed vaccine to all towns within a radius of three leagues from Antigua Guatemala. Esparragosa y Gallardo financed the mission with his own funds, paying the expenses of his lodging, food, servants, and an assistant. On August 8, just as he prepared to lead another expedition to Chimaltenango, he received instructions from the captain general to return to Guatemala City. During his forty-five day sojourn in Antigua Guatemala and its environs, however, Esparragosa y Gallardo vaccinated over nine thousand individuals and trained numerous practitioners and native curanderos. He furthermore dispatched lymph, instructions, and vaccinating needles to León, Trujillo, Granada, and Quetzaltenango—also at his own expense.[38]

While Esparragosa y Gallardo was in Antigua Guatemala, a Franciscan father, Santiago Pérez, from Panajachel in the province of Sololá, conducted two young Indian boys to the city. After observing Esparragosa y Gallardo vaccinate the youths, he returned to the province, conquered the fears of his Indian charges, and widely propagated the vaccine. Pérez vaccinated 784 individuals in Panajachel, San Antonio Palopó, San Andrés, Concepción, and Santa Catalina—the five native villages which comprised his curacy.[39]

The two shipments of lymph which Esparragosa y Gallardo had sent to Dr. José María Ledesma in Trujillo arrived inert. A third shipment from Guatemala City reached the port in late August. Since Dr. Ledesma had died, the vaccine was given to a pharmacist, Don Ignacio Nodal, who, along with practitioners of the Real Hospital, successfully conserved the virus by periodic arm to arm vaccinations.[40]

Also in August, Dr. Ignacio Ruiz de Cevallos, professor of surgery in Guatemala City, led a mission to the province of Totonicapan. Aided by Alcalde Mayor Don Prudencio Cozar, he immunized 871 persons in the district capital. Outside the capital, however, he

[33] Ibid., pp. 347–348.
[34] Ibid., 29 Octubre 1804: p. 487.
[35] Ibid., p. 488.
[36] Ibid., 27 Agosto 1804: p. 409.
[37] Manuel Vela, "Certificación," Nueva Guatemala, 15 Noviembre 1806, AGI, "Indif. Gen.," Leg. 1.558, I, fs. 1–2.
[38] Esparragosa to Junta Central, Guatemala, 15 Noviembre 1806, AGI, "Indif. Gen.," Leg. 1.558, I, fs. 2–4.
[39] Gazeta de Guatemala, 5 Noviembre 1804: p. 495.
[40] Ibid., p. 496.

encountered much resistance to vaccination from "stupid, ignorant Indians and even some whites." [41]

In September, at the request of the Royal Protomedicato, the captain general formalized vaccine distribution to the provinces by naming specific delegates to each major area. The new appointees were Dr. Santiago José Celís (San Salvador), Lic. Luis Franco (Comayagua), Fr. Juan Gómez (León), Dr. Vicente Carranza (Chiquimula and Verapaz), Lic. Manuel Ignacio Lacayo (Costa Rica), and Lic. Manuel del Sol (Sonsonante). Luis Franco would extend his work to the coastal city of Trujillo. The intendant of Petén was ordered to send a delegation to the nearest border with Verapaz to receive the vaccine. Authorities in the district of Omoa were to obtain the lymph from Dr. Vicente Carranza in Chiquimula and then spread the procedure along the Gulf Coast.[42]

THE PASTOR EXPEDITION TO GUATEMALA

While Guatemalan officials busily extended vaccination throughout the captaincy general, a representative of the Royal Expedition had begun an arduous journey from Mérida to the Guatemalan capital. When Balmis reached Havana in May, 1804, he made plans to dispatch the vaccine to Guatemala according to Cavallero's orders of December 16, 1803. The royal instructions stated that, if Balmis chose, he could merely deliver the lymph to a physician sent to meet him at any point along the expedition's itinerary. The director insisted, however, that one of his own aides personally convey the virus to the capital and guide the establishment of a central vaccination board. It is not clear whether Balmis was aware that the vaccine had already reached the area.

Balmis chose Francisco Pastor to lead a subsidiary mission to the Guatemalan capital. In early July Pastor and four boys from Mérida boarded a schooner in Sisal. After making an intermediary stop in Campeche, the mission continued south along the Yucatán Peninsula to Laguna de Términos. From Laguna de Términos, Pastor proceeded inland to Villahermosa, capital of the province of Tabasco.[43]

On July 20 Pastor reached Villahermosa, where he was met by Governor Miguel de Castro y Araoz. The intendant of Yucatán had previously advised Castro y Araoz of the purpose of the expedition and explained his responsibilities. The governor commissioned surgeon Pedro Ramos Reyna to assist Pastor in Villahermosa. Ramos Reyna would therefore gain sufficient practical experience to continue vaccinating after Pastor's departure. In Villahermosa Pastor and Ramos Reyna vaccinated 170 individuals, including Castro y

Araoz's eight-month-old daughter and Lt. Col. Joaquín Fueros, commandant of Ciudad Real de Chiapas, who was visiting Villahermosa.[44]

After a two-day sojourn in Villahermosa, Pastor pushed on to Ciudad Real de Chiapas, located in the dense jungle area of northern Guatemala. Castro y Araoz provided four carriers and paid their father and mothers—Isidro Villegas, Manuela Ortiz, Juana Ortiz, and Francisca Pérez—fifty pesos each in compensation for their children's services.[45] Each child received two jackets, two shirts, two pairs of pants, and a hat. Castro y Araoz charged all expenses incurred by the expedition to the Royal Treasury.[46]

Castro y Araoz commissioned Pedro Ramos Reyna to conserve and propagate the virus in Villahermosa. Ramos Reyna held weekly vaccination sessions in the governor's home and by October 20 had inoculated 520 individuals. Several months after Pastor's departure, Castro y Araoz received the Royal Order of May 20, 1804, instructing him to furnish a room in the local hospital to perpetuate the vaccine. Unable to comply with this directive because of "a number of pitfalls and difficulties," he sought advice from Balmis in Mexico City. The governor promised to continue vaccinating in his own home, and at his own expense, until he received further instructions. The documents do not indicate that Balmis ever replied.[47]

After pausing to renew his supply of carriers in Ciudad Real de Chiapas, Pastor proceeded to Guatemala City. He arrived in the Guatemalan capital a month later.[48] By the time Pastor reached Guatemala, however, there was very little left for him to do. The vaccine had been introduced several months before his arrival. Local practitioners were well instructed in vaccinating techniques. And through the efforts of colonial officials and industrious physicians, the vaccine had reached even the remotest parts of the captaincy general. Pastor left no record of his activities during an apparently extensive stay in Guatemala. He did not rejoin Balmis in Mexico City until January 3, 1805.

Yet Pastor did not make the difficult journey in vain. En route to Guatemala City he introduced the vaccine into many remote villages and instructed numerous

[41] *Ibid.*, p. 495.

[42] *Ibid.*, 29 Octubre 1804: pp. 486–487.

[43] Balmis to Cavallero, México, 4 Enero 1805, AGI, "Indif. Gen.," Leg. 1.558, II, f. 10.

[44] Castro y Araoz to Iturrigaray, Villahermosa, 20 Octubre 1804, AGN, "Epidemias," v. 4, exp. 12, fs. 12–12v.

[45] José Llergo, "Cuenta específica que al Administrador de Real Hacienda de Esta Provincia produce al Sr. Gobernador de ella de los Gastos que de la Real Hacienda se hicieron a la entrada en esta Provincia don Francisco Pastor," Villahermosa, 15 Octubre 1804, AGN, "Epidemias," v. 4, exp. 13, f. 6.

[46] José Suárez, "Cuenta que yo, José Suárez, he llevado de la ropa que de orden del Sr. Governador he hecho para vestir a quatro muchachos que lleva D. Francisco Pastor," Villahermosa, 4 Agosto 1804, AGN, "Epidemias," v. 4, exp. 12, f. 11v.

[47] Castro y Araoz to Iturrigaray, Villahermosa, 20 Octubre 1804, AGN, "Epidemias," v. 4, exp. 12, fs. 12v–14.

[48] Balmis to Cavallero, México, 4 Enero 1804, AGI, "Indif. Gen.," Leg. 1.558, II, f. 10.

native curanderos. Most importantly, however, he delivered Balmis's instructions for the creation of a central vaccination board to the captain general of Guatemala. Consulting Balmis's proposals, Protomédico José Antonio de Córdoba, Archbishop Luis Pañalver y Cárdenas, and Manuel de Castillo Negrete, regent of the Audiencia, created an agency suited to conditions in Guatemala.

Gonzales Saravia authorized publication of the final project, entitled *Reglamento para la Propagación y Estabilidad de la Vacuna en el Reyno de Guatemala,* in January, 1805. Although the instruction was similar to others previously discussed, it did contain important variations. Its principal concern was the creation of the central vaccination board of Guatemala City. The board was composed of three permanent members, three elected members, and a secretary. Permanent members included the archbishop of Guatemala, the regent of the Audiencia, and the royal protomédico. The elected officials included one representative each from the ecclesiastical cabildo, the Ayuntamiento, and the medical community. A secretary would also be chosen to record the board's activities. Elected members would serve two-year terms. The first group of officials would be appointed by the captain general, but after the initial term the board would elect their replacements. No one could refuse to serve on the junta; no one would receive a salary.[49]

The archbishop would preside over board meetings when his duties permitted, and sessions would be held in the Episcopal Palace. When the archbishop was absent, the regent of the Audiencia would replace him and conduct sessions in his own home. Initially meetings would be held weekly; but once vaccination was regularized, the board would meet semi-monthly. During board meetings members would discuss operations performed since the previous session, observations made by physicians, correspondence from provincial juntas, and any particular problems concerning vaccination procedures.[50]

Proceedings would be kept in three separate books. One book would contain minutes of the board meetings; a second would note observations made by Guatemalan physicians; and the third would record observations concerning the vaccine and its effects as reported by foreign physicians. Every six months the secretary would present a complete report to the captain general.[51]

The regulations stipulated that the central vaccination board of Guatemala City foster the creation of provincial juntas in the episcopal cities of León, Comayagua, and Ciudad Real de Chiapas. These regional boards would be composed of the diocesan bishop, the intendant, one member of the ecclesiastical cabildo, one representative from the Ayuntamiento, one physician, and a secretary. These three subsidiary boards would be subordinate to the central vaccination board of Guatemala City, but superior to similar organizations established within the diocese. Local juntas would consist of the principal civil official, one regidor, one ecclesiastic, and the physician or "vaccinator" of the region. Organization and duties of these juntas would be patterned after the central board in the capital. They would submit a report to that body every four months.[52]

Propagation of vaccine in Guatemala City would proceed by weekly inoculations. The board would establish clinics in all urban districts and assign a physician and an assistant to each center. The Royal Protomedicato would license vaccinating physicians and select assistants from priests, regidores, and principal citizens in the capital. The director of each clinic would select the dates for vaccination and proceed according to a roster of non-immune citizens kept by the alcalde. Physicians and assistants were required to visit persons who had been vaccinated, examine their vesicles, and require them to report for the following session in order to communicate the virus. Variolization was strictly prohibited.[53]

To insure perpetuation of an adequate vaccine reserve, an annual birth registry would be kept in each district. Physicians could vaccinate only a number of persons equal to recorded births of the previous year. All priests and neighborhood officials would be issued copies of the regulations of the vaccinating board and Balmis's *Tratado histórico.* It was their duty to convince the public to submit to vaccination in compliance with the general instructions.[54]

The central vaccination board was also required to dispatch periodic expeditions to the provinces. One of the principal duties of these provincial missions was the training of local practitioners. Expedition leaders were directed to instruct whites where possible, but in Indian villages they would train the schoolmaster. In all outlying areas the initial operations would be free; after that, the vaccinator was allowed a just honorarium.[55]

On March 3, 1805, the central vaccination board of Guatemala City met for the first time. No reason is given for the delay in the formal creation of the junta. Perhaps it was postponed because of the serious illness of Protomédico José Antonio de Córdoba, who was to have charge of the essential arrangements, but was permanently incapacitated. Dr. Narciso Esparragosa y Gallardo was named president of the Royal Proto-

49 *Reglamento para la Propagación y Estabilidad de la Vacuna en el Reyno de Guatemala,* Nueva Guatemala, 1805, AGI, "Indif. Gen.," Leg. 1.558, II, fs. 4–5.
50 *Ibid.,* fs. 5–6.
51 *Ibid.,* fs. 7–8.

52 *Ibid.,* fs. 9–11.
53 *Ibid.,* fs. 12–15.
54 *Ibid.,* fs. 19–24.
55 *Ibid.,* fs. 25–26.

medicato and personally directed conservation and propagation of the vaccine until the board was created.[56]

On April 3 Gonzales Saravia, in compliance with the circular of August 4, 1803, presented a full report to the king concerning vaccination in Guatemala. He also sent three copies of the central vaccination board's regulations and requested permission to finance its activities from public rents and community funds.[57] On September 4, 1805, Carlos IV approved the regulations and authorized the appropriation of public revenues to finance the vaccination board.[58]

Under the enlightened leadership of Dr. Narciso Esparragosa y Gallardo, the central vaccination board of Guatemala City had a long and productive existence. Its last formal session was held in July, 1817, after twelve years of effective public welfare service. During that time vaccine was available in both the capital and the provinces. After 1817, however, the junta experienced many changes and irregularities. These difficulties were augmented with national independence and subsequent chronic civil war in the former provinces of the old captaincy general. Such disorders were fatal for public health administration, and the vaccine was often lost.[59]

VII. THE VOYAGE TO THE PHILIPPINES AND BALMIS'S RETURN TO SPAIN

THE ROYAL EXPEDITION IN MANILA

The uncomfortable five-week voyage to the Philippine Islands was marked by strained relations between Balmis and Captain Angel Crespo. The *Magallanes*, as expected, had been crowded. In addition to Balmis, his six assistants, the twenty-six boys, and the vessel's crew, seventy-seven friars from the hospicios of San Jacinto, Santo Tomás, San Agustín de las Cuevas, and San Nicolás, plus an unmentioned number of military officers made the long journey to Manila.[1]

Balmis criticized the inadequate facilities provided aboard the *Magellanes*. Before leaving Mexico City, he had made arrangements for special foods, private cabins for himself and each of his six aides, and a large, well-ventilated compartment with individual cots for the children. While staff members evidently did receive separate quarters, the boys were crammed into a filthy section of the powder magazine. They slept on the floor and were tossed about by the constant roll of the vessel. Despite efforts to keep the children separated, contact during their sleep caused many accidental

vaccinations, including seven at one time. If favorable winds had not shortened the journey, the remaining carriers would have been insufficient to preserve the active virus.[2]

Food provided during the voyage was entirely unsatisfactory. Balmis charged that the children's diet consisted mainly of meat from disease-ridden cattle, beans, lentils, and a few sweets. The director and his aides fared little better. He declared, certainly exaggerating, that all would have starved if they had not shared the extra provisions which each had brought along. According to the director, the captain answered his complaints with rebuffs and insults. Balmis's irritation increased when he discovered that the expedition had been grossly overcharged. While Crespo had demanded three hundred pesos for each child and five hundred pesos for each member of the expedition, all other passengers paid only two hundred pesos for equal and often better accommodations.[3]

On April 15, 1805, the *Magallanes* anchored in Manila Bay. Balmis was annoyed when Rafael María de Aguilar, captain general of the Philippines, failed to greet the expedition. Anxious to get his retinue ashore in order to rest from the arduous voyage, Balmis requested Aguilar's permission to disembark immediately. He also asked the captain general to provide accommodations for the children and his staff. As Aguilar did not reply promptly, Balmis went ashore to discuss the matter with him personally. Although the captain general commissioned the Ayuntamiento to attend to the expedition's needs, the demanding director later complained that their accommodations were "indecent and miserable."[4] This unfortunate beginning augered ill for Balmis's subsequent relations with the captain general. Characteristically, the director had few kind words for Aguilar in his reports to Cavallero.

On April 16 Balmis began vaccinating in Manila. He later alleged that Aguilar was reluctant to help propagate the vaccine, and that he failed to order public announcements of the vaccinating sessions or stimulate the masses to receive immunization.[5] While Aguilar reported that to set an example for the people his own five children were the first to be inoculated in the capital,[6] Balmis charged that they were secretly vaccinated in the captain general's residence. Balmis also complained that he received no support from the bishop of Manila. When the director requested that he urge all parish priests to advocate vaccination, the prelate stated that he had learned on good authority that the

[56] Esparragosa to Junta Central, Guatemala, 15 Noviembre 1806, AGI, "Indif. Gen.," Leg. 1.558, II, f. 4.

[57] Gonzales Saravia to Cavallero, Guatemala, 3 Abril 1805, AGI, "Indif. Gen.," Leg. 1.558, I, fs. 1–2.

[58] "Extracto," fs. 140–142v.

[59] Martínez Durán, 1964: pp. 484–485.

[1] Angel Crespo, "Resumen," Manila, 11 Junio 1805, AGN, "Filipinas," v. 52, exp. 7, fs. 3–4.

[2] Balmis to Cavallero, Manila, 18 Agosto 1805, AGI, "Indif. Gen.," Leg. 1.558, II, fs. 1–2.

[3] *Ibid.*, fs. 3–4.

[4] *Ibid.*, fs. 6–7.

[5] *Ibid.*, f. 8.

[6] Aguilar to Cavallero, Manila, 24 Diciembre 1805, AGI, "Indif. Gen.," Leg. 1.558, II, f. 2.

vaccine was ineffective. Balmis did, however, praise Francisco Díaz Durana, dean of the cathedral; Francisco de Oyuelo, sergeant major of the militia; and Captain Pedro Martínez Cavezón, whose example induced thousands of natives to seek vaccination. By early August over nine thousand people had been immunized in the Philippine capital.[7]

On May 16 Balmis gave Aguilar his proposals for the creation of a vaccination board and a public vaccination center. The captain general readily accepted the plan and authorized its immediate institution.[8] Despite Balmis's claims of Aguilar's indifference, on May 29 the captain general did publish a decree announcing the purposes of the expedition and extolling the benefits of vaccination. He also commissioned surgeon Bernardo Rivera, who had been trained by Balmis, to distribute the vaccine in and around Manila and to instruct local practitioners.[9]

Several clashes with the captain general marked Balmis's stay in the Philippines. The director had complained to Aguilar of the "scandalous" sum Captain Angel Crespo had received for transporting the expedition to Manila and the appalling treatment and accommodations provided on the *Magallanes*. He told Aguilar that Crespo should refund 8,600 pesos which he had unjustly obtained from the Royal Treasury in Mexico. Aguilar instructed Balmis to present his complaint to the naval commandant, who was in charge of such affairs. Balmis interpreted this action as an attempt to protect Crespo and refused to discuss the matter with anyone but the captain general. Aguilar then suggested that he consult the officials of the Royal Exchequer. Balmis insisted, however, that he had already fulfilled his obligation by informing the captain general, who was also general superintendent of the Royal Treasury. Aguilar replied that since Balmis did not wish to follow the suggested procedure, "in the end the king would lose." [10] Evidently Balmis repeated his charges when he reached Madrid, and Crespo eventually was ordered to return the 8,600 pesos.[11]

Balmis's disproportionate sense of self-importance led to another dispute. On June 9, while making initial arrangements to return the twenty-six children to New Spain, Balmis requested that the captain general authorize the purchase of new outfits for them. In his reply Aguilar reported that it was inappropriate to initiate such preparations at that time because the next vessel to Mexico would not sail for several months. He also indicated that Balmis had not followed the proper

procedure in requesting funds from the Royal Treasury. When Aguilar sent this notice to Balmis, he addressed him as "Consulting Director of the Royal Expedition." [12]

Highly offended, Balmis declared that the title of "Consulting Director" was "exceedingly inappropriate." He informed Aguilar that he was not a consultant nor did he intend to act merely in that capacity. He then angrily repeated his request.[13]

Aguilar immediately returned Balmis's letter with a sharp admonition "to reduce it to the decorous terms" that his position as first magistrate of the islands demanded. No one, he declared, no matter how high his position, could address him in such a manner. If Balmis was not acquainted with the "delicate expressions" employed to address superiors or the proper procedures required to request funds from the Royal Treasury, he should consult someone who did. He then ordered Balmis to resubmit his request and modify its language.[14] This harsh reprimand heightened Balmis's criticism of the captain general in his official reports. And the episode provides still another example of Balmis's unfortunately petty character.

Balmis's already broken health became increasingly worse in Manila's sweltering climate. The violent fever he contracted in the New World persisted, and dysentery progressively diminished his ability to perform his duties. His physical state, in addition to poor relations with the captain general and the impossibility of returning immediately to New Spain or Europe, forced him to seek a more salubrious climate.

On July 8 Balmis begged Aguilar to authorize his withdrawal to Macao or Canton, from whence he would return to Spain at the first opportunity. He declared that since the mission was ostensibly completed, his presence was no longer vital. Antonio Gutiérrez could assume direction of the expedition until it returned to Spain. If necessary Balmis would make the trip at his own expense. He also requested passports for himself and for Francisco Pastor, who would accompany him.[15]

Two days later the captain general granted Balmis's petition and provided the passports. Despite the limited resources of the Royal Treasury, Aguilar advanced Balmis six months' salary. He also promised to write letters of introduction to the agents of the Royal Philippine Company and the Portuguese authorities in Macao.[16]

[7] Balmis to Cavallero, Manila, 8 Agosto 1805, AGI, "Indif. Gen.," Leg. 1.558, II, f. 8.

[8] Aguilar to Cavallero, Tierra Alta, 22 Mayo 1805, AGI, "Indif. Gen.," Leg. 1.558, II, fs. 1–2. For the complete text of these documents see Bantug, 1955: pp. 105–115.

[9] Bantug, 1955: pp. 117–119.

[10] Balmis to Cavallero, Manila, 8 Agosto 1805, AGI, "Indif. Gen.," Leg. 1.558, II, f. 8.

[11] Fernández del Castillo, 1960: p. 172.

[12] Balmis to Cavallero, Manila, 8 Agosto 1805, AGI, "Indif. Gen.," Leg. 1.558, II, f. 10.

[13] Balmis to Aguilar, Manila, 15 Junio 1805, AGI, "Indif. Gen.," Leg. 1.558, I, fs. 1–2.

[14] Aguilar to Balmis, Tierra Alta, 17 Junio 1805, AGI, "Indif. Gen.," Leg. 1.558, II, fs. 1–3.

[15] Balmis to Aguilar, Manila, 8 Julio 1805, AGI, "Indif. Gen.," Leg. 1.558, II, fs. 1–2.

[16] Aguilar to Balmis, Manila, 10 Julio 1805, AGI, "Indif. Gen.," Leg. 1.558, II, fs. 1–2.

On July 17 Aguilar appointed Gregorio Zarza Díaz to administer the vaccine in the capital. Apprised of the appointment, Balmis sent Zarza Díaz a brief set of instructions and cautioned him to perform his duties in accordance with the regulation.[17]

Balmis saw his stay in Macao and Canton as another excellent opportunity to spread the vaccine. He explained to Aguilar that not only would his project gain further esteem for vaccination, but it could also advance Spanish political and commercial interests in China. To carry out this scheme he would need only four non-immune boys from Manila and minimal funds from the Royal Treasury. Balmis added that, if no public funds were available, he would finance the mission himself. He also requested that Aguilar advise the governor of Macao and the chief Chinese officials in Canton of his intention to propagate the vaccine throughout the mainland.[18]

On August 1 Aguilar approved the plan and allotted two hundred pesos from the Royal Treasury. He also promised to send requisite notification of the expedition to the governor of Macao and the Chinese governor general in Canton so that they could apprise their respective sovereigns of Balmis's visit.[19] When Balmis encountered difficulty in securing children to convey the lymph to Macao, the priest of the Church of Santa Cruz furnished three boys from his parish.[20]

On August 30, with arrangements for his departure completed, Balmis entrusted the expedition to Antonio Gutiérrez. In his formal instructions Balmis authorized Gutiérrez to assume all duties and obligations of the director until the expedition returned to Spain. Gutiérrez, along with the remaining staff members and the twenty-six Mexican children, would return to Acapulco at the earliest opportunity. He ordered Gutiérrez to restock the dispensary and secure complete outfits for the children, charging all expenses for the expedition's return to Mexico to the Royal Treasury in Manila.[21]

When the expedition reached Acapulco, Gutiérrez would request Iturrigaray to provide complete assistance for their trip to Mexico City. Balmis also suggested that Gutiérrez contact Don Silvestre Díaz de la Vega, who would expedite matters in the secretariat of the viceroyalty. Gutiérrez's initial task in Mexico City was to deliver the children to the viceroy, who would

see to their return to their parents. Gutiérrez should then make arrangements for the expedition's voyage to Spain. During his stay in Mexico City, Gutiérrez would gather information on the status of vaccination throughout the viceroyalty by requesting a detailed report from each provincial intendant.[22]

On September 2, 1805, Balmis and the three carriers departed for the Portuguese colony of Macao on the frigate *Diligencia,* commanded by Captain Miguel López Rodríguez. Although Balmis had made previous arrangements for Francisco Pastor to accompany him, Pastor remained with the expedition.[23]

Since it was still several months before the expedition could return to New Spain, Gutiérrez prepared to disperse the vaccine throughout the Philippine archipelago. On September 24 Captain General Aguilar published a decree which declared that Gutiérrez would select two members of the expedition to convey the vaccine to Misamia, Zamboanga, Cebú, Mindanao, and throughout the Visaya Islands. Community funds of the benefiting villages would finance the mission. Each member of the expedition would receive one hundred pesos per month plus eighteen reales a day for provisions. Each would carry six copies of the *Tratado histórico* for distribution to provincial vicars. Besides vaccinating, they would instruct local priests and physicians in the techniques of conserving and transmitting the lymph. Alcaldes, governors, and parish priests would furnish children to convey the vaccine from island to island. Twelve boys from Manila initiated the chain of inoculations.[24]

Gutiérrez chose Pedro Ortega and Francisco Pastor to lead the island expedition. Few details are available on their activities, but by the time the expedition was ready to return to New Spain in mid-June, 1806, they had vaccinated nearly twenty thousand islanders.[25] Perhaps the outstanding achievement of this enterprise was the extension of vaccine to the Visaya Islands, where fierce, unconquered tribes waged intermittent warfare with the Spanish forces. Just before Pastor and Ortega reached the area, however, a devastating smallpox epidemic struck the islands. The physicians quickly succeeded in impeding further spread of the infection and in a short time had it under complete control. The grateful native chieftains laid down their arms and made peace with their Spanish enemies.[26]

[17] Balmis to Zarza Díaz, Manila, 17 Julio 1805, AGI, "Indif. Gen.," Leg. 1.558, II, fs. 1–2.
[18] Balmis to Aguilar, Manila, 29 Julio 1805, AGI, "Indif. Gen.," Leg. 1.558, II, fs. 1–2.
[19] Aguilar to Balmis, Manila, 1 Agosto 1805, AGI, "Indif. Gen.," Leg. 1.558, II, fs. 1–3.
[20] Balmis to Cavallero, Macao, 30 Enero 1806, AGI, "Indif. Gen.," Leg. 1.558, II, fs. 2–3.
[21] Francisco Xavier de Balmis, "Providencias hechas a D. Antonio Gutiérrez López Robredo, por el Director de la Real Expedición de la Vacuna," Manila, 30 Agosto 1805, AGN, "Epidemias," v. 17, p. 322.

[22] *Ibid.,* fs. 322–323.
[23] Balmis to Cavallero, Macao, 30 Enero 1806, AGI, "Indif. Gen.," Leg. 1.558, II, f. 3.
[24] Rafael María de Aguilar, "Decreto del Govierno Superior de 24 de Septiembre de 1805. Con presencia de lo informado en este expediente por el Subdirector de la Real Expedición de la Vacuna, D. Antonio Gutiérrez Robredo, y de lo que sucesivamente han expuesto los Oficiales Reales," reproduced in Bantug, 1955: pp. 115–116.
[25] Balmis to Cavallero, Macao, 30 Enero 1806, AGI, "Indif. Gen.," Leg. 1.558, II, f. 6.
[26] *Gaceta de México,* 26 Agosto 1807: p. 556.

MACAO

On September 10, after a pleasant eight-day voyage, Balmis and the three boys reached Macao. But because of contrary winds, the *Diligencia* was unable to land immediately. As it lay in the unprotected harbor outside Macao, the ship was caught in a typhoon. The violent winds toppled the mainsail and riggings, destroyed the auxiliary boats, and washed twenty men overboard to their death. Strong gales incessantly lashed the vessel for six days. Despite the storm, Balmis successfully transferred the virus and conserved his precious vaccine. On the afternoon of September 16, after the sea had calmed, Balmis and the boys were taken to Macao by a Chinese fishing boat.[27]

Once Balmis reached Macao he was aided by agents of the Royal Philippine Company, who later introduced him to the principal Portuguese colonial authorities.[28] The bishop of Macao and Oidor Don Miguel Arriaga Brun de la Silveira enthusiastically volunteered to be the first persons in the colony to receive immunization. Their example stimulated hundreds of others.[29]

Balmis, however, was not the first to introduce the vaccine into Macao. During the previous May, a certain Don Pedro Huet had conducted the lymph to the Portuguese colony from the Philippines. Although the virus was quickly spread throughout Macao, Huet did not understand the technique of vaccine preservation. By the time Balmis arrived, it had been lost. The director therefore trained local physicians in the methods of transmitting and safely conserving the virus.[30] On October 5, after firmly establishing the vaccine in Macao, Balmis found a Chinese youth to convey the virus and left for Canton. He paid from his own resources the 311 pesos required to outfit and maintain the boy, provide a small gratuity for his parents, and secure passage to Canton.[31]

CANTON

Encouraged by his success in Macao, Balmis anticipated an equally enthusiastic reception in Canton. He believed that the letters of introduction to the agents of the Royal Philippine Company would ultimately lead to official support of his project. The role of these European commercial agents was extremely important. Since no foreigner was permitted to deal directly with Chinese imperial officials, all correspondence was channeled through the *cohong* (a group of monopoly merchants with exclusive rights to trade with foreigners). The cohong was the only agency authorized to deal with agents of the European companies, who were, in turn, the only recognized representatives of their respective governments in China.

Unfortunately, according to Balmis, the agents of the Royal Philippine Company in Canton showed no interest in his mission. They offered no direct aid and refused to seek the cooperation of local authorities.[32] Merely to preserve active virus, Balmis was forced to beg the poor families living along the banks of the Pearl River to vaccinate their children in return for a few reales. When Balmis implored the Spanish agents to help him, they replied that aiding his scheme was not one of their duties.[33]

Balmis therefore turned to the agents of the British East India Company. The English, who had unsuccessfully attempted to transport the vaccine to Canton from Bombay, Madras, Bengala, and Malaysia, immediately welcomed the director and furnished a temporary vaccination center. Despite the new clinic, however, Balmis was still unable to overcome Chinese resistance. He returned to Macao on November 30. During his fifty-six-day sojourn in Canton he vaccinated only twenty-two persons.[34]

On December 12, 1805, the British East India Company formally established a public vaccination clinic and employed a physician full-time to administer the vaccine. Shortly after creation of the clinic, a devastating smallpox epidemic struck Canton. The Chinese poured into the clinic seeking immunization. From Macao, Balmis caustically observed the irony of British political and mercantile interests being advanced by a gift sent by the Spanish king. In a report to Cavallero he placed direct blame for this unexpected turn of events on Francisco Mayo and Martín Salaverria, chief agents for the Royal Philippine Company in Canton.[35]

Rafael María de Aguilar, captain general of the Philippines, also informed Cavallero of Balmis's misfortunes and repeated most of the director's charges against the company agents. He personally requested that chief agent Francisco Mayo "suffer the full measure of the royal indignation of his majesty." The captain general lamented that his own jurisdiction did not include Canton or he would have personally punished the agents for their lack of cooperation with

[27] Balmis to Cavallero, Macao, 30 Enero 1806, AGI, "Indif. Gen.," Leg. 1.558, II, fs. 2–3.

[28] Mayo and Salaverria to Directores de la Real Compañía de Filipinas en Madrid, Canton, 31 Enero 1806, AGI, "Indif. Gen.," Leg. 1.558, I. f. 2.

[29] Balmis to Cavallero, Macao, 30 Enero 1806, AGI, "Indif. Gen.," Leg. 1.558, II, f. 4.

[30] Mayo and Salaverria to Directores de la Real Compañía de Filipinas en Madrid, Canton, 31 Enero 1806, AGI, "Indif. Gen.," Leg. 1.558, I, f. 2.

[31] Francisco Xavier de Balmis, "Lista de los gastos ocasionados en el viaje de Manila a Madrid de Don Francisco Xavier de Balmis, Director de la Vacuna," Madrid, 4 Diciembre 1806, AGI, "Indif. Gen.," Leg. 1.558, II, f. 1.

[32] Balmis to Cavallero, Macao, 30 Enero 1806, AGI, "Indif. Gen.," Leg. 1.558, II, f. 4.

[33] Aguilar to Cavallero, Manila, 24 Diciembre 1805, AGI, "Indif. Gen.," Leg. 1.558, I, fs. 8–9.

[34] Balmis to Cavallero, Macao, 30 Enero 1806, AGI, "Indif. Gen.," Leg. 1.558, II, fs. 5–6.

[35] *Ibid.*

Balmis and their contemptuous disregard for the king's desires.[36]

Reporting to company directors in Madrid, Mayo and Salaverria told a much different story. They claimed that they had made every effort to persuade the Chinese to submit to vaccination, yet were unable to overcome popular suspicion of the foreign treatment. They had discussed Balmis's project with the leading figure of the Canton cohong, Pan Ke Kua, who informed them that provincial officials were occupied with more important matters. Nor could the agents utilize the Portuguese government's traditional influence with the local Chinese authorities. The murder of a Chinese citizen in Macao had created a political crisis between the ruling Portuguese body and the Chinese government.[37]

The directors of the Royal Philippine Company were extremely embarrassed at their agents' lack of cooperation with Balmis. They promised to conduct a full investigation of the matter after Balmis returned to Madrid. If Mayo was guilty of these accusations, they would remove him from his position.[38] The documents, however, do not indicate that any subsequent action was taken against either Mayo or Salaverria.

Soon after Balmis reached Macao on November 30, he made plans for his return to Spain. The next European-bound ship, the Portuguese *Bom Jesus de Alem,* was scheduled to depart for Lisbon in early February. During his previous stay in Macao, Balmis had formed a close friendship with Dom Francisco Antonio Thobar, an agent for the company which owned the *Bom Jesus.* Aware of the director's limited resources, Thobar offered him passage on the vessel at no immediate cost. Balmis could make arrangements with company officials to pay for his voyage after he reached Lisbon. Balmis, however, declined Thobar's generous offer. He foresaw many problems with the ship's captain, who, without some advance payment, refused to provide the accommodations Balmis required or to transport the many personal effects the director had accumulated.[39]

Balmis faced an acute financial crisis. He had already spent most of the money which Aguilar had advanced him in September, and the depleted Philippine treasury could not afford further disbursements in his favor. Fortunately, however, Don Juan Martín de Ballesteros, former chief agent of the Royal Philippine Company in Canton, was returning to Spain on the *Bom Jesus.* Ballesteros lent Balmis 2,500 pesos with the agreement that the Royal Treasury would reimburse him when he reached Spain.[40]

In the meantime Balmis continued to vaccinate in Macao. He also collected numerous objects of natural history and spent many hours studying Chinese arts and sciences, especially medicine, surgery, pharmacy, botany, physics, and chemistry. He believed that his studies would be valuable in rectifying many common European misconceptions about life in the Far East. He also acquired three hundred detailed sketches of Asian flora and ten large crates of exotic plants for the Royal Botanic Garden in Madrid.[41]

The only report that Balmis submitted from Macao was written one week before his departure. He gave a complete résumé of his activities in the Far East, discussing reasons for his premature return to Spain, his instructions to Gutiérrez, and his disputes with Aguilar and the agents of the Royal Philippine Company.

Balmis also included an emotional tribute to his assistants, especially Isabel Gómez y Cendala. Since this is the only extensive discussion of his personal feelings for his aides, it is worthy of inclusion:

Permit, Your Excellency, the bursting forth of my tears, which I can no longer hold back as I think of the distinguished merits and great sacrifices made in the service of His Majesty. Miserably poor, sick, exhausted, often going without the barest necessities, they have neither diminished their efforts nor avoided any risk. . . . The poor Rectoress, who, from excessive work and the rigors of harsh climates, is completely broken in health. Untiringly, day and night, she has lavished all the tenderness of the most sensitive mother upon the twenty-six little angels she has in her care, just as she did during the voyage from La Coruña to New Spain, and on all the other trips we have made. She has steadfastly watched over them throughout all of her continuous illnesses. . . .[42]

ST. HELENA

On February 7, 1806, Balmis boarded the *Bom Jesus de Alem* and began his long trip home. He had previously learned that the vessel would make a brief stop in the British island of St. Helena and therefore took a portion of vaccine in order to extend vaccination to that area. A little over four months later the ship anchored in St. Helena.

After learning that the vaccine had not yet reached the island, Balmis presented himself to Governor Robert Patton and offered to propagate the lymph. The governor, however, curtly informed Balmis that his subjects did not require vaccination. Undaunted by this initial rebuff, Balmis, with his characteristic determina-

[36] Aguilar to Cavallero, Manila, 24 Diciembre 1805, AGI, "Indif. Gen.," Leg. 1.558, I, fs. 11–12.

[37] Mayo and Salaverria to Directores de la Real Compañía de Filipinas en Madrid, Canton, 31 Enero 1806, AGI, "Indif. Gen.," Leg. 1.558, I, fs. 2–3.

[38] Directores de la Real Compañía de Filipinas to Cavallero, Madrid, 22 Agosto 1806, AGI, "Indif. Gen.," Leg. 1.558, II, fs. 1–5.

[39] Balmis to Thobar, Canton, 16 Noviembre 1805, AGI, "Indif. Gen.," Leg. 1.558, II, fs. 1–3.

[40] Balmis to Cavallero, Macao, 30 Enero 1806, AGI, "Indif. Gen.," Leg. 1.558, II, fs. 1–3.

[41] Balmis to Cavallero, Macao, 30 Enero 1806, AGI, "Indif. Gen." Leg. 1.558, II, fs. 7–4.

[42] *Ibid.*, f. 7.

tion, held a series of conferences with local physicians and leading citizens. He discussed the numerous advantages of vaccination and pointed out that, after all, it was an English discovery. The director's convincing arguments moved many to ask the governor to give the matter more serious consideration. The following day Patton invited Balmis to a dinner in his honor.[43]

Dinner guests included the most influential individuals on the island. The gathering allowed Balmis to expound further upon the merits of the "great British discovery." Patton authorized Balmis to begin vaccinating. On June 15 Balmis held his only vaccination session, during which he inoculated eight individuals— all children or relatives of the island physicians. He also taught Doctors Kay and Dunn to preserve and transmit the virus when more lymph was available.[44]

On June 16, the eve of his departure, Balmis again dined with the governor, who by now was thoroughly convinced of the merits of vaccination. Patton himself proposed a toast to the "universal beneficence of His Catholic Majesty" with the hope that Great Britain and Spain would soon establish friendly relations. Shortly after dinner Patton gave Balmis an unsealed parcel which had arrived in the island several years previously. When Balmis opened the package, he found a portion of lymph and minute handwritten instructions from Edward Jenner himself.[45]

Another sidelight to Balmis's stay in St. Helena was a short report he wrote on June 13, 1806, but could not forward to the Spanish government until his arrival in Lisbon in mid-August:

The English on this island say that on January 6 of this year their troops captured the Cape of Good Hope. They were aided by the traitorous conduct of the Dutch defenders, who deserted and joined the enemy in great numbers. The English, armed with the success of this enterprise, formed an expedition to sail against Montevideo. The expedition, composed of an undisclosed number of English and Dutch soldiers, sailed this past May. It was inferred, however, that the attacking body was not very large, since the British were convinced that they would meet a force of not over 900 men.[46]

The small English army under the command of Colonel William Carr Beresford easily crossed the South Atlantic. On June 25, just twelve days after Balmis wrote his report, the English troops landed on the eastern bank of the Plata estuary and marched on Buenos Aires. The viceregal capital fell two days later.

RETURN OF BALMIS TO EUROPE

On June 17 the *Bom Jesus de Alem* left St. Helena and began the last leg of its journey to Lisbon. The vessel reached the Portuguese capital on the afternoon of August 14. Balmis immediately sent to Cavallero a dispatch discussing his voyage from Macao and requested financial aid for his trip to Madrid. He also stated that the many plants he had brought from Asia would remain in the Spanish embassy until arrangements were made to have them shipped to the Royal Botanic Garden.[47]

Balmis later requested one thousand pesos from the Spanish ambassador to pay expenses occasioned by his trip from the Far East. It is not clear just how he had spent the 2,500 pesos he borrowed from Ballesteros in Macao. But he did receive the money from the ambassador and apparently paid all of his immediate debts.[48]

In addition to the specimens for the Royal Botanic Garden, Balmis also brought a number of personal articles which he had purchased in Canton. He hoped to resell the goods in Spain in order to recoup a portion of the nearly eighty thousand reales which he claimed to have spent from his own resources during the expedition.[49] Among the items he listed were three thousand bolts of nankeen, two quintals of tea, twenty porcelain trays, six cases of chinaware, several tea sets, and eight ivory trays—all of which he wished to bring into Spain duty-free. Since all these items except the nankeen fell outside the monopoly of the Royal Philippine Company, the king granted the request.[50] Freight expenses to Spain, however, probably left little ultimate profit for the director, and it is doubtful whether he ever recovered even a small portion of his purported personal disbursements.

After a brief stay in Lisbon, Balmis hired a coach which took him to Madrid. He soon withdrew to San Ildefonso, where Carlos IV had established his court. Although Balmis still suffered from dysentery and recurrent fevers, the pleasant surroundings of his native land, familiar diet, and special medical care provided by the king soon restored his health.

Balmis's moment of personal glory came on September 7, 1806, when he knelt to kiss the hand of Carlos IV and received the king's personal congratulations for his outstanding service.[51] Balmis later described his "hero's welcome" as the most enthusiastic ever witnessed by Carlos IV's court. Even the Catalans praised him.[52] Balmis could indeed be proud of his achievements. His expedition had successfully ex-

[43] Balmis to Cavallero, Lisboa, 18 Agosto 1806, AGI, "Indif. Gen.," Leg. 1.558, II, fs. 1–2.
[44] *Ibid.*, fs. 2–3.
[45] *Ibid.*, fs. 3–4.
[46] Balmis to Cavallero, Isla de Sta. Helena, 13 Junio 1806, AGI, "Indif. Gen.," Leg. 1.558, II, f. 1.

[47] Balmis to Cavallero, Lisboa, 14 Agosto 1806, AGI, "Indif. Gen.," Leg. 1.558, II, f. 4.
[48] Pedro Cevallos to Cavallero, San Ildefonso, 30 Agosto 1806, AGI, "Indif. Gen.," Leg. 1.558, II, fs. 1–3.
[49] Balmis to Cavallero, Madrid, 4 Diciembre 1806, AGI, "Indif. Gen.," Leg. 1.558, II, f. 1.
[50] Cavallero to Soler, San Lorenzo, Octubre 1806, AGI, "Indif. Gen.," Leg. 1.558, II, fs. 1–2.
[51] *Suplemento a la Gaceta de Madrid,* 14 Octubre 1806: p. 290.
[52] Balmis to Gutiérrez, Madrid, 28 Septiembre 1806, AGN, "Epidemias," v. 17, fs. 276–276v.

tended the life-saving vaccine throughout an empire upon which the sun never set.

EPILOGUE

Little is known about Francisco Xavier de Balmis for the first few years after his return to Spain. In February, 1807, he presented a Chinese-Spanish dictionary to Miguel Cayetano Soler. It is highly doubtful that Balmis himself was qualified to compile it. Four months later he sought the position of chamber surgeon but evidently was unsuccessful. He did, however, serve as medical consultant to the king and retained his position as director of the Royal Expedition.[1]

As a result of Spain's unfortunate involvement in successive armed conflicts with Great Britain and France, Balmis's contact with the expedition was minimal. But he did write to Gutiérrez in August, 1808, after Joseph Bonaparte had arrived in Spain. The director suggested that with "the new order of things" Gutiérrez should consider returning with the expedition. He also requested a report on all vaccination boards which had been established in Mexico and other pertinent information concerning the vaccine.[2]

In late 1808 or early 1809, after French troops occupied the Spanish capital, Balmis's home in Madrid was sacked. Perhaps at this time the detailed diary which he kept during the course of the expedition was lost. This extremely valuable document was never published nor is it among the papers concerning the expedition in the Archivo General de Indias.

Balmis soon fled to Sevilla and allied himself with the Junta Suprema which assumed control of Spain in the king's absence. He later secured appointment as honorary consultant of the Supreme Council of the Royal Treasury.[3] In early December, 1809, Balmis received the first dispatches from the Salvany expedition. The brief reports, written in La Paz, described the spread of the vaccine throughout the viceroyalties of Peru and New Granada. Salvany expressed a desire to go on to Buenos Aires, but declared that he was unable to do so because of failing health. He therefore requested appointment to the position of intendant of La Paz or royal treasurer of Lima, as both offices were vacant at the time.[4]

Balmis was extremely irate that after five years Salvany had yet to send him a personal account of his activities. He accused Salvany of purposely delaying completion of the mission and charged him with attempting to abandon the project altogether. The mere fact that after five years he still had not finished

indicated to Balmis that Salvany was intentionally prolonging the expedition. On the other hand, the director boasted that he had led his half of the mission around the world and had successfully completed all duties in only thirty-three months. Evidently Balmis was ignorant of the vastness of the South American continent, the brutal terrain, and the physical hardships Salvany had undergone. Balmis also seemed to ignore the fact that he, too, had "abandoned" the expedition when his health failed in the Philippines. At any rate, he requested that Salvany be ordered to give a full account of his accomplishments in South America.[5]

Despite the French occupation, on November 30, 1809, the Junta Suprema had authorized Balmis to return to New Spain, review established vaccination boards, examine native sources of cowpox, and further organize administration of the vaccine. He was granted an annual salary of four thousand ducats, which he would draw from the Royal Treasury in Mexico City.[6]

The Mexico to which Balmis returned in June, 1810, was far different from the quiet colony he had left in 1805. Francisco Xavier de Lizanza y Beaumont, archbishop of Mexico, was the new viceroy. José de Iturrigaray, Balmis's old nemesis, had been deposed in September, 1808, after apparently joining an abortive move by Mexico City creoles to establish an autonomous junta. Iturrigaray's replacement, the decrepit Pedro de Garibay, had been a temporary tool of the ruling *peninsulares*. On September 14, 1810, Francisco Xavier de Venegas supplanted Lizanza y Beaumont as viceroy. Two days later the Hidalgo revolt exploded in Dolores. The uprising interrupted Balmis's experiments in Valladolid, the only area where he was able to do any extensive work, and made further organization of the vaccination boards impossible. He left New Spain in August, 1811, without accomplishing any of his original projects. He did, however, stay long enough to become embroiled in two acrimonious disputes, one with Manuel Abad e Queipo, bishop-elect of Michoacán, and another with Antonio Gutiérrez y Robredo.

Balmis had been most active in Valladolid, where he conducted experiments with cowpox on the ranches where Guitérrez had discovered the virus during the northern swing of the expedition in the fall of 1804. In Valladolid he enjoyed the warm hospitality and enthusiastic cooperation of both Intendant Merino and Bishop-elect Abad e Queipo, who had been primarily responsible for popularizing variolization in 1798 and vaccination in 1804. Some time in September, 1810, however, Balmis left Valladolid and returned to Mexico City.

[1] Díaz de Iraola, 1947: p. 103.
[2] Balmis to Gutiérrez, Madrid, 11 Agosto 1808, AGN, "Epidemias," v. 17, fs. 282–283.
[3] Díaz de Iraola, 1947: p. 103.
[4] Balmis to [Hermida?], Sevilla, 6 Diciembre 1809, AGI, "Indif. Gen.," Leg. 1.558, II, fs. 1–2.

[5] *Ibid.*, fs. 3–4.
[6] Hermida to Lizanza y Beaumont, Real Alcázar de Sevilla, 10 Diciembre 1809, AGN, "Reales Cédulas," v. **201**, exp. 335, f. 451.

His dispute with Abad e Queipo began with a letter which the bishop-elect sent to Venegas on November 14, 1810. The prelate complained that the director had been making slanderous statements which impugned his loyalty. He also reported that Balmis had insulted Don Agustín de Ledos, canon of cathedral of Valladolid, and Francisco de Borja Romero y Santa María, prebend in the same church, because they had supported Abad e Queipo's election as bishop.[7]

As the first step to vindicate his honor, Abad e Queipo asked that Venegas request formal declarations from Ledos; Borja; José de Olivares, also a prebend in the cathedral of Valladolid; Guillermo de Aguirre, regent of the Audiencia; Ambrosio Saparzurieta, fiscal de lo civil; Manuel de Flores, fiscal of the Holy Office; Miguel José de Emparán, colonel of the Dragoons of Mexico; and Francisco José Bernal. All of these men, he claimed, had witnessed Balmis's slanderous allegations.[8] Balmis was notified of Abad e Queipo's complaint, and all those cited received copies of the charges.[9]

As the depositions were presented, the case took form. Ledos denied that he had ever heard Balmis say anything directly against the bishop-elect. He did recall, however, that Manuel de Baldovinos, a former resident of Valladolid, reported that Balmis had criticized Abad e Queipo. Ledos admitted only that he had heard Balmis say that the residents of Valladolid "smelled like traitors." He added that he thought the director was "crazy" and had since avoided him.[10]

Ambrosio Saparzurieta declared that he had never heard Balmis accuse the prelate, but added that after the director returned to Mexico City, he did report that there was "much corruption" in Valladolid.[11] Manuel de Flores, Francisco José Bernal, Guillermo de Aguirre, and Miguel José de Emparán presented similar testimony.

Borja and Baldovinos, who was also instructed to submit a deposition, leveled the strongest indictments against the director. Borjas declared that after casually encountering Balmis in Mexico City, the director "pushed him, treated him like an insurgent," and alleged that everyone in Valladolid "smelled like rebels." The irascible director had accosted him in a similar manner on three separate occasions. The third time Balmis had shown a complete lack of respect for his clerical office and "used gross and indecent language" in his address. The prebend stated that while Balmis had not questioned his own loyalty, the director "could not

forgive him for having supported Abad e Queipo's nomination as bishop." [12]

Maunel de Baldovinos avowed that in August, 1810, while taking a drive in Valladolid, Balmis had told him that he suspected the loyalty of both the intendant and the bishop-elect. He claimed that "they had said things which did not sound right." Balmis also stated that only the people of Valladolid could have elected a man of Abad e Queipo's caliber as bishop. Baldovinos remarked that he paid little attention to Balmis's initial accusations because the director had just lost between thirty and forty pesos gambling with two other residents of Valladolid and had impugned their patriotism as well. Balmis, however, had repeated his accusations on several other occasions during his stay in Valladolid. A short time later Baldovinos encountered the director in Mexico City. Balmis accosted him and asked why he had come to Mexico City, since he had nothing to fear from the insurgents. He even suggested that perhaps Baldovinos was needed in the rebel forces. Since that final encounter, Baldovinos declared that he had avoided the director and further confrontations.[13]

Even while the depositions were being gathered, Balmis made preparations to return to Spain. Abad e Queipo, however, learned of his plans and requested that the viceroy instruct Balmis to remain in the capital until the matter was settled. He accused Balmis of "attempting to avoid his responsibility." On December 16, 1810, Balmis received orders to remain in Mexico City.[14] For the next three months Abad e Queipo, through his legal representative, José María de Ortuño, attempted to secure a full confession from the director. No additional implicating evidence was uncovered, however, and Balmis steadfastly refused to confess.

On March 30, 1811, the director made his first formal declaration in a brief letter to Venegas. He flatly denied that he had ever questioned Abad e Queipo's loyalty and alleged that the entire affair was a fabrication of the bishop-elect and his friends. Balmis reminded Venegas of his desire to return to Spain and requested permission to resume preparations for the trip. On April 6 Venegas, upon the advice of the fiscal de lo civil, officially terminated Balmis's commission in New Spain and authorized his departure. Balmis went on to Veracruz, leaving Gervasio del Corral as his legal representative in Mexico City to conclude the affair.[15]

When Abad e Queipo heard of Balmis's departure from the capital, he immediately sought his detention in Veracruz. Ortuño convinced Venegas that Balmis

[7] Abad e Queipo to Venegas, Valladolid, 14 Noviembre 1810, in Rubio Mañé, 1934: 5, 5: pp. 642–643.

[8] *Ibid.,* pp. 643–644.

[9] Francisco Xavier de Balmis, "Statement," México, 20 Noviembre 1810, *ibid.,* p. 644.

[10] Agustín de Ledos, "Statement," México, 21 Noviembre 1810, *ibid.,* pp. 645–646.

[11] Ambrosio Saparzurieta, "Statement," México, 22 Noviembre 1810, *ibid.,* pp. 647–648.

[12] Francisco de Borja, "Statement," México, 22 Noviembre 1810, *ibid.,* pp. 647–648.

[13] Manuel de Baldovinos, "Statement," México, 5 Diciembre 1810, *ibid.,* pp. 652–653.

[14] Francisco Xavier de Balmis, "Statement," México, 16 Diciembre 1810, *ibid.,* p. 656.

[15] Balmis to Venegas, México, 30 Marzo 1811, *ibid.,* pp. 671–673.

should remain in Mexico until the bishop-elect's honor had been completely vindicated.[16] On May 1, 1811, Venegas instructed Carlos de Urrutia, governor of Veracruz, to delay Balmis's sailing.[17]

Irritated by the new postponement, Balmis replied to the new order five days later. He could not understand why the prelate persisted in continuing the case against him, since he had already denied the charges in a certified statement. He noted, however, that Abad e Queipo had twice delayed his trip to Spain and suggested that perhaps the prelate had an ulterior motive for impeding his departure. Balmis must have known that the Inquisition had earlier investigated the bishop-elect for his outspoken criticism of social inequities in New Spain. Perhaps Balmis believed that Abad e Queipo feared he would add new charges once he returned to the peninsula. He agreed to wait in Jalapa while his attorney continued the case, but noted that the bishop-elect was directly responsible for the added expense the delay would cause the Royal Treasury. The director also reminded Venegas that his position as honorary consultant to the Supreme Council of the Royal Treasury entitled him to all privileges and immunities enjoyed by that body. If he was ultimately placed on trial, only that council in Spain could judge him.[18]

By this time, however, steps had been taken to terminate the proceedings. On April 3, 1811, José de Galilea, the assessor general, had reviewed the entire file and declared that no charges against Balmis had been proven. In view of the chaos which swept the country and "in order to avoid more anger, dissention, and problems among distinguished persons," he believed that no further action was required.[19] Venegas agreed and on April 6 notified Balmis and Abad e Queipo of his decision. It will be noted that April 6 was the date on which Balmis was originally authorized to go to Veracruz. Abad e Queipo did not receive the viceroy's notice until May 20, however, and, as we have seen, was able to delay Balmis's departure. When the bishop-elect learned that Venegas had decided to terminate the case, he reluctantly agreed. His letter reached Mexico City on June 12.[20] Two days later the assessor general suggested that Balmis be absolved of all charges, and Venegas accepted his recommendation.[21] On August 17, 1811, Governor Urrutia issued Balmis a passport, and the director departed shortly thereafter.[22]

Most certainly nothing had been proven against Balmis. Only Borja and Baldovinos had presented damaging testimony, and both had been personally insulted by the director. It is most likely that the outspoken director had impugned their loyalty. It appears, however, that they had fabricated the accusations concerning the bishop-elect. After convincing Abad e Queipo that Balmis had made the allegations, they used the prelate's position as a means to retaliate. Venegas, plagued by many more serious problems, soon realized that the charges against Balmis were unsupported. Continued prosecution of the case would only further divide loyalist elements and damage the royalist cause. He took the most diplomatic course of action.

In his dispute with Antonio Gutiérrez, however, Balmis was obviously the aggressor. But before discussing this conflict, it is necessary to examine the course of the Royal Expedition under the assistant. When Balmis left Manila in August, 1805, he ordered Gutiérrez to complete the expedition's work in the Philippines, return the children to Mexico, and gather information on the progress of vaccination in New Spain. The expedition left Manila on June 10, 1806.[23] Pedro Ortega, who had co-directed the outer island mission, died in Manila before the expedition sailed. On August 14, 1807, the expedition reached Acapulco. During the voyage, one of the boys died of "fever"; another died later of "dropsy" in Mexico City.[24] Despite Iturrigaray's earlier order that the expedition not return to New Spain, he welcomed Gutiérrez, provided ample funds for the trip to the capital, and prepared a large residence for the staff and children in Mexico City.[25] The viceroy's surprising change of attitude was probably the result of a harsh reprimand he received from Soler after Balmis had charged him with indifference and obstructionism during his stay in Mexico.[26]

In view of the state of hostilities between Spain and Great Britain, Iturrigaray instructed Gutiérrez to remain in Mexico rather than attempt to lead the expedition back to the peninsula at that time. Upon the viceroy's order, Gutiérrez then took charge of returning the Mexican boys to their homes.[27] After that task was completed in late October, Iturrigaray advised Gutiérrez and the remaining members of his staff, Antonio and Francisco Pastor, Angel Crespo, and Isabel Gómez y Cendala, to find suitable housing elsewhere since they no longer needed the large residence. He allotted them each a monthly subsidy of twelve

[16] Ortuño to Venegas, México, n.d., *ibid.,* p. 677.
[17] Venegas to Urrutia, México, 1 Mayo 1811, *ibid.,* p. 679.
[18] Balmis to Venegas, Veracruz, 6 Mayo 1811, *ibid.,* pp. 679–682.
[19] Galilea to Venegas, México, 3 Abril 1811, *ibid.,* p. 675.
[20] Abad e Queipo to Venegas, Valladolid, 20 Mayo 1811 in Rubio Mañé, 1934: **5**, 6: p. 930.
[21] Galilea to Venegas, México, 14 Junio 1811, *ibid.,* pp. 930–931.
[22] Urrutia to Venegas, Veracruz, 17 Agosto 1811, *ibid.,* p. 947.

[23] *Gaceta de México,* 29 Agosto 1807, p. 570.
[24] Gutiérrez to Venegas, México, n.d., AGN, "Epidemias," v. **17**, fs. 335–336.
[25] Iturrigaray to Gutiérrez, México, 22 Agosto 1807, AGN, "Epidemias," v. **17**, fs. 284–285.
[26] Soler to Iturrigaray, San Lorenzo, 15 Septiembre 1806, AGI, "Indif. Gen.," Leg. 1.558, II, fs. 1–7.
[27] Iturrigaray to Gutiérrez, México, 22 Agosto 1807, AGN, "Epidemias," v. **17**, f. 285.

pesos to pay for their new accommodations.[28] In April, 1808, Iturrigaray granted the rectoress permission to move to Puebla, where she had left her adopted son in the care of the bishop, and instructed the intendant to pay her regular five-hundred-peso salary from the Royal Treasury.[29] The other members of the expedition apparently continued their work in Mexico until improved political conditions would permit their return to Madrid. When Balmis arrived in Mexico in June, 1810, he most certainly discussed the progress of vaccination with Gutiérrez and was satisfied with the assistant's management of the expedition to that point. A letter to Gutiérrez on August 9, 1810, from Valladolid reconfirmed the director's confidence in him.[30]

This ostensibly pleasant relationship dissolved after Balmis's return to Mexico City from Valladolid. On September 28 he informed Venegas that Gutiérrez should have returned to Spain in October, 1807, to give a full report of his activities in Manila and Mexico. He further charged that since the commissions of the members of the Royal Expedition were concluded at that time, Gutiérrez had unjustly accepted his full one-thousand-peso salary for the past three years. Balmis pointed out that the royal instructions of August 4, 1803, clearly stipulated that at the conclusion of the mission, members were to receive only half salary until they found a suitable position. He therefore suggested that Gutiérrez be ordered back to Spain to meet his obligations.[31]

A letter which Balmis received from Gutiérrez on October 3 explains his surprising change of attitude. In the letter Gutiérrez confessed that a few days previously he had gambled away not only his own money but the 575 pesos he had collected from the Royal Treasury to pay for the return passage to Spain of Balmis's nephews, Antonio and Francisco Pastor. He had desperately tried to borrow the money but failed at every turn. Begging Balmis's forgiveness, he offered to give the director his own monthly salary and any additional income he earned in his private medical practice until the debt was paid.[32] Balmis had probably already heard of Gutiérrez's indiscretion from his nephews and had made the initial charges on that basis.

Gutiérrez's letter of confession apparently caused Balmis to remember additional infractions. In a letter to Venegas he explained Gutiérrez's misuse of the funds and repeated that he was obligated to return to Spain immediately. He added that Gutiérrez must "answer

charges pending in the Ministry of Grace and Justice" concerning his personal conduct and management of the Royal Expedition. He also accused Gutiérrez of misappropriating the estate of Pedro Ortega in Manila, thus leaving Ortega's two orphaned children destitute. He declared that Gutiérrez should return to Spain at his own expense since he no longer deserved any official consideration.[33] Despite this suggestion, on October 3 Venegas instructed the ministers of the General Treasury to advance Gutiérrez three months' salary and sufficient funds for his passage to Spain.[34]

Gutiérrez was informed of Balmis's charges, apparently only those of September 28, and agreed to comply with the viceroy's orders.[35] Before he returned to Spain, however, Gutiérrez believed that certain aspects of the case required clarification. He explained that he was not required to give an account to the Ministry of Grace and Justice concerning the expedition because he had never been ordered to do so. Balmis, as director, had that responsibility. He stated that he had complied with all of Balmis's instructions and had remained in Mexico City at the order of Iturrigaray. The unfortunate series of events in Spain, he added, would have impeded his return anyway. His initial defense, and the one he would maintain throughout the case, was that he had not illegally delayed his departure and therefore had not unjustly drawn full pay from the Royal Treasury. He concluded that Balmis's charges of personal misconduct should have no bearing on the case.[36]

Although the viceroy had previously ordered the General Treasury to advance Gutiérrez funds for his trip to Spain and three months' salary, on October 5 he informed them that Gutiérrez had misused 575 pesos which rightfully belonged to the Pastors. He therefore authorized them to give the money to Balmis. On the following day the director received 520 pesos, which he declared was partial payment of the 575 pesos Gutiérrez owed his nephews. Balmis evidently gave this money to his nephews, who returned to Spain shortly thereafter. When Gutiérrez attempted to collect the money at the General Treasury on October 6, he discovered that it had already been given to Balmis.[37]

Without funds and apparently deprived of his salary, Gutiérrez was still in Mexico City in mid-December. He informed Venegas that although the instructions of August 4, 1803, had stated that at the end of the expedition the members should return to Madrid, conditions

[28] Iturrigaray to Gutiérrez, México, 27 Noviembre 1807, AGN, "Epidemias," v. 17, fs. 286–286v.
[29] Iturrigaray to Gutiérrez, México, 8 Abril 1808, AGN, "Epidemias," v. 17, fs. 288–288v.
[30] Balmis to Gutiérrez, Valladolid, 9 Agosto 1810, AGN, "Epidemias," v. 17, fs. 280–28v.
[31] Balmis to Venegas, México, 28 Septiembre 1810, AGN, "Epidemias," v. 17, fs. 224–224v.
[32] Gutiérrez to Balmis, México, 27 Septiembre 1810, AGN, "Epidemias," v. 17, fs. 231–232.

[33] Balmis to Venegas, México, 3 Octubre 1810, AGN, "Epidemias," v. 17, fs. 228–230.
[34] Venegas to Ministros de la Tesorería General, México, 2 Octubre 1810, AGN, "Epidemias," v. 17, f. 226.
[35] Antonio Gutiérrez, "Statement," México, 4 Octubre 1810, AGN, "Epidemias," v. 17, f. 227.
[36] Gutiérrez to Venegas, México, 5 Octubre 1810, AGN, "Epidemias," v. 17, fs. 237–238v.
[37] José Monter and Diego Mandobel, "Statement," México, 6 Octubre 1810, AGN, "Epidemias," v. 17, fs. 239–239v.

on the peninsula had changed. He could not go to Madrid because the capital was occupied by the French. In addition, the Royal Treasury in Spain was unable to pay his salary. He noted, however, that under similar circumstances many military physicians and surgeons were allowed to draw their pensions in Mexico. Gutiérrez requested that he also be permitted to receive his salary in Mexico City or any other part of the viceroyalty.[38] This request was then sent to Balmis and the assessor general for their opinions.

Balmis refused to accept the suggestion and insisted that the original orders had obliged Gutiérrez to return to Madrid when his commission was terminated. He contended that Gutiérrez could be paid legally only in Spain.[39] According to the assessor general's interpretation of the royal orders, Balmis, as director, not Gutiérrez, merely a subordinate, was responsible for giving an account of the expedition in Spain. Gutiérrez could personally inform the director concerning the expedition, and Balmis could later make a full report. Galilea reasoned that, since Gutiérrez need not return to Spain to deliver his report, he need not return to Spain to draw his salary. He did suggest, however, that the assistant be given one year in which to secure permission to remain in Mexico. He also suggested that a portion of the two hundred pesos already allotted for his return to Spain be discounted from his monthly salary until the total amount was repaid. He concluded that only the Spanish Cortes was empowered to rule on Balmis's charges of personal misconduct.[40]

Balmis refused to accept Galilea's interpretation of the original orders and insisted that they required Gutiérrez to return to the peninsula. To strengthen his case, he brought further charges against his aide. Balmis now declared that Gutiérrez was personally responsible for the deaths of the two Mexican children during the voyage from Manila because of their "total abandonment and lack of care." He re-emphasized that Gutiérrez had to answer in Spain for the misappropriation of Pedro Ortega's estate and other unspecified funds. These actions, Balmis declared, had merited the Spanish government's extreme displeasure. He concluded that, if Gutiérrez was allowed to remain in Mexico, he should receive no salary at all until the case was settled.[41] Although the assessor general did not change his initial interpretation, he did recommend that the entire file be sent to Ambrosio Saparzurieta, now fiscal of the Royal Treasury, for an opinion.[42]

Saparzurieta reviewed the case and supported Balmis on every count. He declared that Gutiérrez should have returned to Spain in October, 1807, and that the director's charges indeed merited careful consideration. He therefore recommended that Gutiérrez be given one week in which to repay one-half of all sums he had received from the Royal Treasury since October, 1807, and begin his trip to Spain. If Gutiérrez did not do so, he should be taken to Veracruz in chains and put on the first vessel sailing for the peninsula. On June 17 Venegas accepted the fiscal's recommendations and gave the corresponding orders.[43] In the meantime, the ministers of the General Treasury determined that Gutiérrez's total debt was 1,354 pesos.[44] Informed of the ruling, Gutiérrez declared that he could not comply because he "had neither money, goods, nor credit," and that he was living in the home of a friend because he was completely without means.[45]

The latest orders did move Gutiérrez to make his first energetic defense. He announced his respect for superior orders but complained that up to that point he had not been formally charged, nor had his legal right to a hearing been granted. All action taken against him was based solely on Balmis's word. And Balmis, he declared, was motivated by personal resentment and was not at all concerned with adherence to royal orders. He added that the director's charges of personal misconduct should in no way affect his rights as a member of the Royal Expedition.[46]

He insisted that he deserved his full salary, and that he had not been able to return to Spain because of the war. He declared that he would prove with letters from Balmis that the director had sanctioned his actions until the gambling episode. Gutiérrez also asserted that if he had illegally drawn full salary since October, 1807, all other members of the expedition, including Balmis's own nephews, were equally guilty. In addition, he pointed out that his presence in Mexico could be of value. Other less qualified physicians were receiving public funds for administering the vaccine. He could assume these duties at no additional expense to the Royal Treasury.[47] This document was then passed on to Saparzurieta.

Saparzurieta, completely convinced by Balmis's arguments, refused to alter his earlier opinions. He charged that Gutiérrez had willfully delayed his departure and indicated that he had done nothing in Mexico to qualify him for the salary he had received. The fiscal noted

[38] Gutiérrez to Venegas, México, 14 Diciembre 1810, AGN, "Epidemias," v. 17, fs. 242–243v.

[39] Balmis to Venegas, México, 9 Enero 1811, AGN, "Epidemias," v. 17, fs. 245–246.

[40] Galilea to Venegas, México, 31 Enero 1811, AGN, "Epidemias," v. 17, fs. 247–249v.

[41] Balmis to Venegas, México, 31 Enero 1811, AGN, "Epidemias," v. 17, fs. 250–253v.

[42] Galilea to Venegas, México, 6 Febrero 1811, AGN, "Epidemias," v. 17, fs. 254–255.

[43] Saparzurieta to Venegas, México, 6 Abril 1811, AGN, "Epidemias," v. 17, fs. 256–262v.

[44] Ministros de la Tesorería General, "Auto," México, 28 Junio 1811, AGN, "Epidemias," v. 17, f. 264.

[45] Antonio Fonseca, Antonio Gutiérrez, and Manuel Dávila Galindo, "Diligencia," México, 2 Julio 1811, AGN, "Epidemias," v. 17, fs. 264v–265.

[46] Gutiérrez to Venegas, México, n.d., AGN, "Epidemias," v. 17, fs. 335–338.

[47] Ibid., fs. 338v–339.

that since French troops had not occupied Madrid until December, 1808, Gutiérrez had had ample time to return to the peninsula. If Gutiérrez was allowed to remain in Mexico, however, he should receive only half salary, one-third of which should be withheld each month until his debt to the Royal Treasury was paid.[48] Venegas accepted this recommendation and gave the corresponding orders.[49]

Without remaining to learn the outcome of the case, Balmis had returned to Spain in August, 1811. Gutiérrez meanwhile continued to press the case in Mexico City in order to exonerate himself of the director's charges. On January 8, 1812, he presented his most complete statement of defense and included royal orders and several letters from Balmis to support his position. He limited his defense to maintaining his legal claim to a full annual salary of one thousand pesos until January 19, 1811, when Venegas had officially terminated his commission, and five hundred pesos per year after that time.

He pointed out that both Angel Crespo and Isabel Gómez y Cendala were bound by the same orders, and yet they had received full salary until January 19, 1811, and half salary thereafter. Gutiérrez insisted that he should be no exception and suggested that he was entitled to additional pay since he had served as assistant director since August, 1805. To prove that his work had been completely satisfactory until the gambling incident, he produced letters from Balmis praising his management of the expedition. Gutiérrez claimed that certified statements from local magistrates would absolve him of all blame in connection with the deaths of the two children. He re-emphasized that he had remained in Mexico City legally. Iturrigaray had given him verbal instructions to stay in Mexico and review the results of vaccination in the viceroyalty. No one had ever notified him that his commission had been terminated. To prove that Balmis had previously approved his remaining in Mexico, he included the director's letters from Madrid in 1808 and Valladolid in 1810.[50]

On January 27 his statement and supporting documents were sent to Ambrosio Saparzurieta. Apparently without reading them, Saparzurieta sent the complete file to the ministers of the Royal Treasury and the Royal Tribunal of Accounts for their opinions.[51] On February 13, 1812, the ministers of the Royal Treasury ruled in favor of Gutiérrez. They declared that he was

entitled to full pay until January 19, 1811, and half pay thereafter. They further declared that Balmis's charges concerning Gutiérrez's alleged personal misbehavior should have no bearing on the case. They then sent the file to the Royal Tribunal of Accounts. When it seemed that at last Gutiérrez would be completely exonerated, the file was mislaid and remained in the Royal Tribunal seven and a half years![52]

During that long delay, however, Venegas, convinced of Gutiérrez's innocence, had nominated him for the position of professor of surgery in the Hospital Real in Mexico City. The appointment was ultimately approved on November 14, 1818.[53] Finally on July 16, 1819, the Royal Tribunal of Accounts "rediscovered" the Gutiérrez case. In their belated opinion the ministers declared that Balmis had been clearly motivated by personal resentment and his accusations were totally unfounded. They agreed with the ministers of the Royal Treasury that Gutiérrez had been entitled to his salary and should immediately receive all funds previously withheld from him.[54]

The file was then returned to Saparzurieta. This time the fiscal did consider Gutiérrez's side of the conflict and acknowledged the "surprising turn of events in the case." He accepted the consensus that Balmis had unjustly accused Gutiérrez, and that the assistant was innocent on all counts. Weighing heavily upon his decision, of course, was Fernando VII's appointment of Gutiérrez as professor of surgery. The appointment alone confirmed Gutiérrez's merit.[55]

Viceroy Juan Ruiz de Apodaca accepted the decision and recommended that the case be officially closed. He did send a harsh reprimand to the ministers of the Royal Tribunal of Accounts and pointed out that their "excessive . . . scandalous delay had severely prejudiced Gutiérrez." He informed them that if a similar case of negligence should occur they would face sharp disciplinary action.[56] On September 20, 1819, Gutiérrez was informed of the final decision and received 1,169 pesos from the Royal Treasury.[57]

The Gutiérrez episode closes the story of the Royal Vaccination Expedition in New Spain. The turmoil

[48] Saparzurieta to Venegas, México, 22 Julio 1811, AGN, "Epidemias," v. 17, fs. 269–271.

[49] Venegas to Ministros de la Tesorería General, México, 6 Agosto 1811, AGN, "Epidemias," v. 17, f. 272.

[50] Gutiérrez to Venegas, México, 8 Enero 1812, AGN, "Epidemias," v. 17, fs. 292–298.

[51] Saparzurieta to Venegas, México, 27 Enero 1812, AGN, "Epidemias," v. 17, fs. 299–299v.

[52] José Monter and Antonio de Batres, "Statement," México, 13 Febrero 1812, AGN, "Epidemias," v. 17, fs. 300–300v.

[53] Lozano to Apodaca, Madrid, 14 Noviembre 1818, AGN, "Reales Cédulas," v. 219, exp. 322, f. 322.

[54] Ramón Martínez, "Statement," México, 16 Julio 1819, AGN, "Epidemias," v. 17, fs. 302–304.

[55] Saparzurieta to Apodaca, México, 11 Agosto 1819, AGN, "Epidemias," v. 17, fs. 306–310v.

[56] Apodaca to Real Tribunal de Cuentas, México, 6 Septiembre 1819, AGN, "Epidemias," v. 17, fs. 314–314v.

[57] José Monter and Antonio de Batres, "Liquidación que con arreglo al Superior Decreto de 6 del corriente forma la Tesorería General de los sueldos que deben abonarse al Sub-Director que fue de la Expedición de la Vacuna D. Antonio Gutiérrez Robredo," México, 20 Septiembre 1819, AGN, "Epidemias," v. 17, fs. 315–315v.

of the wars of independence destroyed the network of vaccination centers throughout the viceroyalty. Conservation of the vaccine was sporadic thereafter, and active serum was often unavailable even in the major cities.

While Francisco and Antonio Pastor had returned to Spain late in 1810, and Balmis followed them one year later, the other members of the expedition remained in Mexico. Miguel Lerdo de Tejada, who was personally acquainted with Antonio Gutiérrez and Angel Crespo, related that they lived in Mexico City until their deaths at mid-century. He reported that Gutiérrez, "the dean, although certainly not the best of Mexico City's physicians," had received a small pension from the National Treasury as director emeritus of one of the wards of the Hospital de San Andrés. Angel Crespo had held a minor bureaucratic position with the Mexican government.[58] Isabel Gómez y Cendala apparently remained in Puebla.

There is scant information concerning the last years of Francisco Xavier de Balmis. Although documents in the Mexican National Archives indicate that he left Veracruz in August, 1811, Díaz de Iraola declares that Balmis did not reach Cádiz until February 15, 1813. He states that on February 26 Balmis delivered his report on the vaccination in New Spain to the Cortes. The following month Balmis informed the Cortes that he had received news that Salvany had died in La Paz and requested that his remaining staff in South America be ordered home.[59] Francisco Xavier de Balmis died in Madrid on February 12, 1819, at the age of sixty-six.[60]

[58] Lerdo de Tejada, *op. cit.,* I, 343–344.
[59] Díaz de Iraola, *op. cit.,* p. 103.
[60] Martínez Durán, *op. cit.,* p. 477.

BIBLIOGRAPHY

PRIMARY SOURCE MATERIAL

Manuscripts

I. Archivo General de Indias (Sevilla, Spain).

   A. Indiferente General, Legajo 1.558. This material may be found on two rolls of microfilm (I and II) in the Mary Couts Burnett Library, Texas Christian University.

II. Archivo General de la Nación (México, D.F.).

   A. Ramo de Epidemias.
     1. v. 1, exps. 1–5.
     2. v. 2, exp. 3.
     3. v. 3, exp. 1.
     4. v. 4, exps. 1–16.
     5. v. 6, exps. 5–7.
     6. v. 7, exps. 1–10.
     7. v. 9, exp. 4.
     8. v. 10, exps. 7–15.
     9. v. 12, exp. 6.
     10. v. 16, exps. 2–10.
     11. v. 17.

   B. Ramo de Filipinas.
     1. v. 52, exp. 7.
     2. v. 53, exp. 15.

   C. Ramo de Historia.
     1. v. 44, exps. 14–17.
     2. v. 195, exp. 2.
     3. v. 222, exps. 12, 14.
     4. v. 430, exp. 1.
     5. v. 460.

   D. Ramo de Impresos Oficiales.
     1. v. 21, exp. 6.
     2. v. 22, exp. 64.
     3. v. 26, exps. 42–46.

   E. Ramo de Reales Cédulas.
     1. v. 130, exp. 168.
     2. v. 187, exp. 216.
     3. v. 189, exp. 64.
     4. v. 193, exp. 44.
     5. v. 196, exp. 232.
     6. v. 197, exps. 168, 237.
     7. v. 201, exps. 53, 335.
     8. v. 219, exp. 322.

   F. Ramo de Virreyes.
     1. v. 214, exp. 349.
     2. v. 235, exp. 487.

III. Biblioteca Nacional de Antropología e Historia (México, D.F.).

   A. Fondo de Micropelícula, Serie "Guatemala," #51.

Printed Works

ALAMÁN, LUCAS. 1942. *Historia de Méjico* (5 v., México, D.F.).

BALMIS, FRANCISCO XAVIER DE. 1794. *Demostración de las eficaces virtudes nuevamente descubiertas en las raíces de dos plantas de Nueva España, especies de agave y de begonia para la curación del vicio venéreo y escrofuloso y de otras graves enfermedades que resisten al uso de mercurio, y demás remedios conocidos* (Madrid).

BENAVENTE, TORIBIO DE (MOTOLINÍA). 1914. *Historia de los indios de Nueva España* (Barcelona).

DÍAZ DEL CASTILLO, BERNAL. 1928. *The Discovery and Conquest of Mexico, 1517–1521* (New York).

HERRERA Y TORDESILLAS, ANTONIO DE. 1934–1952. *Historia general de los hechos de los castellanos en las Islas y Tierra Firme del mar Océano* (10 v., Madrid).

HUMBOLDT, ALEJANDRO DE. 1941. *Ensayo político sobre el Reino de la Nueva España* (5 v., México).

JENNER, EDWARD. 1789. *An Inquiry into the Causes and Effects of the Variolae Vaccinae* (London).

LAS CASAS, BARTOLOMÉ DE. 1812. *Breve relación de las Indias Occidentales* (London).

SAHAGÚN, BERNARDINO DE. 1956. *Historia general de las cosas de Nueva España* (4 v., México, D.F.).

TORQUEMADA, JUAN DE. 1943. *Monarquía Indiana* (3 v., 3rd ed., México, D.F.).

Newspapers

Diario de México.
Gaceta de México.
Gazeta de Guatemala.
Mercurio de España.

SECONDARY SOURCE MATERIAL

Books

ALVAREZ AMEZQUITA, JOSÉ, *et al.* 1960. *Historia de la salubridad y de la asistencia en México* (4 v., México, D.F.).

BORAH, WOODROW. 1951. *New Spain's Century of Depression* (Berkeley).

BRAU, SALVADOR. 1966. *La colonización de Puerto Rico* (3rd ed., San Juan).

CLAVIJERO, FRANCISCO XAVIER. 1844. *Historia antigua de México y su conquista* (2 v., México).

COOPER, DONALD B. 1965. *Epidemic Disease in Mexico City, 1761–1813* (Austin).

FERNÁNDEZ DEL CASTILLO, FRANCISCO. 1960. *Los viajes de don Francisco Xavier de Balmis* (México, D.F.).

FIGUEROA MARROQUÍN, HORACIO. 1957. *Enfermedades de los conquistadores* (San Salvador).

FLORES, FRANCISCO A. 1886. *Historia de la medicina en México desde la época de los indios hasta la presente* (3 v., México, D.F.).

GIBSON, CHARLES. 1964. *The Aztecs Under Spanish Rule* (Stanford).

GUERRA, FRANCISCO. 1953. *Historiografía de la medicina colonial hispano-americana* (México, D.F.).

HAYWARD, JOHN A. 1956. *Historia de la medicina* (México).

LAFUENTE, MODESTO. 1930. *Historia general de España desde los tiempos primitivos hasta la muerte de Fernando VII* (22 v., Barcelona).

LANNING, JOHN TATE. 1953. *Dr. Narciso Esparragosa y Gallardo* (Caracas).

LERDO DE TEJADA, MIGUEL. 1850. *Apuntes históricos de la heroica ciudad de Veracruz* (3 v., México).

LÓPEZ SÁNCHEZ, JOSÉ. 1950. *Vida y obra del sabio médico habanero Dr. Tomás Romay y Chacón* (La Habana).

MARTÍNEZ DURÁN, CARLOS. 1964. *Las ciencias médicas en Guatemala, origen y evolución* (3rd ed., Guatemala).

OCARANZA, FERNANDO. 1934. *Historia de la medicina en México* (México).

OSLER, WILLIAM. 1927. *The Principles and Practice of Medicine* (10th ed., New York).

ROSENBLAT, ANGEL. 1954. *La población indígena y el mestizaje en América* (2 v., Buenos Aires).

SOMOLINOS D'ARDOIS, GERMÁN. 1964. *Historia de la medicina* (México, D.F.).

VALLE, RAFAEL HELIDORO. 1942. *La cirujía mexicana del siglo XIX* (México, D.F.).

VILLACORTA CALDERÓN, JOSÉ ANTONIO. 1942. *Historia de la Capitanía General de Guatemala* (Guatemala).

Articles and Periodicals

BANTUG, JOSÉ. 1955. "Carlos IV y la introducción de la vacuna en Filipinas." *Anuario de Estudios Americanos* **12**: pp. 75–129.

BERMÚDEZ, SALVADOR. 1946. "La vida y obra de Eduardo Jenner." *Gaceta Médica de México* **66**,5: pp. 297–310.

COOK, SHERBURNE F. 1942. "Francisco Xavier Balmis and the Introduction of Vaccination in Latin America." *Bulletin of the History of Medicine* **12**,5: pp. 543–560.

———. 1942. "Francisco Xavier Balmis and the Introduction of Vaccination in Latin America." *Bulletin of the History of Medicine* **12**,6: pp. 70–101.

DÍAZ DE IRAOLA, GONZALO. 1947. "La vuelta al mundo de la Expedición de la Vacuna." *Anuario de Estudios Americanos* **17**: pp. 103–266.

FERNÁNDEZ DEL CASTILLO, FRANCISCO. n.d. "El doctor Francisco Xavier de Balmis y los resultados de su expedición vacunal a la América." *Salud Pública de México* **2**,1: pp. 189–200.

———. 1946. "La introducción de la vacuna en México." *Gaceta Médica de México* **66**,5: pp. 311–324.

RUBIO MAÑÉ, JOSÉ IGNACIO (ed.). 1934. "El obispo Abad e Queipo y el doctor Balmis." *Boletín del Archivo General de la Nación* (México) **5**,5: pp. 641–682.

———. 1934. "El obispo Abad e Queipo y el doctor Balmis." *Boletín del Archivo General de la Nación* (México) **5**,6: pp. 923–947.

MEMOIRS

OF THE

AMERICAN PHILOSOPHICAL SOCIETY

TRANSACTIONS

OF THE

AMERICAN PHILOSOPHICAL SOCIETY

———————

Lewis Evans and His Maps. WALTER KLINEFELTER.
Vol. 61, pt. 7, 65 pp., 1 map, 1971. $2.50.

The Diplomacy of the Mexican Empire, 1863–1867. ARNOLD BLUMBERG.
Vol. 61, pt. 8, 152 pp., 15 figs., 1971. $5.00.

Maurus of Salerno: Twelfth-century "Optimus Physicus" with his Commentary on the Prognostics of Hippocrates.
    MORRIS HAROLD SAFFRON.
Vol. 62, pt. 1, 104 pp., 1972. $4.00.

Joseph Eötvös and the Modernization of Hungary, 1840–1870. PAUL BÖDY.
Vol. 62, pt. 2, 134 pp., 7 figs., 1972. $5.00.

Respiration and the Lavoisier Tradition: Theory and Modification, 1777–1850. CHARLES A. CULOTTA.
Vol. 62, pt. 3, 41 pp., 2 figs., 1972. $2.00.

Prehistoric Research in Afghanistan (1959–1966). LOUIS DUPREE et al.
Vol. 62, pt. 4, 84 pp., 157 figs., 1972. $5.00.

The Major Political Issues of the Jacksonian Period and the Development of Party Loyalty in Congress, 1830–1840.
    DAVID J. RUSSO.
Vol. 62, pt. 5, 51 pp., 1972. $2.00.

The Scientific Papers of James Logan. Edited by ROY N. LOKKEN.
Vol. 62, pt. 6, 94 pp., 14 figs., 1972. $4.00.

Burmese Earthworms: An Introduction to the Systematics and Biology of Megadrile Oligochaetes with Special
    Reference to Southeast Asia. G. E. GATES.
Vol. 62, pt. 7, 326 pp., 2 figs., 1972. $12.00.

The Painful Labour of Mr. Elsyng. ELIZABETH READ FOSTER.
Vol. 62, pt. 8, 69 pp., 1972. $3.00.

Tepexi el Viejo: A Postclassic Fortified Site in the Mixteca-Puebla Region of Mexico. SHIRLEY GORENSTEIN.
Vol. 63, pt. 1, 75 pp., 30 figs., 4 maps, 1973. $3.50.

Theodore Roosevelt and His English Correspondents: A Special Relationship of Friends. DAVID H. BURTON.
Vol. 63, pt. 2, 70 pp., 1973. $3.00.

Origin and Evolution of the Elephantidae. VINCENT J. MAGLIO.
Vol. 63, pt. 3, 149 pp., 50 figs., 19 pls., 1973. $8.00.

The Austro-Slav Revival: A Study of Nineteenth-century Literary Foundations. STANLEY B. KIMBALL.
Vol. 63, pt. 4, 83 pp., 1 map, 1973. $3.50.

Plains Cree: A Grammatical Study. H. CHRISTOPH WOLFART.
Vol. 63, pt. 5, 65 pp., 1973. $4.00.

Arms Across the Border: United States Aid to Juárez During the French Intervention in Mexico. ROBERT RYAL
    MILLER.
Vol. 63, pt. 6, 68 pp., 9 figs., 1973. $2.50.

F. A. Smitt, Marine Bryozoa, and the Introduction of Darwin into Sweden. THOMAS J. M. SCHOPF and EDWARD
    L. BASSETT.
Vol. 63, pt. 7, 30 pp., 1 fig., 1973. $2.50.